The Cambridge Introduction to the
Short Story in English

The short story has become an increasingly important genre since the mid-nineteenth century. Complementing *The Cambridge Introduction to the American Short Story*, this book examines the development of the short story in Britain and other English-language literatures. It considers issues of form and style alongside – and often as part of – a broader discussion of publishing history and the cultural contexts in which the short story has flourished and continues to flourish. In its structure the book provides a chronological survey of the form, usefully grouping writers to show the development of the genre over time. Starting with Dickens and Kipling, the chapters cover key authors from the past two centuries and up to the present day. The focus on form, literary history and cultural context, together with the highlighting of the greatest short stories and their authors, make this a stimulating and informative overview for all students of English literature.

Adrian Hunter is Lecturer in English at the University of Stirling.

Cambridge Introductions to Literature

This series is designed to introduce students to key topics and authors. Accessible and lively, these introductions will also appeal to readers who want to broaden their understanding of the books and authors they enjoy.

- Ideal for students, teachers, and lecturers
- Concise, yet packed with essential information
- Key suggestions for further reading

The Cambridge Introduction to the
Short Story in English

ADRIAN HUNTER

CAMBRIDGE
UNIVERSITY PRESS

CAMBRIDGE UNIVERSITY PRESS
Cambridge, New York, Melbourne, Madrid, Cape Town, Singapore, São Paulo, Delhi

Cambridge University Press
The Edinburgh Building, Cambridge CB2 8RU, UK

Published in the United States of America by Cambridge University Press, New York

www.cambridge.org
Information on this title: www.cambridge.org/9780521681124

First published 2007

Printed in the United Kingdom at the University Press, Cambridge

A catalogue record for this publication is available from the British Library

ISBN 978-0-521-86259-2 hardback
ISBN 978-0-521-68112-4 paperback

Contents

Acknowledgements

Thanks are due to the University of Stirling and the Arts and Humanities Research Council for funding the period of research leave that allowed me to complete this book. I am likewise indebted to John Coyle for overseeing my early work on the short story and for continuing to hear me out on the subject. For advice, pointers and support of various other sorts I am grateful to Allison Bow, Glennis Byron, Valentine Cunningham, Jennifer Ellis, Scott Hames, Jacqui Harrop, Donald Mackenzie, Robert Miles, Adam Piette, Chris Powici, James Procter, Angela Smith, Joanne Thomson and Rory Watson.

Introduction

What is it that makes a short story short?

Once upon a time, no one thought of asking that question. The cave-dwelling storyteller, as E. M. Forster imagines him, simply *told*, and if he was lucky and able enough to hold his hearers' attention, then they might not kill or eat him.[1] It was incident and excitement, anticipation and suspense, and above all the provision of a satisfying ending that characterized the story as it was embedded in oral culture, and as it prevailed in the short printed prose narrative up until the end of the nineteenth century, at which point something changed, and the question was asked: what is it that makes a short story short?

This book introduces the reader to a broad selection of English-language writers who, in one way or another, whether directly or indirectly, have taken up that question and whose work has been decisive in shaping our understanding of what the modern short story is, and what it is capable of. These writers come from diverse places – England, Scotland, Ireland, Australia, New Zealand, Nigeria and Canada (for reasons of space, authors from the United States of America have been excluded, and interested readers are directed instead to Martin Scofield's complementary volume in this series, *The Cambridge Introduction to the American Short Story*); what connects them to one another can be summed up in the words of the Anglo-Irish writer Elizabeth Bowen: they have understood the 'shortness' of the short story to be something more, something other, than 'non-extension';[2] they have treated 'shortness', that is to say, as a 'positive' quality.

What Bowen was referring to when she made this discrimination in her landmark 1936 introduction to the *Faber Book of Modern Short Stories* was the change that occurred in the latter decades of the nineteenth century, a change that, as she saw it, signalled the short story's breaking free from the grip of novel and the novelistic imagination. Up until that point, the short story had been treated as a condensed novel, and the art of writing it lay in the skill with which the author could squeeze the machinery of plot and character into the reduced frame of a few thousand words. The short story was a doll's house, a fully realized world in miniature. What suddenly occurred to writers like Henry James, however, was the notion that writing 'short' might be less a matter of shrinking the novel into a tiny space than of making more artful and strategic economies, cutting away the kind of material we normally depend upon for narrative continuity and coherence, for example, and working with these tactical omissions to *suggest* and *imply* meaning, rather than stating it directly. What James and others saw was that the short story could achieve great richness and complexity – or 'multiplicity' to use James's own word – *as a result of*, rather than in spite of, its brevity.

James himself, it must be said, was keener to observe such reticence in others' writing than practise it in his own; nevertheless, the idea of a creative trans-action between brevity and complexity – the art of saying less but meaning more – took hold among the emergent literary avant-garde at the turn into the twentieth century, and as we shall see in Part II, became the basis of modernist experimentation in the short form. Yet this new-found property of the short story was always more than just a matter of form and technique. James had come upon it through his reading of Russian and European writers like Ivan Turgenev and Guy de Maupassant, and, as he recognized at the time, these were authors likely to baffle and perplex the 'moralists' among their English readers. In other words, James descried a potential connection between an elliptical, ambiguous, evasive, non-didactic story style and the breakdown of certain cultural and moral certainties.

Many agreed with James, among them G. K. Chesterton, for whom the attraction to short stories was a reflection of the 'fleetingness and fragility'[3] of modern existence. Throughout the twentieth century we encounter the idea that the short story form is somehow specially amenable or adaptable to the representation of an increasingly fragmented social character under the condi-tions of technological, industrial modernity. This is perhaps most in evidence in the modernist period, but contemporary writers too like to claim that the short story is ideally calibrated to the experience of modern life. Here is the South African author Nadine Gordimer, writing in 1968:

> Each of us has a thousand lives and a novel gives a character only one. *For the sake of the form.* The novelist may juggle about with chronology and throw narrative overboard; all the time his characters have the reader by the hand, there is a consistency of relationship throughout the experience that cannot and does not convey the quality of human life, where contact is more like the flash of fire-flies, in and out, now here, now there, in darkness. Short story writers see by the light of the flash; theirs is the art of the only thing one can be sure of – the present moment. Ideally, they have learned to do without explanation of what went before, and what happens beyond this point.[4]

This is shortness as a 'positive' quality, in the sense that the form, handled right, is able to embody an experiential condition of modernity – a sense of chronic uncertainty, historical sequestration and social isolation.

In the classic accounts of the short story – by Bowen, H. E. Bates, and Frank O'Connor – one repeatedly encounters the idea that the short story is somehow 'up to speed' with the realities of modern life. Bates, for example, citing Bowen, claims that the form is 'a child of this century' in the same way that cinema is. Like film, it conducts narrative not by extended exposition, as the novel does, but 'by a series of subtly implied gestures, swift shots, moments of suggestion, an art in which elaboration and above all explanation are superfluous and tedious'.[5] In this respect it is the literary form readily adaptable to the experience of modernity and the accelerated pace of life 'that travels so fast that we even attempt to anticipate it and play at prophets'.[6] It is for this reason too that Bates thinks the short story has played so prominent a part in the literature of America in an age where people are 'talking faster, moving faster, and apparently thinking faster'.[7]

The idea that American writers have raised the short story to the level of 'a national art form' is reiterated by Frank O'Connor in *The Lonely Voice*, a book that remains for many the landmark work in criticism of the short story. Like Bates, O'Connor considers the short story to be both an essentially 'modern art', attuned to 'modern conditions – to printing, science, and individual religion',[8] and, in its anti-traditionalist versions, a distinctly literary one that will persist for as long as 'culture' survives the onslaught of 'mass civilization'. The reason for its pre-eminence in the twentieth century, O'Connor argues, is that it manages to embody 'our own attitude to life'.[9] What that attitude is has something to do with the experience of social dislocation in the modern world – what he calls the 'intense awareness of human loneliness'.[10] In the short story's fascination with 'submerged population groups', O'Connor sees the reflection of a society 'that has no sign posts, a society that offers no goals and no answers'.[11]

Whether or not one agrees that the short story is uniquely or specially equipped to do the kind of cultural work that these commentators suppose, it is certainly the case that the form has remained a vital and valid one in the twentieth century, and has served as the medium for much that has been new or innovative in modern fiction. This book is organized in such a way as to reflect both the formal and contextual aspects to the short story's development and to explore the interactions between them. Each chapter presents close analyses of stories alongside comments writers and critics have made on them, attending both to what is happening in the language, structure and form of the texts, and to the cultural, social and material *con*texts in which they were produced and to which they contribute. These principles have also dictated the organization of the book into four sections. The first of these examines the 'rise' of the short story in the nineteenth century and the emergence of a body of critical and creative work that reflects the new 'literary' status of the form. Part II deals with the modernist period. In many respects modernism has been, and remains, the short story's centre of gravity – and not only in academic criticism. For many readers, James Joyce and Katherine Mansfield are the first names that come to mind in any roster of the modern form; and the innovations they introduced, most notably the 'epiphany', have assumed the status of first principles for aspiring writers of short fiction, not to mention the professionals who teach them on creative writing courses throughout the English-speaking world. Part III considers the afterlife of modernism, as the form was absorbed into different writing contexts and became a fixture of the academic study of literature. This is the period of classic statements on the story by Bates, Bowen, O'Connor and Sean O'Faolain, in all of which a central concern is how to deal with the legacy of modernism. This is also the period that sees the consolidation of the modernist aesthetic in the values and practices of academic criticism, and the establishment of 'creative writing' in the university – both of which contexts are apparent in the work of Angela Carter and Ian McEwan. Part IV enlarges the focus of this book to take in the short story as it has featured in Anglophone literatures from beyond England and Ireland. Once again, it is the relationship between text and context that is the main interest of this section, and in particular the question of why the short story has played such a prominent role – disproportionately so – in cultures that have experienced colonial disruption.

Part I

The nineteenth century

Introduction: publishers, plots and prestige

It is a commonplace of short story criticism to assert that English writers were slow taking to the from in the nineteenth century. Where Russian and American authors excelled in the dramatic 'single-incident' narrative, the English culti-vated, as V. S. Pritchett would later put it, a 'national taste for the ruminative and disquisitional': 'we preferred to graze on the large acreage of the novel and even tales by Dickens or Thackeray or Mrs Gaskell strike us as being unused chapters of longer works'.[1] Among commentators of the time one finds a good deal of support for Pritchett's claim, not least from Henry James who, in an essay on the French writer Guy de Maupassant, suggested that the English pre-ferred their fiction 'rather by the volume than by the page'.[2] It was not until the last two decades of the nineteenth century, as the novel began to lose com-mand of the literary marketplace and the periodical publishing industry began to boom, that circumstances were finally propitious to the development of the short story.

To a great extent, the 'rise', albeit belated, of the form in England had to do with commercial factors. The 1880s and 1890s saw the dramatic expansion of a magazine market that had been growing exponentially since the 1840s. Improved technologies in printing, such as machine-made paper and half-tone illustrations, the repeal of mid-Victorian free-trade duties on paper and changes in copyright law had all conspired to make periodical publishing one of the most accessible and lucrative sectors of the modern economy. Book pub-lishers such as George Smith and Macmillan quickly got involved, launching their own story-based journals as low-capital testing grounds for fresh talent and a ready means of securing new writers for their lists. Meanwhile, the gath-ering pace of periodicals – monthlies, weeklies, dailies, evening dailies – meant a vast increase in demand for material that was as easy for the jobbing writer to produce as it was for the time-pressed commuter to consume. Penny-press titles like Alfred Harmsworth's *Answers* began to favour stand-alone stories over seri-alized fiction, while George Newnes's hugely successful *Tit-Bits* (the model for Harmsworth's journal) and his *Strand Magazine* ran short story competitions and provided instruction to their readers in how to write winning submissions.

By 1891 penny and six-penny journals alike were no longer carrying serialized novels at all but were instead publishing an original short story by a distinguished writer in every number. According to the historian Peter Keating, it is unlikely that the short story would have developed much at all in this period 'if the market had not been so desperate to fill periodicals columns with fiction'.[3] As Henry James put it at the time, 'Periodical literature is a huge open mouth which has to be fed – a vessel of immense capacity which has to be filled'.[4]

The 'rise' of the short story also brought with it a new interest in the internal workings of the form. In commentary by James, Frederick Wedmore and Brander Matthews, among many others, we see developing the idea that the 'shortness' of the short story might be conceived of as, in Elizabeth Bowen's suggestive phrase, a 'positive' quality, rather than a matter merely of 'non-extension'. Whereas for Dickens and Mrs Gaskell the short story had been little more than a highly condensed novel, not governed by any aesthetic principles of its own, later Victorian authors began to think more strategically about the art of writing 'short'. Instead of shrinking down novelistic tropes and conventions, they experimented with more artful methods of omission, compression, aperture and ellipsis. Out went traditional methods of plotting and characterization, and in came a new roster of narrative concepts: implication, ambiguity, suggestion, dilation and, above all, *plotlessness*.

More thoroughly than any critic of the time, it was Henry James who explored the art of writing short (though it has to be said that James's own stories did not much reflect his thinking on this matter). The short story, he told his English readers, was less a matter of condensing some preconfigured narrative unit to fit a lesser word count, as the mid-Victorian novelist had thought, than of learning to manage without the orientational structures of plot and exposition on which the novel was based. For instruction in the matter he looked abroad – to Maupassant, of course, but also to the Russian writer Ivan Turgenev, for whom, James said, 'the germ of a story . . . was never an affair of plot – that was the last thing he thought of: it was the representation of certain persons . . . The thing consists of the motions of a group of selected creatures, which are not the result of a preconceived action, but a consequence of the qualities of the actions'.[5] James's choice of the word 'motions' indicates a quality of action without definable consequence, 'purposiveness' without purpose, where brevity takes the form of a suggestive and implicatory method of characterization and a marked de-emphasis of plot. In his preface to 'The Lesson of the Master', James described the ideal short story in similar terms, as the form in which one might 'do the complicated thing with a strong brevity and lucidity – to arrive, on behalf of the multiplicity, at a certain science of control'. Of essence was the idea that a disparity of extent could emerge between utterance and meaning: though material statement be curtailed, diversity and complexity of sense need not. Where in the past the short story had been governed by action and incident, providing 'adventure[s] comparatively safe, in which you [had], for the most part, but to put one foot after the other', the new 'plotless' form dealt in 'exposures' and 'glimpses', creating the 'impression . . . of a complexity or a continuity'. It was the 'rarer performance' and made 'the best of the sport' by being 'as far removed as possible from the snap of the pistol-shot'.[6] It was also the form that quickened the *literary* sensibility by revealing that 'liberal *more*'[7] of which the short story was capable.

Other critics picked up on James's idea that 'plotlessness' was a marker of literariness, and that this was what distinguished the short story proper from the mass-market popular tale. The 'plotless' form, Frederick Wedmore argued, 'with its omissions' and 'the brevity of its allusiveness', was beyond the grasp of the common consumer schooled in the 'convenient inexactness' of the Victorian story; rather, it needed to be 'met half way' by the 'alert, not the fatigued, reader'. The proper home of the short story, therefore, was the highbrow literary magazine where its art could be practised 'upon exalted lines' and the writer freed of the burden of 'appealing to, at all events of having to give sops to, at one and the same moment, gallery and stalls'. Only in so discerning a venue could the 'true' short story thrive, 'not as a ready means of hitting the big public, but as a medium for the exercise of the finer art – as a medium, moreover, adapted peculiarly to that alert intelligence, on the part of the reader, which rebels sometimes at the *longueurs* of the conventional novel'.[8]

A similar blend of aesthetics, economics, and reception sociography features, in more anguished form, in G. K. Chesterton's reading of turn-of-the-century literary culture. Looking back on the career of Charles Dickens, Chesterton explained the contemporary taste for the short story by way of contrast with the high-Victorian era of the great and heroic novelist:

> Our modern attraction to short stories is not an accident of form; it is the sign of a real sense of fleetingness and fragility; it means that existence is only an impression, and, perhaps, only an illusion. A short story of to-day has the air of a dream; it has the irrevocable beauty of a falsehood; we get a glimpse of grey streets of London or red plains of India, as in an opium vision; we see people – arresting people with fiery and appealing faces. But when the story is ended, the people are ended. We have no instinct of anything ultimate and enduring behind the episodes. The moderns, in a word, describe life in short stories because they are possessed with the sentiment that life itself is an uncommonly short story, and perhaps not a true one.[9]

That sense of 'fleetingness and fragility' contrasted for Chesterton with the mid-Victorian period of progress and hope and, of course, of the three-decker novel. His imagery recalls Walter Pater's conclusion to *The Renaissance*: not only is modern experience fissiparous, formed of tenuous, infinitely divisible impressions, but we are each confined within our own perceptual ambit. What was lacking in this condition, Chesterton lamented, was the continuity of vision, the faith in public knowledge, the assurance of certain certainties that permitted the Victorian novelist's art. And the destruction of these values was directly expressed in literary form, as a retreat into smallness and 'minor' style.

Chesterton saddles the slight frame of the short story with a great deal of moral and circumstantial lumber here, but he voices assumptions and anxieties that lay embedded in the comments of many of his contemporaries. For James, Wedmore and others, fretful encounters with publishers and with the rapidly fragmenting marketplace for fiction triggered worries about literary value and status and, in particular, the composition of the contemporary readership, anxieties that intersected with broader cultural and social controversies in the 1890s around mass education and the spread of literacy, the effects of democratization and the impact of technological change and urbanization. By conceiving of the short story as a 'finer art', beyond the comprehension and consumption habits of the 'big public', James and his fellows drew the form directly into these debates.

As we shall see later, this positioning of the short story as a 'literary' as opposed to a 'popular' fictional form would pave the way for its absorption into modernism in the early decades of the twentieth century; but more of that in Part II. For now, the chapters in this section trace three distinct stages in the short story's development during the Victorian era. The first looks at Charles Dickens and Thomas Hardy and shows how both writers reserved the short story, or the 'tale' more properly, for treating material of a supernatural or sensational nature, drawing heavily on the traditions of oral folk culture. Chapter 2 moves forward to the 1890s and the work of Rudyard Kipling and Joseph Conrad, both of whom exploited the conventions of the popular magazine story while at the same time experimenting with enigmatic and frequently ironic narrative structures. Chapter 3 examines the circle of writers associated with John Lane and Henry Harland's notorious decadent journal *The Yellow Book*, among them Hubert Crackanthorpe and George Egerton. This chapter shows how the new 'plotless' form became associated with avant-garde literary values, and by extension with the radical cultural criticism of the 'New Woman' feminists.

Chapter 1

Charles Dickens and Thomas Hardy

In his apologetic preface to the 1852 edition of *Christmas Stories*, Charles Dickens remarked on how much harder he found it writing short stories than long ones:

> The narrow space within which it was necessary to confine these Christmas Stories when they were originally published, rendered their construction a matter of some difficulty, and almost necessitated what is peculiar in their machinery. I could not attempt great elaboration of detail, in the working out of character within such limits, believing that it could not succeed.[1]

While he recognized that condensed narrative forms 'necessitated' a different approach from longer fiction, Dickens was unable to think of this as other than a 'confining' or 'limiting' of his full expressive capacity; that short stories did not allow him to individuate character through 'great elaboration of detail' was a privation rather than a stimulus to a new concept of characterization. The impression Dickens gives here, as throughout his career as a short story writer, is of a master builder labouring to construct a doll's house from the plans to a mansion.

Like most of his English contemporaries, Dickens considered the 'shortness' of the short story to be a matter largely of length. What defined the form was, simply, that it contained fewer words than a novel, not that it did anything the novel didn't, or couldn't, do. To invoke Elizabeth Bowen again, 'shortness' was not regarded as a 'positive' quality; it was at best a hindrance, a technical obstacle to the exercise of one's full expressive capacity. Early in his career, Dickens tended to compose short stories as parts of larger projects, or as fillers for spare pages in the serial instalments of his novels. *Pickwick Papers* (1836–7), for example, contains nine 'inset' tales within its narrative framework, while two stand-alone stories, 'The Baron of Grogzwig' and 'The Five Sisters of York', feature in chapter 6 of *Nicholas Nickleby* (1838–9). H. E. Bates, in his classic study of the short story in English, suggests that these novelistic preoccupations caused Dickens to 'underestimate the reader', a flaw that is lethal to success in the short form.[2] By adopting a declarative, authoritarian style of narration more properly belonging to the novel, Dickens left little to the co-productive imagination of the reader: he *told* rather than *showed,* stated rather than implied, with the effect that his short stories, like those of his contemporaries Thackerary and Mrs Gaskell, seemed like 'unused chapters of longer works'.[3]

Dickens himself didn't think much of his early efforts in the short form either, dismissing *Sketches By Boz* (1836–7), in the preface to the 1850 Cheap Edition, as 'extremely crude and ill-considered', full of youthful 'haste and inexperience'. More than crude technique, *Boz* reveals the extent to which Dickens's narrative practice was orientated around the novel. Although it is composed of seemingly separate tales and sketches, the book is held together by a cohesive, novelistic centre of consciousness which functions as a privileged voice within the stories, an elevated discourse able to interpret and rationalize all that it surveys. While we may get only glimpses and snapshots of the inhabitants of Seven Dials or Monmouth-street, the narrator is nevertheless able to render the incoherence and ignorance of the lives he depicts as symptoms of a broad social condition which is then held up for scrutiny and entertainment:

> Now anybody who passed through the Dials on a hot summer's evening, and saw the different women of the house gossiping on the steps, would be apt to think that all was harmony among them, and that a more primitive set of people than the native Diallers could not be imagined. Alas! the man in the shop ill-treats his family; the carpet-beater extends his professional pursuits to his wife; the one-pair front has an undying feud with the two-pair front persisting in dancing over his (the one-pair front's) head, when he and his family have retired for the night; the two-pair back *will* interfere with the front kitchen's children; the Irishman comes home drunk every other night, and attacks everybody; and the one-pair back screams at everything. Animosities spring up between floor and floor; the very cellar asserts his equality. Mrs A 'smacks' Mrs B's child for 'making faces'. Mrs B forthwith throws cold water over Mrs A's child for 'calling names'. The husbands are embroiled – the quarrel becomes general – an assault is the consequence, and a police-officer the result.   ('Seven Dials')

To adopt some terms from narratology for a moment, the *énonciation* in this passage – that is, the narrator – is empowered to impart information that transcends the comprehension of the subjects it describes – the characters, or subjects of the *énoncé*.[4] This hierarchy of discourses, in which the narrating voice signals over the heads of the characters, is a fixture of the Victorian classic realist novel, and it finds its way into Dickens's short fiction in more or less undiluted form. The particular events and occurrences in his stories are less significant than the general condition or point of social analysis they exemplify. Unable to portray character through 'great elaboration of detail', as he could in his novels, Dickens in his short fiction adopts a highly compressed, summary form of characterization, to the extent that when characters are given leave to speak, they merely reproduce what the *énonciation* has already declared to be the case about them. Thus, when the ex-churchwarden makes his hustings address to the parishioners in 'The Election for Beadle' (*Sketches by Boz*), for example, his speech, both in manner and substance, enters unproblematically into the consensus of opinion about him that the narration has already established with the reader. He emerges, as the narrator has told us he would, as a man of 'confined' rather than 'extensive', 'narrow' as opposed to 'liberal', views, who 'prides himself, not a little, on his style of addressing the parishioners in vestry assembled'. The 'Dickensian catalogue', as Bates called it, leaves the reader with little interpretative room to manoeuvre.

It is easy to see why so many critics, Bates among them, should have come to the conclusion that Dickens's treatment of the short story was arbitrary, that he had little coherent idea of what the form was or what it could do, and that he was drawn to it at particular moments as a matter merely of commercial convenience. Yet this is rather misleading, for it suggests that Dickens did not develop as a story writer over the course of his career. In fact, we can detect a shift in his treatment of the form around 1850. Where the bulk of his short fiction had, until that point, taken the form of impressionistic sketches, such as those in *Boz*, from the time he began contributing to the magazine *Household Words*, he reserved the form almost exclusively for material of a supernatural or fantastic nature.

In part Dickens was answering here to a long-held ambition of presenting his own version of the *Arabian Nights* tales, which had been a staple of his childhood reading. As early as 1839, when he was drawing up plans for his miscellany *Master Humphrey's Clock*, he had expressed the hope that, alongside the satirical sketches, political squibs and imaginary letters that would take up the bulk of the journal, he would be able to run a series of 'stories and descriptions of London as it was many years ago, as it is now, and as it will be many years hence, to which I would give some such title as The Relaxations of Gog and Magog, dividing them into portions like the *Arabian Nights*, and supposing Gog and Magog to entertain each other with such narrations . . . all night long'.[5] (According to the novelist George Gissing, Dickens made 'more allusions throughout his work to the *Arabian Nights* than to any other book or author').[6] Yet there was another, more profound reason for Dickens's attraction to tales of the exotic, the preternatural or the uncanny, and that is that it provided a means of staging resistance to the sort of rational-scientific materialism that was coming increasingly to dominate Victorian cultural conversation. It was this, I would suggest, more than a propensity to the novel, that conditioned the kind of short story Dickens wrote, and that furthermore explains why he treated the form in the apparently mechanistic way he did.

To take an example, 'To Be Read At Dusk' (1852), composed during the period of Dickens's greatest productivity in the short form, is a story that, for all its resolute plotting, manages to convey a sense of unsettling *ir*resolution. The story contains a double frame, beginning with the narrator remembering a conversation he overheard among a group of couriers seated outside a convent in Switzerland. Within that conversation, two stories are then retailed on the theme of the supernatural and the difficulty of distinguishing truth from fiction. The first story is told by a Genoese courier, Giovanni Baptista, who recounts his experience working for an Englishman whose young bride was troubled by the vision of a 'dark, remarkable-looking man' who came to her in dreams. In this story, the newly wed couple visit Italy, where they meet a friend of the husband's Signor Dellombra. The young bride immediately recognizes him as the man she has dreamed of, and faints at his feet. In the days that follow, she attempts to accustom herself to Dellombra's presence, but despite her husband's assurances she continues to fear him. One day she disappears. Her husband and the courier ride out in search of her, only to learn from a posthouse that Dellombra had passed several hours earlier with a terrified English lady crouching in his carriage. She is never seen again.

In the second story, this time told by the German courier, we find a similar mingling of the inexplicable and the coincidental. An English gentleman by the name of James one night experiences a vision of his brother John dressed in white. He is uncertain of the meaning of the vision, but resists the temptation to attribute it to supernatural forces, believing it instead to be a symptom of some physiological malady. At that very moment, however, news arrives that his brother is gravely ill. He immediately travels to his brother's house, where he finds him lying close to death and dressed, as the vision had foretold, all in white. John raises himself in bed: '"JAMES, YOU HAVE SEEN ME BEFORE, TO-NIGHT – AND YOU KNOW IT!" And so died!'

The clunking machinery of both these plots will no doubt strike the modern reader as fanciful and superficial. Yet that is Dickens's point: he is using the sensational and supernatural as a means of exposing the limitations and blind-spots in our rational thinking. At the conclusion of the second story, the couriers mysteriously disappear, 'so noiselessly that the ghostly mountain might have absorbed them into its eternal snows', leaving the narrator alone and baffled, not only as to the meanings of the tales he has heard, but as to the very existence of the couriers themselves. To the scientific mind, such events are explicable as coincidence or as the products of distorted imagining, but the open-endedness of Dickens's story preserves at least the possibility that they are the result of supernatural agency at large in the world. And this was the role that Dickens always envisaged for the short story – to recapture for the modern, grown-up reader the fantastic world of the fairy tale read in childhood. Throughout his short fiction from the 1850s on, we find Dickens dramatizing such encounters between the citizens of a technological, industrial modernity and the inexplicable forces of chance, fate, the imagination and the supernatural. As he put it in an article called 'Frauds on the Fairies', published soon after 'To Be Read At Dusk', his interest was in staging the 'fairy literature of . . . childhood' in the midst of the contemporary 'utilitarian age'.[7]

The collision between utility and fancy, physic and metaphysic, is clearly evident in the *Mugby Junction* stories of 1866, a series of narratives set around a fictionalized version of Rugby Junction, whose complex of railway lines are said, in one of the stories, to look like 'a great Industrial Exhibition of the works of extraordinary ground spiders that spun iron'. 'No. 1 Branch Line. The Signalman' tells of the narrator's encounter with a railway signalman and the latter's death beneath the wheels of a passing train. The story is structured around an opposition between the rational, enquiring narrator and the troubled signalman who is convinced he is haunted by a spectre foretelling imminent death on the railway line. The narrator is sceptical and seeks plausible explanations to counter the signalman's distress, arguing that 'remarkable coincidence' can 'deeply . . . impress' the fallible human mind. But throughout the story, Dickens invests the phenomenal world of the railway, including its modern paraphernalia of electricity and telegraphy, with a mysterious agency and power. For all his rationality, the narrator is concerned that in the signalman he might be dealing with a 'spirit' rather than a man, and soon superstitious fears of his own begin to shape his encounter with the railway: 'Just then, there came a vague vibration in the earth and air, quickly changing into a violent pulsation, and an oncoming rush that caused me to start back, as though it had force to draw me down.' At the end of the story, the narrator resiles entirely from any attempt to explain the remarkable series of coincidences that attended the signalman's death, preferring instead to list these without presuming to know their meaning or significance.

What 'The Signalman' reveals is the extent to which Dickens conceived of the short story as an essentially anti-modern form – anti-modern both in the sense that it was an opportunity for him to reproduce the ancient pleasures of storytelling through a melodramatic repertoire of heightened sensation, coincidence, suspense and sudden revelation, and in that it provided a means of testifying to dimensions of phenomena and experience that lie beyond the comprehension of the modern, materialistic mind. In the way that they resist the plausible, reasonable, credible version of events, making room always for the uncanny and the spiritual, Dickens's short stories can be read, then, as gestures of resistance to the dominant tide of the mid-Victorian era of industrial development and scientific progress.

A similar back-formation is observable in the short fiction of Thomas Hardy. Powered by improbable coincidence and dramatic convolution, Hardy's stories too deal with the supernatural and with dimensions of experience rooted in the pre-modern past. As he put it in a letter of 23 February 1893, 'We tale-tellers are all Ancient Mariners, and none of us is warranted in stopping Wedding Guests (in other words, the hurrying public) unless he has something more unusual to relate than the ordinary experience of every average man and woman.'[8]

Hardy's conception of the short story as first and foremost a mode of popular entertainment bespeaks a wish to preserve and revitalize the form's attachment to oral, communal tale-telling traditions – traditions he believed were rapidly vanishing in an urbanized, print-literate culture. Repetitive, formulaic and dependably emphatic in nature, Hardy's tales of supernatural and occultish forces, far-fetched coincidence and numinous awe, violent passion and high adventure are typically structured around a series of suspenseful enigmas which are then resolved by some dramatic and highly visible contrivance in the action. In 'The Three Strangers' (1883), for example, events are set in motion with the arrival at a lonely country cottage one stormy night of the three eponymous, enigmatic strangers. Uncertainty about their motives and identities ensues among the guests at the cottage. The first stranger arouses mild suspicion on account of his rough attire and his request for some tobacco, despite his obvious lack of a pipe to smoke it in. The second stranger, dressed in cinder-grey, foregrounds his enigmatic status by composing riddles as to his identity. Just as it is discovered that he is a hangman there to carry out an execution at the neighbouring jail, the third stranger comes to the door. 'Can you tell me the way to – ?' is all he says before fleeing, apparently at the sight of the hangman. News then breaks that a prisoner has escaped from the jail, and it is deduced that the third stranger must be the escapee. The guests give chase, and the third stranger is caught. However, he proves not to be the escapee, but the escapee's brother who had come to visit the condemned man on the night before his execution. The condemned man is now identified as the first stranger, who has by this time fled the cottage.

At the level of plot, the story is clearly organized towards closure, that point of *dis*closure which functions to dissolve the enigma surrounding the identity and purpose of each of the strangers. The disruption that their presence causes is healed by a settling reinstatement of intelligibility both for the characters in the story, who now have answers to their questions – 'But what is the man's calling, and where is he of . . . ?' – and for the reader in whom anxiety was created by the initial reticence of the text in supplying the solution (which the text, of course, always 'knows') to its enigma. Consequently, we are able to attribute function retrospectively to every narrative detail: we now know why the first stranger had no tobacco, pipe or tin; we know why he was so poorly dressed; we can even supply the destination sought by the third stranger, 'Can you tell me the way to – ?': he was looking for the prison. Revelation of the 'truth' about the strangers is the *raison d'être* of the story; in Roland Barthes's terms, it is 'what is *at the end* of [the] expectation' generated by the narrative.[9]

As with Dickens, the only things that remain inexplicable in Hardy's stories are the forces of coincidence or supernaturalism that intervene in human affairs – 'spectres, mysterious voices, intuitions, omens, dreams, haunted places, etc. etc.',[10] as Hardy himself described them. As befits the tradition of the oral tale, in which, as E. M. Forster once remarked, the cave-dwelling teller had to hold the attention of his auditors lest they grow weary and kill him,[11] extraordinary, fantastical, and coincidental pleasures proliferate. In 'The Withered Arm' (1888), for example, a young wife is instructed to touch with her afflicted limb the neck of a recently hanged convict in order to lift the curse that has been placed on her, while 'Fellow-Townsmen' (1880) turns on several outrageous coincidences and equally unlikely near-misses. At one point in that story, the central character learns of the death of his loathed wife, determines, on the eve of her departure for India, to propose to the woman he *should* have married in the first place, and discovers that she is in fact about to be wed in private to his best friend – all this in the space of a morning, and as part of a narrative that has included the miraculous resuscitation of a woman declared dead by drowning. Intent on rendering the implacable forces of chance and fate, Hardy grants his characters little by way of agency or an effectual inner life: rather, what happens to them, or upon them, proves decisive and irresistible. When a character does take matters into his or her own hands, their efforts are more often than not undone by some outlandish contrivance of ill-luck. In 'The Grave by the Handpost' (1897), a sergeant-major takes his own life only to have the suicide note, in which he states his wish to be buried beside his father, accidentally overlooked until after his funeral in a remote churchyard, while in 'Interlopers at the Knap' (1884), fate is similarly compelling, intervening to ensure that a young man's intention to marry is shaken by the sudden vision, in the dress he has purchased for his fiancée, of the woman he once loved.

If it is fate that governs the lives of Hardy's characters in the short stories, it is history that controls the authorial imagination. In the prefaces he attached to his collections, Hardy often stresses the material accuracy and factual basis of the stories, offering clarifications and corrections wherever his fiction appears to conflict with the historical record. The preface to *Wessex Tales*, for example, contains the following statement about 'The Withered Arm':

> Since writing this story some years ago I have been reminded by an aged friend who knew 'Rhoda Brook' [the name of a character in the story] that, in relating her dream, my forgetfulness has weakened the facts out of which the tale grew. In reality it was while lying down on a hot afternoon that the incubus oppressed her and she flung it off, with the results upon the body of the original as described. To my mind the occurrence of such a vision in the daytime is more impressive than if it had happened in a midnight dream. Readers are therefore asked to correct the misrelation, which affords an instance of how our imperfect memories insensibly formalize the fresh originality of living fact – from whose shape they slowly depart, as machine-made castings depart by degrees from the sharp hand-work of the mould.

That final image, of the flaws that inevitably accumulate in any reproductive process, is a telling indication of how Hardy views his stories – less acts of literary invention than heirlooms, vessels transmitting, albeit imperfectly, the precious 'originality' of the rural past to a modern, and by implication less authentic, 'machine-made' world.

It is this mission to testify, as precisely as possible, to an all-but-vanished time and place that can make Hardy's story style appear so novelistic and over-blown, 'like a baby fed on a diet of two-inch steaks and porter', as H. E. Bates so memorably put it.[12] To return to 'The Three Strangers' for a moment, consider the opening paragraph:

> Among the few features of agricultural England which retain an appearance but little modified by the lapse of centuries, may be reckoned the long, grassy and furzy downs, coombs, or ewe-leases, as they are called according to their kind, that fill a large area of certain counties in the south and south-west. If any mark of human occupation is met with hereon, it usually takes the form of the solitary cottage of some shepherd.

This passage would seem to bear out H. E. Bates's theory that Victorian story writers were in thrall to novelistic conventions. The narrative is given its longitudinal and latitudinal coordinates here, its place within a particular rural history and topography, in an effort to attain the compass of the novel.[13] That privileged discourse reappears at the end of the story, completing the narrative frame:

> The grass has long been green on the graves of Shepherd Fennel and his frugal wife; the guests who made up the christening party have mainly followed their entertainers to the tomb; the baby in whose honour they all had met is a matron in sere and yellow leaf. But the arrival of the three strangers at the shepherd's that night, and the details connected therewith, is a story as well known as ever in the country about Higher Crowstairs.

The events in this story are here placed within a conclusive historical narrative. Just as the enigma of the strangers was resolved for the characters in the story, so the frame offers to resolve any indeterminacy, tie up any conceivable loose ends, that the brevity of presentation might have created. It is as though the short story form presents a danger in that its very shortness tends towards enigma, momentariness, open-endedness, ahistorical sequestration – as though the threat to order in the lives of the characters is mirrored by the threat of an ultimately inconclusive narrative and so must be recuperated for the classic realist novelistic enterprise whereby closure is ensured, historical continuity established and interpretative uncertainty eradicated.

Reading both Dickens's and Hardy's stories, one is reminded of Samuel Beckett's comment about the French novelist Honoré de Balzac:

> To read Balzac is to receive the impression of a chloroformed world. He is absolute master of his material, he can do what he likes with it, he can foresee and calculate its least vicissitude. He can write the end of his book before he has finished the first paragraph, because he has turned all his creatures into clockwork cabbages and can rely on their staying put wherever needed or going at whatever speed in whatever direction he chooses.[14]

Like Balzac's, Hardy's fiction world is rigorously teleological, or end-orientated. The details of character and action are entirely subordinated to their plot functions. The difficulties Dickens describes above of achieving effective characterization in the short story are writ large in Hardy: unable to grant them a cumulative reality, he reduces his characters to 'clockwork cabbages' serving a pre-determined plot trajectory. Closure, coherence and unity govern his aesthetic of the short form. Hence the reinforcement of the deterministic plot by the historical and topographical contextualization of the adventure of the strangers in a narrative frame. Hardy's need to place the action of his story within a long-range continuum of events, people, places suggests that he considered the short story a potentially atomistic and discontinuous form.

Such a view of the short story contrasts tellingly with Henry James's praise of the French author Guy de Maupassant and his gifts of characterization: 'These are never prolonged nor analytic,' says James, 'have nothing of enumeration, of the quality of the observer, who counts the items to be sure he has made up the sum . . . His eye selects unerringly'.[15] As James recognized, the short story could be something more, something other than a cut-down novel. The true art of it lay in the skill with which the writer could handle techniques of selection, distillation and suggestion. Though James himself rarely practised what he preached, other writers were, by the 1890s, beginning to explore the art of writing 'short' in ways that he suggested. It is with these writers, the subject of the next two chapters, that the short story enters its decisively modern phase in England.

Chapter 2

Rudyard Kipling and Joseph Conrad

In a career spanning some six decades, Rudyard Kipling authored in excess of 350 short stories. His first collection, *Plain Tales From the Hills*, appeared in 1888, his last, *Limits and Renewals*, in 1932. In the early 1890s, when his stories of India first reached a mass audience, he was hailed as the coming man of English letters. His contemporaries credited him with having reinvented the short story, raising it to the status of a serious art form. He persisted through the high-tide of European modernism and the First World War, continuing to develop in his writing themes and ideas that had detained him in his early work: the relationship between creativity and the imagination, the boundaries between the real and the supernatural, the ideology and workings of empire, the personal and emotional costs of war. He wrote many poems as well as novels, essays and criticism, but the best of his creative energies he saved for the literary form best suited to his particular constellation of talents: the short story.

It is all the more remarkable, then, that the two most influential and eloquent critics of short fiction in the twentieth century, H. E. Bates and Frank O'Connor, should have been so damning of Kipling and his achievement in the form. O'Connor, to be fair, at least pays close attention to the work, identifying the failings of what he calls Kipling's 'oratorical' narrative style, his manner of addressing the reader 'as an audience who, at whatever cost to the artistic properties, must be reduced to tears or laughter or rage'.[1] Bates, on the other hand, is unguarded in his contempt not just for the 'moral pseudo-Biblical tone' of Kipling's writing, but for the man himself. He attacks Kipling as an apologist for empire who used his talent 'to make palatable both episodes and the creeds inspiring them, when otherwise they would have been wholly disgusting'. Writing in the early years of the Second World War, Bates found particularly repellent what he took to be Kipling's 'almost mystical' sublimation of the biases of 'blood, creed, and class' that underlay right-wing imperialist ideology. Comparing him with his European contemporaries Anton Chekhov and Guy de Maupassant, he considered him wanting in essential qualities of humane 'affection' and 'tolerance', and guilty of peddling 'a harsh, confused, egotistical mysticism [. . .] vulgar and cruel in its class intolerance'.[2]

In recent years, Kipling has met with more sensitive, less tendentious appraisers. The ironic complexity of his work, and the textual manifestations of his ambivalence towards empire and about war, have been brought to the fore, qualifying the portrait of a right-wing ideologue that George Orwell, another wartime author, suggested had reduced Kipling, by the time of his death, to little more than a 'by-word'.[3] Yet for the student of the short story, there remains the nagging difficulty of assessing Kipling's contribution to the development of the form. He seems at once an inveterate traditionalist and a bold experimenter, a writer as fond of familiar story structures as he was elsewhere determined to break them down. Widely celebrated for his popular tales of adventure and exoticism, he at the same time crafted beguilingly enigmatic and disturbing insights into human consciousness and its encounters with the apparatus of technological modernity. Such range and inconsistency gives rise to critical hesitation, for depending on which stories one refers to, it is as easy to champion Kipling as a peripheral modernist as it is to dismiss him, *pace* Bates and O'Connor, as an outmoded conventionalist, faltering well into the new century under the artistic and ideological burdens of the old.

Yet if Kipling's inconsistency and eclecticism are frustrating, they are also illuminating, for they reveal much about the changing character of the short story in the period from the 1890s to the 1930s. During these decades, the span of Kipling's working life, the short story underwent a profound transformation, emerging from the shadows of the Victorian novel to occupy a place at the very centre of British literary culture. Kipling's oeuvre, in its sheer variety, helps us to narrate that transformation. Embodying simultaneously the spirit of oral tale-telling traditions while breaking new ground in narrative technique, for example by mimicking cinematic devices, his stories look both forward and back. Moreover, they straddle the divide between popular 'middlebrow' entertainment, and high-literary experimentalism, a divide that, as we shall see later, was fundamental to modernism and its self-definitions.

These two tendencies, the innovative and the preservative, are in evidence throughout Kipling's work. Sometimes, as in 'The Wish House' (1924), they combine to thrilling effect. In that story, a dying woman tells her friend of how, through the supernatural agency of a 'wish house', she has transferred to herself all the pain and suffering of the man she loves but whom she cannot possess. Her mortal sickness is the price she pays for his continuing life and well-being. What is remarkable about the story is the way Kipling folds this extraordinary scenario into a study in social and psychological realism. The gothic mysteriousness of the 'wish house' is not what motivates the narrative or intrigues the reader; indeed, the house itself figures only briefly, and what happens in it is only cursorily sketched out. The enigmatic centre of 'The Wish House' is, rather, the two elderly women, Mrs Ashcroft and Mrs Fettley, whose conversation, over tea and muffins, composes the bulk of the story. Kipling goes to some lengths to embed the women, through their language and behaviour, in a specific social and class milieu. They converse in regionally marked speech, discussing such trivialities as Mrs Ashcroft's new church visitor and indulging in the kind of platitudes, for example about the laziness of contemporary youth and its obliviousness to the value of money, that women of their generation might be expected to make. With the same matter-of-factness, however, they also discuss the powers of the 'wish house'. At one point, Mrs Ashcroft wonders if the pain she suffers on behalf of the man she loves will be counted in her favour by the supernatural forces should he try to marry anyone else. 'It ought to be, dearie', Mrs Fettley remarks. 'It ought to be'. That the women accept it as a part of ordinary experience focuses our attention beyond the paranormality of the 'wish house' and on to the women themselves.

And it is here, in the women's histories and motives, that the real puzzle of 'The Wish House' resides. Kipling's presentation of the women is disturbingly elliptical, the narrative withdrawing into silence and impercipience at crucial moments. One blatant ellipsis is apparent near the beginning of the story, where a lengthy account of Mrs Fettley's past life is cleaved away, leaving only a brief and ambiguous trace for the reader to ponder. Kipling teases us by alluding to the emotional seriousness of Mrs Fettley's revelation – 'Mrs. Fettley had spoken very precisely for some time without interruption, before she wiped her eyes' – but what moved her so we are never told. The narrative, that is, advertises what it leaves unsaid. Equally enigmatic is Mrs Ashcroft's character, even though she provides a much fuller account of herself than her companion. Various motives for her obsessive passion are hinted at, but none prevails as definitive. Indeed, the reader frequently lurches between admiration, intrigue and repulsion regarding Mrs Ashcroft's behaviour. A psychopathology is hinted at more than once. For example, she thinks that if she had let Harry (the man she loved) die, rather than taking his ailments upon herself, then she would have been able better to possess him: ''Arry bein' *dead*, like, 'e'd ha' been mine, till Judgment'. At other times she seems almost manically self-involved, pulling away from Mrs Fettley when the other offers a comforting hand on her arm. At the end of the story, she assumes an almost emblematic stature, as an exemplar of human forbearance in the face of suffering. 'It *do* count, don't it – de pain?' she asks her friend, a question that goes right to the ambiguous heart of the Kipling's narrative.

Combining the suspenseful intrigue and plot-based intricacy of the traditional tale with the elliptical austerity of a modern realist narrative technique was the dominant design in Kipling's fiction. One sees it in the early stories of imperial India, such as 'In the House of Suddhoo' (*Plain Tales from the Hills* (1888)), 'Without Benefit of Clergy' and 'On Greenhow Hill' (*Life's Handicap* (1891)), as well in later, more expansive works such as 'Mary Postgate' (*A Diversity of Creatures* (1917)), 'The Wish House' and 'Dayspring Mishandled' (*Limits and Renewals* (1932)). In all these stories, the sequential action, rich in decisive incident, coexists with a complex and frequently ambiguous narrative discourse. In 'In the House of Suddhoo', for example, the narrator, who confidently and humorously exposes the workings of a clairvoyant sorcerer as so many tricks and deceptions, finds himself caught up in a situation he cannot control, critically implicated in a scenario of vengeance and, more than likely, bloodshed. Initially declaring himself 'the chorus who comes in at the end to explain things', he is by the end of the story able only to testify to his own helplessness in the face of the destructive forces of human darkness that surround and threaten to surmount him. In 'Dayspring Mishandled', similarly, what starts out as an ornate revenge plot, a melodramatic tale of literary jealousy involving a forged medieval manuscript, becomes a disturbingly enigmatic portrait of obsession and moral duplicity. While the revenge plot, in which a failed writer, Manallace, seeks to ruin his more successful associate Castorley, a literary critic, by duping him into believing that he has discovered a lost manuscript by Chaucer, is brought to a conclusion with the premature death of Castorley, the story is replete with unresolved questions, particularly concerning the motives and behaviour of Manallace and Castorley's wife, and of the narrator. Again, it is Kipling's elliptical presentation that gives rise to these complications, for he has the story told by an unnamed first-person narrator who is studiedly impercipient when it comes to commenting upon the conduct of the main players, even though he is intimately involved with them, and is even implicated in the lies that Manallace tells. The major events of the narrative – the unravelling of Manallace's scheme, Castorley's sickness and dying, Lady Castorley's taking up with her dead husband's physician – are conveyed with little or no evaluative commentary, so that the reader is left to puzzle over the motives and morality not only of the characters, but of the narrator too. The tale that is told can be easily recounted, but the question of who tells it, and why, is impossible to determine.

Of course, creating a sense of the mysterious and inexplicable was, as we saw in the previous chapter, a characteristic of the oral tale-telling tradition that Hardy and, to a lesser extent, Dickens drew upon in their short stories. The difference with Kipling, however, is that the interrogative quality of his writing is produced not by the strangeness of what is described, but by estrangement in the narrative discourse itself. That is to say, while inexplicable things might happen in a Hardy story, the narration remains stable, secure in its omniscience. Kipling, on the other hand, deliberately generates inconsistency and provisionality by withholding the crucial orientational material that we require in order to make sense of the story. He describes this discovery of the intensifying effects of strategic omission in his notoriously gap-ridden autobiography, *Something of Myself* (1937):

> A tale from which pieces has been raked out is like a fire that has been poked. One does not know that the operation has been performed, but everyone feels the effect. Note, though, that the excised stuff must have been honestly written for inclusion. I found that when, to save trouble, I 'wrote short' *ab initio* [from the beginning] much salt went out of the work.[4]

Some years later, Ernest Hemingway would offer an almost identical formulation of his own short story technique. Describing how he had omitted the original ending of his story 'Out of Season', Hemingway outlined his 'theory that you could omit anything if you knew what you omitted and the omitted part would strengthen the story and make people feel something more than they understood'.[5] In both cases, the shortness of the short story is being treated as a 'positive', i.e., positively disruptive, quality; the act of excising makes for a creative strengthening of the narrative. It is an insight that the modernists, Hemingway among them, would pursue to ever more adventurous ends.

Given Kipling's sensitivity to the aesthetics of narrative fiction, it is all the more curious that successive generations of critics should have been so determined to exclude him from the mainstream modernist canon. It is worth remembering that Kipling wrote and published in the same period as James Joyce, Katherine Mansfield, T. S. Eliot and Virginia Woolf; and while his fiction continued to utilize established story-telling conventions, pieces like 'Mrs. Bathurst' (1904), 'Mary Postgate' (1917), 'The Wish House' (1924), 'On the Gate' (1926) and 'Dayspring Mishandled' (1932) are every bit as restless and innovative as the stories in *Dubliners*. The reasons for Kipling's neglect as a writer of 'serious' literature in the modernist period can be traced back to the 1890s and the alignment of realist modes of fiction with avant-garde literary values (for more on this see chapter 3). Crudely stated, his fondness for the extraordinary, the magical and the exotic marked him out as a writer inclined to mass-market populism. Meanwhile, his reputation as an apologist for imperialism lost him favour with the liberal intelligentsia, who, in the early decades of the twentieth century, were responsible for establishing literary criticism as a professional academic discipline.

For the present-day reader, however, and especially for the student of the short story, it is Kipling's engagement, through both content and form, with the experience and conditions of modernity that is the most striking and significant thing about his work. If one were pressed to single out a story that exemplifies Kipling at his most intrepid and innovative, it would be 'Mrs. Bathurst' (1904). Set in 1902, around the end of the Boer War (1902), it takes the form of a conversation among four men in a bar in South Africa, two of whom, Pyecroft and Pritchard, relate their acquaintance with the woman of the title. Pritchard tells of his encounter with Mrs Bathurst, a hotel-keeper, while on shore leave near Auckland, New Zealand, but this soon gives way to Pyecroft's lengthy narrative about her relationship with Vickery, a sailor who has deserted the navy and whose whereabouts, as Pyecroft embarks on his story, are unknown. He remembers how in Cape Town he would accompany Vickery to viewings of a visiting cinematograph (a new invention of the time), where an early film of passengers alighting a train in London was showing. In the film, Mrs Bathurst would appear, walking down the platform towards the camera and passing out of shot. After numerous nightly viewings, Vickery, on the verge of insanity with longing, guilt and regret (we infer that he deceived Mrs Bathurst about his being married), goes absent-without-leave from his ship.

The question of what Mrs Bathurst was doing in London when the film was shot (Vickery claims she was looking for him) is but one of the many mysteries that Kipling's story sets in motion and only partially resolves for the reader. Equally unclear is what precisely takes place between Vickery and Mrs Bathurst and what subsequently becomes of them. Precisely what does Vickery disclose to his ship's captain before deserting? And why, moreover, does he desert when, if what he says is true, he is close to pensionable retirement, widowed and presumably free to marry? Does he stop to see Mrs Bathurst after he absconds? And what is the memento that the railway employee Hooper reaches into his pocket for at the end of the story, but does not show to the others? One could go on like this, listing the enigmas Kipling's text instates and conspicuously refuses to dispel. The narrative drive of 'Mrs. Bathurst' is produced in precisely the same way as Hardy's 'The Three Strangers', but where the point of Hardy's tale is the resolution of the questions that the story itself prompts us to ask, Kipling provides only fragments and glimpses of the 'whole truth' of what happened. In this respect, his narrative resembles the cinematographic technology it so memorably depicts. Just as Mrs Bathurst disappears off the side of the screen, 'walk[s] right out o' the picture', so Vickery is lost to view in Pyecroft's account of him after he deserts. It is reasonable to infer that it is his corpse that Hooper describes encountering at the end of the story, but this fact, if that's what it is, is just one more partial sighting, one more intriguing glimpse, of Vickery. It is the most superficial of resolutions as it neither confounds nor confirms a single detail about him, nor breaks the 'silence' into which he has withdrawn. He is no more tangible in Hooper's telling than was the figure of Mrs Bathurst on the cinema screen. 'Mrs. Bathurst' confirms Kipling's intuition about the suggestive power of elliptical writing, about the importance of withholding as much as one discloses in a short story. Meaning is not curtailed by the artfully compressed narrative in the way that Dickens had feared, but in fact multiplies and resonates: as the critic William Empson put it, 'ambiguity is a phenomenon of compression'.[6]

It is sometimes easy to overlook the interrogative complexity of Kipling's narratives, so full of incident are they and so accustomed have we become to thinking of plot and dramatic action as the hallmarks of superficiality and populism in modern fiction. Something similar can be said about Joseph Conrad, a writer who, like Kipling, adopted many of the familiar conventions of the mass-market magazine story, but who embedded these in enigmatic and frequently ironic narrative structures.

Conrad came to the short story during the periodicals publishing boom of the 1890s (of which more in chapter 3). He wanted to make money, principally, but he was also eager to court the good opinion of influential editors like William Ernest Henley and break into avant-garde literary circles. Most of the stories he wrote during the 1890s were composed with a particular journal in mind, whether it be Henley's conservative *National Observer* and *New Review*, John Lane and Henry Harland's decadent *Yellow Book*, or Arthur Symons's wilfully avant-garde *Savoy*. His early efforts in the form reflect both his uncertainty about what the short story could do and the range and variety of fiction that the vast periodicals market could at that time accommodate. Likewise, his first volume of stories, *Tales of Unrest* (1898), betrays both a great gift for the form and considerable confusion about what do with it. In 'The Return', for example, Conrad tries unsuccessfully to mimic the 'bad marriage' story that was a fixture of the *Yellow Book*. Here, a melodramatic study of domestic conflict centring on a man's discovery that his wife is having an affair becomes the occasion for a heavy-handed, high-minded discourse on the 'impenetrable duplicity' of modern women and the cosmic workings of the 'Inscrutable Creator of good and evil . . . the Master of doubts and impulses'. Equally arch is 'The Idiots', a lurid, semi-mythical narrative which tells of a married couple, Jean-Pierre and Susan Bacadou, and the series of outrageous misfortunes and improbable back luck that besets them, culminating in his murder and her suicide. As in 'The Return', Conrad uses the story as a platform on which to set out his tragic-comic vision of humanity and the pointlessness of suffering beneath a 'high and impassive heaven'.

'The Idiots' is in many respects about indeterminacy and the absence of meaning, but it is in no sense an indeterminate story. The precariousness it records is not a feature of its narration, which remains robustly objective and uncompromised. Elsewhere, however, in the more successful parts of *Tales of Unrest*, Conrad's narrators exhibit an exhilarating *lack* of purchase over what they describe. 'Karain: A Memory' marks a decisive moment of development in Conrad's short story art, for it is there that he first begins to explore the destabilizing consequences of the frame-narrator, a device that would come to dominate his mature fiction. As we have seen in the case of Hardy and Dickens, the tale-within-a-tale was one way in which the nineteenth century short story retained the appearance of a direct connection to oral narrative traditions. Conrad, on the other hand, saw how the framing device could be used to draw attention to the partial, provisional nature of storytelling. What Henry James called Conrad's 'wandering, circling, yearning, imaginative faculty'[7] found formal expression in elaborate, indirect narrative structures where two, or sometimes more, narrators would present the story, each inside the other, creating a Chinese-box effect. In such stories, the reader is constructed as an auditor, a listener-in to various and often discrepant 'oral' accounts, and his or her task is to mediate among these and get to the truth of what happened. Of course, we never get to that truth: to adopt a typically Conradian metaphor, we never get to the 'heart' of the matter, for the stories we hear are partial, subjective, impressionistic and always insidiously qualified.

'Karain' is composed from three points-of-view: the anonymous frame narrator, the titular character and, in a coda to the story, the narrator's companion Jackson, who has also heard Karain's tale of vengeance, betrayal and guilt. From the outset, our attention is drawn not to the story Karain tells, but to the manner of the telling and, by extension, to the man himself. His narrative is described as a 'performance', an 'illusion', an 'accomplished acting of [. . .] amazing pretences', and his behaviour – his rhetorical gusto and staged dignity – as an 'elaborate front', 'ornate and disturbing', hiding what the narrator fears is a 'horrible void'.

Yet if the narrator means to raise doubts and questions about Karain's authority and sincerity, both as a storyteller and as a ruler of men, then he fails, for his own narrative authority leaks away in precisely the same doubts and questions. The portrait of Karain as pompous and performative, we must realize, is a construct of the narrator, and as the story unfolds it is the biases and prejudices shaping that portrait that come into focus. Foremost among these is the narrator's belief in Western rational empiricism. He considers Karain a 'wanderer coming suddenly from a world of sunshine and illusions'; faced with his passionate insusceptibility to reason, he feels 'a protection and relief' in the 'firm, pulsating beat of the two ship's chronometers ticking off steadily the seconds of Greenwich time'; and when at the end of the story Jackson admits to a lingering belief in the tale Karain told, the narrator laughs at his credulousness, directing his attention instead to the tangible, material reality of the busy urban street on which they are standing, with its hansome cabs and omnibuses and helmeted policemen, and concluding that his friend has 'been too long away from home'. Yet Jackson is unconvinced and persists in feeling that the city and the technological modernity of which it is part is 'no more real' to him than 'the other thing . . . say, Karain's story'.

The effect of this ending is not simply to expose the biases of the narrator, but to undo the very concept of narrative closure itself. The narrator fancies that he can capture the meaning of Karain by revealing him to be a man of 'primitive ideas' whose self-exulting rhetoric masks a 'profound ignorance of the rest of the world'. Yet Conrad ensures that this account of Karain, while it may be the dominant one in the story, is far from determinate. The central character floats free, so to say, of the narrator's attempt to narrativize him. This spectacle of an emasculated narration recurs throughout Conrad's mature work and, as with Kipling, it cuts against the powerful desire that his incident-rich stories inevitably excite in the reader for closure and resolution. In 'Amy Foster' (1903), we are treated to the elaborate story of a Polish sailor, Yanko Goorall, who, shipwrecked off the coast of England, is found dazed and wandering in Romney Marsh, Kent. In an act of 'impulsive pity', Amy Foster feeds him bread, so beginning the process of his gradual assimilation to the local community. After the two marry and have a child, however, his foreign habits and behaviour begin to trouble Amy, and she fears he may be harming their son. When Yanko is struck down with a mysterious lung condition, Amy withdraws from him further still, refusing to nurse him and instead harbouring an 'unaccountable fear' of him. When at the height of his fever he begs her for water in his native tongue, she believes he is trying to attack her and flees the cottage with her child. Yanko collapses with dehydration and dies from heart failure.

Such an account conveys nothing, however, of the interrogative complexity of Conrad's narrative, which again deploys the frame-narrator device in order to place the story at two removes from the reader. The frame-narrator gets the story of Amy and Yanko from a Dr Kennedy, the village physician, who in turn tells the tale as a series of unanswered questions, conjectures and speculations. The predominant mood of Kennedy's narrative is subjunctive, particularly where Amy's 'unreasonable terror' of her husband is concerned. Her attitude to him is as much a puzzle to Kennedy as it is to the reader: 'I wondered

whether his difference, his strangeness, were not penetrating with repu
that dull nature they had begun by irresistibly attracting. I wondered . . .' ....
Yanko's fate accounted for, the main focus of Kennedy's narrative falls on Amy
herself; but she proves wholly inscrutable. Kennedy finds it 'impossible' to
say what Amy thinks or feels about anything relating to her husband's death,
thereby leaving in play any number of possible explanations of what nestles
in that 'dull nature'. Is she malevolent, callous, indifferent, ignorant, envious,
hysterical or genuinely afraid? All of these accounts of Amy are supported by
the text. Kennedy, for his part, makes no attempt at the end to settle on any one
of them, preferring instead merely to state the questions about Amy as he sees
them, and to wonder at the tragedy of human isolation, 'the supreme disaster
of loneliness and despair'.

Trepidatious narrators like Kennedy are to be found throughout Conrad's
mature fiction, from 'The Anarchist', 'Il Conde' ('The Count') and 'The
Informer', published together in *A Set of Six* (1908), through 'The Secret Sharer'
(1912) to 'The Tale' (1925), the last short story he wrote. With increasing bold-
ness, Conrad omitted determinate material from his narratives, leaving more
and more to the reader's imagination and further complicating our response
to his frame-narrators. In one of his 'Author's Notes', he made the following
comment on 'Il Conde':

> Il Conde . . . is almost a verbatim transcript of the tale told me by a very
> charming old gentleman whom I met in Italy . . . Anyone can see that it
> is something more than a verbatim report, but where he left off and I
> began must be left to the acute discrimination of the reader who may be
> interested in the problem . . . What I am certain of, however, is that it is
> not to be solved, for I am not at all clear about it myself by this time. All
> I can say is that the personality of the narrator was extremely suggestive,
> quite apart from the story he was telling me.[8]

'Il Conde' is one of Conrad's most beguiling and intricately structured narratives. As these comments suggest, the challenge of the story lies in our response
to the narrator who relates the tale given to him by the Count. As the Count tells
it, he has suffered the most 'abominable adventure', being robbed at knife-point
and subsequently stalked by a young man whom he has encountered while trav-
elling alone in Southern Italy. The narrator is sympathetic and apparently so
convinced of the 'fundamental refinement of nature about the man' that he is
happy to conclude that there was nothing 'disreputable' about his encounter
with the young man, and that the Count was simply a victim of a predator. Yet
in voicing the possibility that there may be elements of the Count's conduct that
could, in certain quarters, be construed as disreputable, the narrator reveals a

deliberate bias in his account. I say 'deliberate', but it is not at all clear how far we can take the narrator's obvious collusion with the Count's story as evidence of an attempt to cover over impropriety in the Count's behaviour (in which case he is an unreliable narrator) or a genuine, gullible belief that what he is being told is the truth. Either way, a gap quickly opens up between the reader's response to the Count's story and the narrator's, for there is much to suggest that the Count is homosexual and that he is victimized, not randomly, but on account of his susceptibility to attractive young men. How far the narrator knows or understands this is impossible to determine. He recognizes that he is relating a 'deucedly queer story', but whether that comment, with its obvious homosexual overtones, is offered knowingly or innocently we cannot say. Once again, we advance through the layers of Conrad's narrative only to find an ungraspable enigma at its centre.

Similarly intangible is the conclusion to 'The Informer', the convoluted account of a 'conspiracy within a conspiracy' involving an anarchist terrorist group in London. Here, the unnamed frame-narrator reports what he was told by a third party, the mysterious 'Mr X', whom a friend of the narrator's has recommended as 'the greatest rebel . . . of modern times'. In the manner of a detective fiction, Mr X's narrative describes the series of events by which a young member of the anarchist group, Sevrin, is uncovered as an informer. The unmasking of Sevrin provides the dramatic climax to the tale, but in the short coda which follows Conrad performs a characteristic ratio upon the narrative, abruptly opening up new perspectives on the story we have just been reading and casting doubt on the status and motives of those engaged in telling it. In the final scene, the frame-narrator describes a meeting with the friend who had introduced him to Mr X, at which he gives vent to feeling that X's 'cynicism was simply abominable'. The friend agrees, but also cautions that X 'likes to have his little joke sometimes'. The narrator admits that he 'fail[s] to understand the connection of this last remark' and that he has since been 'utterly unable to discover where in all this the joke comes in'. For the reader, however, the possibility exists that X's cynical treatment of the anarchists in his tale has all been a ploy designed to outrage the sensibilities of his auditor, the gullible frame-narrator, whose subsequent outrage is evidence that he has 'fallen' for the joke. Then again, perhaps the narrator is not as gullible as he seems, and by his comment that he is 'unable to discover where in all this the joke comes in' he means that he is conscious of, but not amused by, the manipulations of X – that is to say, he 'gets' the joke, but sees beyond it, into the pitiless heart of X's cynicism. Either way, we find ourselves in the presence not of an unreliable narrator as such, but of a narrator the ambivalence of whose closing remarks reflects the impossibility of disentangling the truth of what happened from the act of telling it.

Like Kipling, Conrad's relationship to the literary avant-garde of his day was problematic. To a great extent, as I implied earlier, this is because his fondness for traditional story forms brought him into conflict with a cultural elite that increasingly defined itself in terms of its difference from, and opposition to, popular modes of entertainment. From early in his career, Conrad was conscious of his position as an outsider and regarded with a mixture of envy and suspicion the activities of the London literati. As we saw in the case of 'The Return', he struggled to imitate the introspective domestic dramas that had by the 1890s come to dominate highbrow magazines like *The Yellow Book*, and it was not until he earned the imprimatur of William Ernest Henley that he felt he had achieved recognition as a writer of serious literary fiction. That such recognition was bound up in the cultural politics and commercial intrigues of periodical publishing tells us a good deal about the circumstances surrounding the formation of modernist values and attitudes. In the next chapter, I will explore more fully the relationship between the 1890s avant-garde magazine and the short story in order to show how the form came to occupy so prominent a position within British literary culture at the turn of the twentieth century.

Chapter 3

The *Yellow Book* circle and the 1890s avant-garde

Ever since it first appeared in 1894, the *Yellow Book* has been a by-word for *fin-de-siècle* decadence and literary avant-gardism in England. Published by John Lane and edited by Henry Harland, it was marketed from the outset as a product for the discerning consumer, its bright yellow hardback casing, high-quality, spaciously margined paper and risqué illustrations making it look and feel distinctly 'adult', and quite unlike any other title on the crowded late-Victorian magazine shelf. Lane's wish, somewhat forlorn in retrospect, was for a periodical that would appeal to a highbrow readership but which would sell widely enough to return a profit against its exorbitant production costs. Harland's overriding concern, on the other hand, was for the quality of the content, especially the verse and prose fiction – so much so that he was willing to subsidize the venture out of his own pocket. The reality that quickly faced both men was a magazine market more complex and fickle than they had ever imagined, and while Lane delighted in the strong sales that notoriety and the whiff of licentiousness early brought, it was precisely the suggestion of luridness that caused the serious writers whom Harland wished to attract (among them Henry James) to want to distance themselves from the journal, and this would eventually prove fatal to the venture.

The problem with the *Yellow Book* in the end was that it fell between two stools, being neither attractive to a popular readership (unwisely, Harland ran several editorial columns attacking the reading habits of the masses), nor sufficiently reputable to secure the work of established writers. For the bulk of the numbers, Harland was forced to depend on lesser-known names such as Hubert Crackanthorpe, Ella D'Arcy, Evelyn Sharp and Netta Syrret, writers whose reputations were never able to generate sales sufficient to make as costly an enterprise as the *Yellow Book* a viable concern in the long run. The journal folded in 1897 after some thirteen issues; yet for all that it was misconceived as a commercial proposition, and for all that its featured authors were, and have remained, relatively obscure, the *Yellow Book* nevertheless played an important role in the development of the short story, raising the status and visibility of the form by aligning it with avant-garde values and interests and, by extension, with broader forces of political and cultural radicalism.

One reason why the short story may have come to play so important a part in the *Yellow Book* was because Harland's personal literary ambitions were centred in it. In his wilfully controversial 'Yellow Dwarf' column, introduced in 1895, he formulated a crude set of aesthetic principles that clearly had in mind the kind of short story he himself aspired to write:

> Some books, in their uncouthness, their awkwardness, their boisterousness, in their violation of the decencies of art, in their low truckling to the tastes of the purchaser, in their commonness, their vulgarity, in their total lack of suppleness and distinction, are the very Dogs of Bookland. The Average Man loves 'em. Such as they are, they're obvious.
>
> And other books, by reason of their beauties and their virtues, their graces and refinements; because they are considered finished; because they are delicate, distinguished, aristocratic; because their touch is light, their movement deft and fleet; because they proceed by omission, by implication and suggestion; because they employ the *demi-mot* and the *nuance*; because, in fine, they are Subtle – other books are the Cats of Bookland. And the Average Man hates them, or ignores them.[1]

The division Harland draws here, between a vulgar popular fiction pandering to the debased judgement of a mass readership and the rarefied activities of the literary avant-garde, was widely observed in the 1890s, and, as I have already suggested, this would become a central plank of modernist self-definition. What is particularly pertinent to the short story, however, is Harland's description of how the avant-garde text proceeds – 'by omission, by implication and suggestion', employing 'the *demi-mot* and the *nuance*'. Harland's vocabulary here echoes that of his hero Henry James and the many other highbrow commentators who, throughout the 1890s, were striving to define a new species of literary short fiction. James was among the first to descry this new form as it drifted in from foreign shores. Writing in 1888 about Ivan Turgenev, James remarked on how for the Russian 'the germ of a story . . . was never an affair of plot – that was the last thing he thought of: it was the representation of certain persons. . . . The thing consists of the motions of a group of selected creatures, which are not the result of a preconceived action, but a consequence of the qualities of the actions'.[2] For James, the point of such stories lay not in the dramatic resolution of the action, but in representation of character, motive and psychology. He drew a distinction between the story that had been governed by incident – the 'adventure comparatively safe, in which you have, for the most part, but to put one foot after the other' – and the new 'plotless' form which deals in 'exposures' and 'glimpses' and which creates instead the 'impression . . . of a complexity or a continuity'. It was this latter, James averred, that was the 'rarer performance', making 'the best of the sport' by being 'as far removed as possible from the snap of the pistol-shot' and so capable of quickening the *literary sensibility*.[3]

James's privileging of psychology over plot, character interiority over external action, and his making this the basis of a discrimination between literary and popular forms of short fiction, was replicated by many other commentators at the time, among them Frederick Wedmore, Daniel Greenleaf Thomson, Brander Matthews (author of the first book-length study of the short story) and, as we have seen, Henry Harland. James's initial enthusiasm for the *Yellow Book* arose because of the journal's willingness to publish short stories of any length – a decisive step, as James saw it, towards freeing the form from generic convention. As he would put it later, Harland's 'small square lemon quarterly' single-handedly 'opened up the millennium to the "short story" in England'.[4] While James himself published only two pieces in the *Yellow Book*, and both of those early in the journal's life, his influence is felt not only in Harland's editorial expostulations but in the work of writers who became the mainstay of the magazine for the duration of its short life.

The most obviously Jamesian of the *Yellow Book* circle was Hubert Crackanthorpe, whom James praised in a posthumous tribute for his willingness to forswear the 'inane' tricks and formal mannerisms of the popular tale – the 'miraculous coincidence', 'hairbreadth escape' and 'simplified sentiment'.[5] Crackanthorpe made a habit of cultivating such influential admirers as James: while in France in the early 1890s he met Emile Zola, Stéphane Mallarmé, André Gide, Henri de Régnier, Paul Bourget and Guy de Maupassant. In England, Arthur Symons, W. B. Yeats and Richard Le Gallienne were among his acquaintances, while as co-editor of the short-lived *Albemarle* magazine he sponsored work by James McNeill Whistler, Walter Sickert and Henri Fantin-Latour. He also became involved at the *Albemarle* with feminist activists such as Elizabeth Holland Hollister and the Countess of Malmesbury and developed an interest, through his reading of George Meredith and the French author Henri Frédéric Amiel, in questions of sexual and gender identity.

By the time he met Harland, Crackanthorpe had already published a volume of stories, *Wreckage* (1892), and was making a name for himself as a writer willing to deal with the seamier, sordid aspects of life, so much so that he had been christened 'the English Zola'.[6] To the second number of the *Yellow Book* he contributed an essay, 'Reticence in Literature', in which, like James, he lauded the achievements of his French contemporaries while setting out the case for a fiction in which the interrogative complexities of character and personality were preferred over the simplistic determinations of plot and action. '[E]very narrative of an external circumstance,' he argued, 'is never anything else than the transcript of the impression produced upon ourselves by that circumstance, and, invariably, a degree of individual interpretation is insinuated into every picture, real or imaginary, however objective it may be.' The writer's task was to represent the inner experience of reality, and that meant abandoning the 'popular' assumption that 'in order to produce good fiction, an ingenious idea, or "plot," as it is termed, is the one thing needed'. This in turn meant that a new audience for fiction would need to be cultivated and educated to appreciate that the 'business of art is, not to explain or describe, but to suggest'.[7]

In the wider cultural context of the 1890s, psychological realism of the sort Crackanthorpe advocated was indissolubly associated with the perceived 'feminization' of social and political life in Britain. The so-called New Woman was a familiar target of misogynistic ridicule throughout the nineties, typically appearing in *Punch* magazine cartoons as a bespectacled androgyne bicycling in bloomers. Women's struggle, however, was not just for political enfranchisement and social equality, but for cultural expression and a literature of their own. For many commentators, the literary avant-garde's fondness for introspective realism was evidence of this spreading, and deleterious, influence of the feminine. Critics such as George Saintsbury, Andrew Lang and H. D. Traill bemoaned the retreat from a masculine literature based around 'exciting events and engaging narrative' into the 'unrelentingly minute portraiture of modern life'. It was a tendency that would leave the 'Coming Man', Lang warned, 'bald, toothless, highly "cultured," and addicted to tales of introspective analysis'.[8] Just as the de-emphasis of plot and action marked off the literary popular forms of fiction, so the same distinction was used to separate out masculine and feminine narrative practices: 'With the story . . . man is mainly concerned,' another reviewer wrote, 'and the character-studies, the descriptions of scenery, and the irrelevant chatter he incontinently skips'.[9]

The rise of 'plotless' psychological realism in the 1890s, then, was closely bound up with gender-political debate, and in particular with anxiety about the diminishment of male cultural authority. And it is precisely this anxiety that is played out in Crackanthorpe's 'bad marriage' stories, as it is in the work of several other *Yellow Book* writers. In 'Modern Melodrama' (1894), his first contribution to Harland's journal, Crackanthorpe portrays a middle-class married couple at the moment when they discover that the woman, Daisy, is terminally ill. He uses this lugubrious scenario to explore the condition of a modern marriage in which the threat of ultimate separation by death is distorted by the couple's already being profoundly distant from one another on so many points in life. The story contains very little action and nothing by way of a peripeteia or revelatory conclusion – indeed, it breaks off abruptly while the couple are in mid-conversation. Instead, Crackanthorpe focuses on Daisy's irritation at the homosocial conspiracy of silence her husband and her male physician perpetrate against her, and on her search for an authentic discourse with which to account for her own death. At the same time, the story dramatizes the husband's inadequate attempts to embrace and reassure his wife, and his hapless fumbling over simple tasks in the domestic arena to which he is confined. By the time Daisy asks the question with which the story ends – 'Is that doctor a good man?' – all confidence in the husband's ability to answer it, or even to detect the irony with which it is asked, has leaked out of the story. The couple are left rehearsing the disunion that will soon become absolute.

Inadequate men – emasculated, domesticated and wrestling with their own conflicted mentalities – figure throughout Crackanthorpe's fiction. When his male characters do try to assert themselves in the old ways, through seduction or domination of women, for example, they are confronted with antagonists no longer biddable to their wishes or amenable to their desires. Stories like 'A Study in Sentimentality', 'The Hazeltons', 'Dissolving View' and 'Embers' dramatize the collapse of male authority, more often than not by revealing what it is composed of. In 'The Hazeltons', for example, the caddish central character, Hillier, is exposed not only as an adulterer but as a self-pitying, self-dramatizing sentimentalist whose power over women is a sham of rhetorical suavity. Other members of the *Yellow Book* set explored similar issues in their short stories, portraying unhappy marriages and faltering relationships in which male characters struggle to control and contain their increasingly restive and powerful womenfolk. Ella D'Arcy (who served as unofficial sub-editor to Harland), Frances E. Huntley, George Egerton, Evelyn Sharp and Victoria Cross (Vivian Cory) all authored stories of this sort, laying particular emphasis on the challenge that female assertiveness presented to traditional notions of competent masculinity. In Huntley's 'A Pen-and-Ink Effect', for example, Luttrell imagines how the young girl he has seduced, then rejected in favour of marriage to another woman, will feel when she learns of his betrayal. 'She would mind – mind horribly,' he imagines. 'Her mouth would set itself, her eyes would look bright and pained – oh! she was brave enough; but she would be silent, sadder than her wont, and – envious? His smile grew broader. Poor little dear!' But in fact the girl, retreating to her room at the end of the story, enjoys a thrilling sense of freedom and release when she discovers her power to resist, through mimicry of his language, Luttrell's arrogant presumptions about her:

'Poor girl! oh, the poor girl, poor girl!' The mirror looked clouded, vanished quite, grew clear again.

'To think I could ever have loved him!'

For a moment she hid her shamed, white face.

'Feel up for a game of tennis, Ronald, Sydney, Edith!' her voice pealed out.

One must do something to work off this mad joyous thrill of freedom, liberty. . . . looking forward!

She dashed down the stairs with a wild whirl of frills and lace-edges.

More profoundly, Ella D'Arcy explores the psychological basis of these male presumptions about women. In her first *Yellow Book* story, 'Irremediable', she probes the character of Willoughby, a young clerk who marries a country girl, Esther Stables, whom he meets while on holiday from his job in London. A dabbler in Socialism, Willoughby is drawn to Esther as 'a working daughter of the people', but when the couple return to London she quickly falls into idleness and, as he would have it, depravity. Willoughby's progressive ideals evaporate as he bemoans his 'irremediable' misfortune in finding himself bound to a companion who has no wish to 'improve' herself and who, worse still, exhibits all the deplorable 'self-satisfaction of an illiterate mind'. D'Arcy's technique in the story, however, is to undermine Willoughby's self-pitying assertions by probing his motives in marrying Esther. She reveals, for instance, that he was once in love with another woman, the educated and sophisticated Nora Beresford, whose rejection of him 'indissolubly associated in his mind ideas of feminine refinement with those of feminine treachery'. We discover that Nora was in fact nothing like Willoughby had imagined her to be, and that he had fantasized her 'with the wholeheartedness of the true fanatic'. Suddenly a quite different impression of Willoughby begins to impose itself. There is the suggestion of a vengefulness against women: 'he had said to himself that even the breaking of stones in the road should be considered a more feminine employment than the breaking of hearts'. His attraction to Esther, it follows, may reflect not so much his Socialist principles as his need for a woman whom he can fictionalize and shape around his desires – a woman quite different from the literate, resistant Nora. Far from a straightforward story about an unfortunate misalliance that it at first appears to be, 'Irremediable' develops into a complex study of male psycho-sexual discomposure.

By far the best-known member of the *Yellow Book* circle, though she didn't publish much in the journal itself, was George Egerton. More strongly than any other writer Egerton was identified with 1890s New Woman feminism, even appearing as a cartoon, 'Borgia Smudgiton', in *Punch* magazine. Like D'Arcy and others of the *Yellow Book* group, she was as much concerned with the psychology of masculinity as of femininity in the new age of gender politics, and her portrayals of sexually emancipated women are focalized as frequently through male as female characters. A common trope of Egerton is to transplant her couples from the oppressive domestic interiors favoured by Crackanthorpe to the more determinately masculine space of the open countryside. There her women participate in such male pursuits as hunting and fishing, not as tolerated guests of men but as their imposing equals. When, in 'A Cross Line', a man out fishing comes across a woman doing the same, he finds himself adopting an unfamiliar role in the ensuing conversation:

> He met the frank, unembarrassed gaze of eyes that would have looked with just the same bright inquiry at the advent of a hare, or a toad, or any other object that might cross her path, and raised his hat with respectful courtesy, saying, in the drawling tone habitual with him –
> 'I hope I am not trespassing?'
> 'I can't say; you may be, so may I, but no one has ever told me so!'
> A pause. His quick glance has noted the thick wedding ring on her slim brown hand, and the flash of a diamond in its keeper. A lady decidedly. Fast? perhaps. Original? undoubtedly. Worth knowing? rather.
> 'I am looking for a trout stream, but the directions I got were rather vague; might I –'
> 'It's straight ahead, but you won't catch anything now, at least not here, sun's too glaring and water too low, a mile up you may, in an hour's time'.

In this exchange it is the man whose speech and manner are deferential, decorous, and plaintive; the woman, on the other hand, has knowledge and speaks in a factual, informative, unemotional way. He is concerned with rules and boundaries, while she flaunts these, meeting his gaze directly, fishing without regard for laws of trespass, and interrupting him when he speaks. Egerton is fond of staging disorientating encounters of this sort where women not only invade male spaces, but assume male codes of behaviour too. Elsewhere she debunks the conventions of the masculine adventure narrative of the kind popularized by H. Rider Haggard and Robert Louis Stevenson. In 'A Little Grey Glove', for example, her male character sets off in pursuit of the 'life of a free wanderer' only to find himself literally hooked by a woman who is fishing. The force of her intellect and personality, and the account she gives of her life as an adulteress, captivate him; but the effect of his desire is a kind of paralysis and emasculation. He abandons his adventuring, preferring to remain indoors, ruminating and awaiting the woman's return. In an inversion of the Homeric narrative, where the woman awaits her heroic husband's homecoming, the story ends with him sitting dreaming 'in the old chair that has a ghost of her presence', longing for the moment when she will 'come to me across the meadow grass, through the silver haze, as she did before'.

Egerton's tactical inversions and reversals of the narrative tropes of popular romance are the textual embodiments of a much broader set of convictions shared with many avant-garde writers, not just concerning women's sexual and social liberation, but about the role of art in an age of widespread literacy and mass mediation. Her antagonism towards the popular romance reflects a more general impatience with what she called the 'humbug' of bourgeois morality and its cultural expression in such mainstream magazines as George Newnes's family-orientated *Strand* – organs 'Englishly nice and nicely English', as she put it a letter of 1891. For Egerton, the kind of generic conventionalism sponsored by the *Strand* and its ilk (Newnes's journal was responsible for bringing Sherlock Holmes to the world) was coterminous with ideological conservatism. An alliance of sorts therefore emerged in her mind, and the minds of her fellows, between avant-garde cultural production, experimental writing and publishing practices, and political radicalism. The short story, as we have seen, was one of the central literary forms through which that cluster of values found expression. In part this was because so much avant-garde activity was, by economic necessity, centred around the magazine, and the short story was a staple of that format. But the form also appealed precisely because it was so much a fixture of popular culture: that is to say, with so clearly defined a set of generic expectations attaching to it, it could be very readily and visibly subverted.

As we have seen, Egerton performed that subversion in her treatment of the masculine romance, but for avant-garde writers not directly associated with the *Yellow Book* the 'plotless' short story offered a means of challenging other familiar fictional modes of representation. Arthur Morrison was perhaps the most successful writer of his generation when it came to understanding the subversive potential of the short form. He was also extraordinarily adept at fashioning short stories to satisfy the demands of specific magazine editors and readerships. In his day he scored a number of commercial successes, for example providing the *Strand* with a successor to Sherlock Holmes in the shape of the modest but brilliant amateur detective Martin Hewitt. At the same time, however, Morrison also wrote fiction for the upper end of the periodicals market, forming a relationship early in his career with the highly influential William Ernest Henley, then editor of the *National Observer* (formerly the *Scots Observer*). Henley was responsible for publishing most of the stories that composed Morrison's first book *Tales of Mean Streets* (1894). In these graphic and candid pieces, Morrison explores the squalid reality of slum life in London's East End; but the stories are significant more for the manner in which they represent that reality than for the shocking nature of what they describe. For unlike the urban detective fiction he wrote for the *Strand*, Morrison's *Observer* stories refuse to bring the city and its inhabitants to any sort of narrative order. Where the classic detective story is predicated on the principle that it will provide a resolution to the enigmas and puzzles it sets up (the point of a who-dunnit is to answer the question who *did* do it?), Morrison's slum fiction deals in loose ends, unanswered questions and irresolvable complexes. His stories are 'plotless' in the sense that they contain no emphatic moment of discovery, revelation or disclosure, nor do they provide any interpretative vantage point from which the reader can descry the coherence of the whole. If the function of the detective story, at least as it operated in the case of the *Strand* magazine, was to reassure its largely metropolitan readership that the supernumerary dangers of the city could be contained and annulled by the superordinate deductive intelligence of the detective, then Morrison's slum fiction serves quite different ends, conjuring up a social space and a feral citizenry neither amenable to narrative convention nor susceptible to the rule of law.

Morrison was particularly drawn to the figure of the middle-class altruist or philanthropist intent on making his corrective intervention in the slum. Several of his stories for Henley's *Observer* dramatize the failure of religious do-gooders and medical professionals to ameliorate the social problems they encounter. What is particularly provocative about Morrison's writing, however, is that he determines to grant the slum inhabitants their own ethnographic singularity, their own complex patterns of social hierarchization and value systems. The well-meaning interventionists fail because they are incapable of recognizing this singularity and try instead to impose their ethical and behavioural norms on the slum underclass. The young medical student who, in 'Lizer's First', attempts to save the pregnant Lizer Hope from another beating by her drunken, slovenly husband, only to find himself physically attacked by both Lizer and her mother for his meddling, is guilty of the kind of charitable presumptuousness and class impercipience that Morrison would attack at length in his novel *A Child of the Jago* (1896). Likewise, in 'On the Stairs', the mother who saves the five shillings given to her by a young doctor (to buy medicine for her dying son) in order that she can pay for a 'respectable' funeral for him, is acting in accordance with social and ethical codes that exceed what the physician, bound to his medical oaths, is able to comprehend.

'On the Stairs' is a story rich in irony and ambiguity, not least because Morrison conducts its climactic death-bed scene literally behind a closed door, keeping the reader from seeing what transpires between the mother and son. Such interstitial, interrogative conclusions are a feature of Morrison's slum stories, and he (and indeed Henley) were sensitive to the effects that could be produced by tactical omission and creative 'shortness'. When he came to revise 'Without Visible Means', the first story of his published in the *Observer*, for inclusion in *Tales of Mean Streets*, Morrison cut a summary paragraph rounding out the fate of the central character, thereby leaving the outcome of the story open to speculation. Similarly indeterminate is the ending of 'In Business'. There, the motives behind Ted Munsey's decision to abandon his family when debts on the business he and his wife run grow to unmanageable proportions, are entirely hidden from view, even though it is Ted's actions that provide the dramatic crux to the story. Before he departs the family home, in the dead of night, Ted writes two letters which he leaves on the kitchen table for his wife to find, one publicly declaring his liability for all monies owed by the failing business, and the other privately addressed to his wife, giving his reasons for leaving. The first of these documents serves the obvious purpose of saving his family from ruin, but the content of the personal letter greatly complicates the reader's understanding of Ted's decision, for in it he contradicts much of what the narrative has previously told us about Mrs Munsey and the couple's relationship. For example, he declares in the letter his confidence that his wife will make the business succeed in his absence; but the narrative up to that point has detailed her incompetence in running the shop and managing money: indeed, no matter how cheaply she priced her goods, we are told, 'none of the aprons nor the bows nor the towels nor the stockings nor any other of the goods were bought – never a thing beyond a ha'porth of thread or a farthing bodkin'. Much has been implied, too, concerning Mrs Munsey's maltreating her husband, whom she blames and peevishly punishes for the sorry state of the business when it is she who is largely responsible for burdening them with debt. All of this puts in question the real reason for Ted's leaving. He says in the letter to his wife, 'if you do not see me again will you pay the detts when [the business] is pull round as we have been allways honnest and straght'. The implication is that his absence will be permanent, and that his departure is as much an act of escape for him personally as it is salvation for his family. This crucial ambiguity arises because Morrison has prohibited access to Ted's thoughts and feelings prior to his writing the letter and departing. Portrayed as 'a large, quiet man of forty-five, the uncomplaining appurtenance of his wife', he is viewed for the majority of the story through the eyes of others, including his wife, daughter, neighbours and workmates. The 'truth' about Ted is invariably just the opinion of those around him, and is communicated throughout the story in free indirect discourse: 'There was no guessing what would have become of [the money] in Ted's hands; probably it would have been, in chief part, irrecoverably lent; certainly it would have gone and left Ted a moulder at Moffat's, as before'. At the first decisive words and actions that come from Ted, his letter and his leaving, the narrative voice maintains this distance from him, leaving the issue of his motives and intentions as uncertain as the future Mrs Munsey faces in the story's concluding sentences: 'Upstairs the girls began to move about. Mrs Munsey sat with her frightened face on the table'. The 'solution' that Ted presents to his wife is really no solution at all, as his removal takes from the family their only dependable prospect of an income. Likewise for the reader, kept from knowing why Ted left and by extension whether or not he will return, the narrative refuses to provide answers to the questions it has itself prompted us to ask.

In the contribution he made to a symposium on the short story published in the *Bookman* magazine in 1897, Morrison stressed the importance of 'the things that are not written in the story as well as those that are'.[10] Where the detective story works by rendering visible and articulate that which is hidden and suppressed, Morrison's slum fiction refuses to disintricate the complex social, ethical and behavioural reality of the city. Like his *Yellow Book* contemporaries, he was scathing of the popular romance tradition (see his essay 'What Is a Realist?'), and he saw how the short story, by breaking with generic convention, could offer a more authentic representation of the experience of urban modernity. As we will see in the next section, this interest in destabilizing familiar narrative structures, both as a way of identifying one's work in contradistinction to popular, mass-market fare and creating a fictional form adequate to the representational demands of the modern world, would come to dominate the work of the succeeding generation of modernist writers, among them James Joyce, Katherine Mansfield and Virginia Woolf.

Part II

The modernist short story

Introduction: 'complete with missing parts'

When Thomas Hardy finished reading Katherine Mansfield's story 'The Daughters of the Late Colonel', one day in 1921, he assumed that there would be a sequel. He didn't recognize the ending as an ending, or the story as complete in itself. He told Mansfield as much. She was bemused. 'I put my all into that story,' she wrote to a friend, 'and hardly anyone saw what I was getting at . . . As if there was any more to say!'[1]

Was Hardy missing something? Up to a point he was. But then so too, we might say, was Mansfield's story. Elliptical and wilfully enigmatic, 'The Daughters of the Late Colonel' is a superlative example of the 'plotless' short story, which, as we have just seen, was now firmly aligned with 'literary' or avant-garde writing and cultural values in Britain. Hardy's bafflement at Mansfield's interrogative, irresolute narrative was by no means unusual, and reflects the extent to which this new species of story ran against the precepts and expectations readers customarily brought to a piece of narrative fiction. Far from its origins in the popular tale-telling tradition, the short story had become, by the time Hardy died in 1928, a focus for modernist experimentation, a fixture of high-culture publishing venues and the subject of a growing body of aesthetic theory.

For many readers, the decisive moment in the short story's history is 1914, the year James Joyce published *Dubliners*. That book, more than any other, has become synonymous with our idea of what a modern short story is like. *Dubliners* bequeathed two concepts, meanwhile, which have become mantras both for those who would write short fiction and, until recently, for those who would write about it. The first of these concepts is the 'epiphany', by which Joyce (or, rather, his character Stephen Hero) meant a 'sudden spiritual manifestation, whether in the vulgarity of speech or gesture or in a memorable phase of the mind itself.'[2] The other is the belief that the proper prose style for short stories is one of 'scrupulous meanness'.[3] I shall explore what Joyce meant by both of these things in chapter 4, and, given their ubiquity, we shall have occasion to return to them in subsequent chapters. But for now we might note that Joyce's ideas are really formulations and developments of trends we witnessed in the previous section – the 'epiphany' standing in place of the conventional resolution of plot, and the scrupulously mean style producing an indirect, elliptical and ambiguous narrative discourse. What this suggests is that *Dubliners*, far from being a moment of superlative transition, of profound change in the development of the form, was a further evolution of the 'plotless' short story of the 1890s. Likewise, Joyce's proximity to the *fin de siècle* needs to be borne in mind, because while *Dubliners* was not published until 1914, the stories that compose it were begun in 1904 and completed, with the exception of the otherwise exceptional 'The Dead', by 1906.

It is also worth remembering that Joyce's landmark novel *Ulysses* (1922) started life as a short story. So too did Virgina Woolf's *Mrs Dalloway* (1925), while her novel *Jacob's Room* (1922) is composed of chapters that Woolf thought of as individual stories. What this suggests is that the short story, while we may tend to think of it as the lesser fictional form, the apprentice piece to the novel, in fact played a fundamental role in the development of experimental modernist fiction. In Woolf's case, as chapter 4 describes, it was in the short story that she first began to devise the techniques of narration and characterization by which she hoped to render, more authentically than her Victorian or Edwardian predecessors, the texture of human consciousness and the nature of experience. To this she was abetted by the example of the Russian writer Anton Chekhov, whose stories were then appearing in English, superbly translated by Constance Garnett. It was in Chekhov's work that Woolf first heard the 'note of interrogation'[4] that showed her a way out of the moribund conventionalism of the English novel.

What Woolf also found in Chekhov's stories was a means of conducting in fictional form a broadly anti-materialist critique of modern mass culture. Woolf famously accused her fellow novelists Arnold Bennett and John Galsworthy of 'materialism' in their writing, by which she meant their preoccupation with the superficial material, economic and behavioural dimensions of existence, rather than what she considered the 'proper stuff of fiction', the study of character consciousness and what she unblushingly called 'soul'. Again, it was in the short story that she first devised an alternative to the materialist nomenclature by creating a sense of indeterminacy and open-endedness that allowed her to allude to the existence of realities that lay beyond the comprehension of the culturally authoritative, superintendent 'masculine point of view', as she called it in one story, 'The Mark on the Wall'.

Many of the same concerns are evident in the work of Katherine Mansfield, who, like Woolf, was also greatly influenced by the example of Chekhov. Mansfield is a rare thing among modern writers in that she dedicated herself to the short story form. But this does not mean that she has had any less of an impact on the subsequent development of fiction in the twentieth century, nor that her contribution to the creation of the modernist aesthetic was any less significant than Woolf's. As chapter 5 shows, Mansfield's boldly indeterminate stories reflect far more than just an impatience with the superficial conventionalism of contemporary fiction. They are also indicative of a deeper and characteristically modernist hostility towards bourgeois culture and its infatuation with what she called, in an echo of Woolf, 'purely external value'.[5] What Mansfield termed the 'question put'[6] – her description of the interrogative, open-ended Chekhovian story – cleared a space for the self beyond the confines of an inauthentic, mass-mediated, commodity-saturated modern culture.

It will be clear from the above that I think the short story needs to be considered in the context of the whole culture of modernism in Britain, rather than just in formalist terms. Indeed, a case can be made that the short story enjoyed such prominence among the avant-garde because it was calibrated to the conditions and experience of modernity itself. That is a bold claim and demands some elucidation. In 'The Work of Art in the Age of Mechanical Reproduction', Walter Benjamin suggests that art does not simply reflect modernity, it inhabits and produces it too.[7] Benjamin's case in point is cinema. By utilizing its technologies, entertainments, social spaces and practices, cinema was obviously a *participant* in modernity, but it was also a *result* of it, the sheer intensity of experience having disposed the modern subject towards the hyperkinetic stimulation that film provided. At the same time, cinema *resembled* modernity in its privileging of visual over other sorts of experience. Taking an analogous approach to the short story, it is possible to argue that the new 'plotless' form was brought into being in part because of technological advances in printing that facilitated the late-Victorian boom in periodical publishing. But it was also, by its very brevity, recognized as a form capable of answering to the demands of an increasingly time-pressed modern readership – hence its attraction to magazine editors keen to fill their pages with material that could be both quickly produced and readily consumed. Moreover, the rapidity and ephemerality of the short story's disclosures were felt to reproduce in narrative form the exigency and immediacy, the 'fleetingness and fragility', as G. K. Chesterton called it, of modern life itself.

Benjamin's multi-dimensional, multi-directional model of the relationship between cultural production and modernity opens the way for us to think of innovation in literary form less in terms of superlative gestures of nonconformist genius, and more as the result of interactions between the creative imagination and the material, ideological and technological conditions prevailing at a particular historical moment. Read in this way, the formal characteristics of the 'plotless' short story – the way it privileges the experiential fragment over the eventful sequence, for example, or the arbitrarily subjective moment over the historical totality – become more than just examples of writerly ambition to 'make it new'. Rather, they are aspects of what Fredric Jameson describes as modernism's specialist function, namely to make us feel 'increasingly at home in what would otherwise . . . be a distressingly alienating reality'. The modernist text performs this function, Jameson claims, by effectively 'retraining' us 'culturally and psychologically . . . for life in the market system'.[8] In the way that it makes an aesthetic virtue out of social phenomena of fragmentation, dislocation and isolation, the short story participates in this process of acclimatizing the subject to the experience of technological modernity. To adopt Georg Lukács's term, in its 'negation' of the features of traditional narrative art, it mimics the very forces of estrangement it describes.[9]

Throughout the modernist corpus we see conscious acts of resistance – and not always in the form of a recrudescent archaism or primitivism – to the defining modern trends of urbanization, massification and commoditization. Indeed, the notion of an 'elite' or 'high' literary culture itself in this period depends upon the construction of a value-nexus antithetical to that of the market-oriented contemporary society Jameson envisages. James Joyce's sentiment that 'No man . . . can be a lover of the true or the good unless he abhors the multitude'[10] was, of course, widely echoed among his contemporaries, but such characteristically modernist high-handedness amounts to more than just a blanket contempt for the masses and their cultural entertainments. Rather, it reflects the modernists' desire to establish a readership and niche market of their own – a qualified community of the like-minded that could participate in 'a cultural space set apart from mass culture [and] from commercial "pressures"'.[11] Through the coterie press and the 'little magazines', and through the system of aristocratic patronage that freed writers and publishers from dependence on the market, modernism attempted to clear that space for itself. Which is not to imply that it was successful in its aims, or that those aims were ever straightforward: as much recent criticism has shown, modernism was, in many of its guises, deeply and contentedly complicit with the forms, genres and values of the mass culture it claimed to abhor. Rather, it is to make the point that, while the short story seems to impose itself as a distinctly 'modern' form, it appealed to the avant-garde as much for the way it could be used to critique capitalized, mass-mediated modernity as for the expression it might give to it. As this and the previous section make clear, the short form became one of the key literary battlegrounds on which modernism's struggle to establish its values and identity was played out from the 1890s onward. From Frederick Wedmore's insistence that the 'plotless' story was 'not . . . a ready means of hitting the big public, but . . . a medium for the exercise of the finer art',[12] to

Virginia Woolf's belief that the form could embody both the anti-commercial ethos of the coterie press and the anti-materialist principles of 'modern fiction', the short story answered to the modernists' conflicted desire to forge an artistic idiom adequate to modernity, while absenting their art from the degrading spectacle of mass activity.

That the short story, very much the lesser fictional form and still rooted, at the end of the nineteenth century, in oral tale-telling and generic conventionalism, should have taken hold so rapidly among the literary avant-garde is perhaps the less surprising when one considers the form in the context of modernism's valorization of *difficulty*.[13] Although we may be more accustomed to thinking of difficulty, in the modernist text at least, as the product of multiplicity, superabundance and allusive excess, it was also recognized that obscurity could be generated through radically curtailed or laconic modes of expression where these broke down the logical connections in narrative and semantic sequence. It is to the modernist period that Umberto Eco dates the emergence of what he calls the 'open' work, that is, the text that is markedly reticent or even materially incomplete and in which the artist strives to 'prevent a single sense from imposing itself at the very outset of the receptive process'. Eco cites Verlaine's *Art Poétique* and Mallarmé's celebration of the pleasures of 'guessing' as the first statements in Western art of a programmatic, self-conscious 'openness', of an effort to produce works that indulge the free play of interpretative possibility, that seek out the 'free response of the addressee' to their 'halo of indefiniteness . . . pregnant with infinite suggestive possibilities'.[14] Similarly, the demands that interrogative, elliptical short stories make on their readers becomes a validating factor for modernists. Henry James's discrimination between stories that leave their readers wrestling with the 'impression . . . of a complexity or a continuity', and those that merely satisfy curiosity with the 'snap of the pistol-shot'[15] is the token of a more profound separation between different sorts of cultural election and activity. The 'open' text emerges as a powerful embodiment of the anti-commercial, autonomous work of art, the work whose very difficulty is the measure of its symbolic value – a value that is not set by the market. The 'mechanical thrill' and 'base pleasure' of plot and story, by contrast, come to be regarded as signs of commercial flippancy, cultural immaturity, and, in some more apocalyptic modernist jeremiads, a 'barbarous residue' in our nature.[16]

These are some of the broader cultural issues and questions that circulate in this section on the modernist short story. But as this book serves also as a history of literary *form*, I conclude the discussion with Samuel Beckett, a writer who helps us to mediate the transition, if that is what it is, from modernism to the subject of Part III, 'post-modernism'. Beckett is a fitting writer to close with because throughout his career he is preoccupied with the question of how to 'go on' from modernism, how to take the next step. In his early collection of stories, *More Pricks Than Kicks*, we find him experimenting with short story form as he inherited it from Joyce. Later, he returns to short fiction to carry out his singular exploration of the limits of writing and the sayable at the border with silence. In this respect, he takes to new depths the notion of 'shortness' and its relationship, through narrative, to experience in the modern world.

Chapter 4

James Joyce

For many readers, the short story enters its distinctively modern phase with the publication of James Joyce's *Dubliners* (1914). Certainly, the book has garnered more attention than any other volume of short fiction in the English language; meanwhile the descriptions Joyce gave of his own aesthetic principles and compositional practices – in particular the concept of the 'epiphany' and the development of an ascetic prose style of 'scrupulous meanness' – have come to occupy a central place in scholarly accounts of the short form in the twentieth century. Yet while the publication date of *Dubliners*, 1914, may locate the text within the high-tide of European modernism, it is important to remember that work began on the stories as early as 1904, and that the book was complete, but for 'The Dead', by 1906. The literary environment in which *Dubliners* was composed, then, was not that of the high-modernist literary manifesto, the 'little' magazine, T. S. Eliot and Ezra Pound; rather Joyce's reading was concentrated (often antagonistically) in the literature of the Irish Cultural Revival and, as the decidedly decadent-sounding title he gave to an early project, *Silhouettes*, suggests, the British *fin-de-siècle* avant-garde.

By relocating *Dubliners* to the period in which it was composed we are able to take a more measured appraisal of it than is usual in modernist criticism. For it is a mistake to think of the book as a one-off, stand-alone work of superlative genius that came from nowhere and changed the course of short fiction. In fact, Joyce was conversant in the recent history of the form, reading not only the work of his fellow countryman George Moore, but also that of Arthur Morrison, George Gissing and the *Yellow Book* circle. What is more, he took to the short story for that most ignoble (in literary history, at least) of reasons: to make some money. The impetus came from George Russell, a leading figure in the Irish Cultural Revival. Joyce had visited Russell in 1902, impressing the older man with his intelligence, breadth of reading and, above all, infectious arrogance (at that first meeting Joyce passed judgement on Yeats and declared openly his scepticism about Russell's literary values and theosophical beliefs). In the summer of 1904, Russell wrote suggesting to Joyce that he try submitting a short story to the *Irish Homestead*, a mainstream family paper and the official organ of the Irish Agricultural Organization Society, of which Russell was shortly to take over the literary editorship. He recommended that Joyce think of offering something 'simple, rural?, livemaking?, pathos?', adding that story writing was 'easily earned money if you can write fluently and don't mind playing to the common understanding and liking for once in a way'.[1] Following Russell's advice, Joyce familiarized himself with a story in the most recent number of the *Homestead*, 'The Old Watchman' by Berkeley Campbell, and set about composing the first of the narratives that would later make up *Dubliners*. It was called 'The Sisters'.

'The Sisters' is important not just because it was Joyce's first venture in the short story, but because it brings together several of the elements that would prove crucial to the form's rise within the culture of high-modernism. As we have already seen, the short story became a fixture of literary avant-gardism in the 1890s as writers began to explore the aesthetic possibilities of 'shortness', turning away from the plot-orientated populism of detective fiction and the imperial adventure romance to produce disturbingly irresolute, 'plotless', open-ended narrative structures. 'The Sisters' does something similar in the way it perverts the conventions of the typical *Irish Homestead* story. Joyce's story takes the basic situation of Berkeley Campbell's 'The Old Watchman' – in which a young boy perceives an old, dying man – and contorts it, not just by undermining the sense of a conclusive ending (though he certainly does that) but by attacking the very moral structure of Campbell's narrative, and by extension the editorial values of the *Homestead* itself. Where 'The Old Watchman' reads as a clumsily obvious and sanctimonious life-lesson to its young narrator on the dangers of drinking, gambling and profligacy, 'The Sisters' is replete with enigma, salacious suggestion and moral ambivalence. Joyce's story of the death of an aged priest, Father Flynn, narrated by a young boy whom he had befriended and mentored, is notable more for the questions it raises than the answers it provides. A vocabulary of imprecision and evasion stalks the narrative. It is said, for instance, that there was 'something' wrong with the priest, but what that 'something' was is never revealed. We learn too that he seemed 'nervous', but no explanation for this is offered. At the same time, suggestions build up that the priest may have been harbouring some dark secret. He is described as 'queer' by some, too 'scrupulous' by others, while still others suggest that he 'read too much'. Of particular significance seems to be an incident late in his life that resulted in the breaking of a chalice. Precisely what happened, and who the boy was who was with him at the time, are not revealed, but the event is said to have left his mind 'a bit affected'. To this is added, finally, the mystery of why the priest's body is not taken to the chapel to rest before his funeral.

When Joyce came to revise 'The Sisters' for inclusion in *Dubliners*, he further intensified the suggestions of impropriety or disgrace surrounding Father Flynn, having him described as 'uncanny', 'one of those . . . peculiar cases', even, in one cancelled draft, 'bad for children', and introducing a trio of curious words on the first page – *paralysis, gnomon* and *simony* – at least one of which indicates illicit conduct. He furthermore stressed the complexity in the narrator's relationship with the old man, hinting that he may have known what the 'something' was that ailed the priest.

Both the epistemological ambivalence and moral evasiveness of 'The Sisters' were intended to subvert the *Irish Homestead*'s editorial values. Neither Russell nor the editor at the time, H. F. Norman, appears to have picked up on Joyce's ulterior designs, for another story, 'Eveline', was soon accepted for publication. Again, however, Joyce used his story to parody and critique the *Homestead* and the kind of work it published. In the case of 'Eveline', his target was the didactic anti-emigration fiction that the magazine frequently ran – fiction designed to warn the Irish citizenry, especially impressionable young women, of the dangers and the inevitable unhappiness attendant upon emigration.[2] The *Homestead* published this material as part of its broader campaign to stem the flow of Irish youth abroad, especially to the Americas. Joyce's offering was designed both to disturb the artistic conventions of this fiction and to compromise the moral message it sought to convey.

'Eveline' does this by leaving its heroine trapped between the wish to escape Ireland for Buenos Aires and a life with her suitor Frank and the obligation she feels to stay at home and care for her father. Yet even that brief summary is misleading, for Joyce renders Eveline Hill with such a degree of discursive complexity and contradictoriness that it is impossible to say for sure that she ever does intend to leave with Frank, or equally that she feels the pull of home quite as strongly as she makes out. To a great extent, the difficulty of making determinations about 'Eveline' arises from Joyce's use of free indirect discourse, where the thoughts of his character and the voice of the impersonal third-person narrator blend indistinguishably into one another. We feel the effect of this intrigue in the narrative point-of-view particularly at the climax of the story, as Eveline stands at the quayside in Dublin with Frank, preparing to board ship:

> She stood among the swaying crowd in the station at the North Wall. He held her hand and she knew that he was speaking to her, saying something about the passage over and over again. The station was full of soldiers with brown baggages. Through the wide doors of the sheds she caught a glimpse of the black mass of the boat, lying in beside the quay

wall, with illuminated portholes. She answered nothing. She felt her cheek pale and cold and, out of a maze of distress, she prayed to God to direct her, to show her what was her duty. The boat blew a long mournful whistle into the mist. If she went, to-morrow she would be on the sea with Frank, steaming towards Buenos Ayres. Their passage had been booked. Could she still draw back after all he had done for her? Her distress awoke a nausea in her body and she kept moving her lips in silent fervent prayer. A bell clanged upon her heart. She felt him seize her hand:

– Come!

All the seas of the world tumbled about her heart. He was drawing her into them: he would drown her. She gripped with both hands at the iron railing.

– Come!

No! No! No! It was impossible. Her hands clutched the iron in frenzy. Amid the seas she sent a cry of anguish!

– Eveline! Evvy!

He rushed beyond the barrier and called to her to follow. He was shouted at to go on but he still called to her. She set her white face to him, passive, like a helpless animal. Her eyes gave him no sign of love or farewell or recognition.

Saying what, if anything, Eveline 'decides' here – and by extension, what the story's moral message is – is fraught with difficulty. The blank passivity she adopts in the final paragraph may strike us as a kind of emotional paralysis, brought on by the intensity of the dilemma she faces. But that is to reckon without Joyce's adventurous use of free indirect discourse in retailing Eveline's thoughts to us. For when we look in more detail at this passage (and, indeed, at the many other passages of inner dialogue Eveline has in the story), we may come to question the authenticity of her reflections. Particularly significant here are Eveline's deliberations at the climactic turning point in the story: 'A bell clanged upon her heart . . . All the seas of the world tumbled about her heart . . . Amid the seas she sent a cry of anguish!' Dominic Head has argued that 'the exaggerated language of romantic fiction' that Joyce deliberately adopts in this passage has the effect of falsifying, or at least raising doubts about, the authenticity of this apparent moment of insight. The suggestion is laid that Eveline's epiphany can be read as 'a strategy of self-preservation, a wilful act of self-delusion' in which she protects herself from a dreadful acknowledgement of the unreality of her elopement.[3]

One can easily see how Joyce's *Homestead* stories can be read as early instalments in what he termed his 'battle with every religious and social force in

Ireland'. And if it was his intention to offend the sensibilities of the journal's readership he certainly succeeded, for so many letters of complaint were received following the publication of his third story, 'After the Race', that the *Homestead* refused to take any more contributions by him. Yet the early stories are significant for more than just their subversiveness. They also show Joyce in the process of assembling what would become the narratological repertoire of *Dubliners* as a whole: a prose style of 'scrupulous meanness', the extensive use of free indirect discourse in preference to first- or unflected third-person narration, and the structural device of the 'epiphany'. It is worth spending some time considering each of these aspects of Joyce's narratology in order to understand why *Dubliners* represents, if not the emphatic breakthrough in the development of the short story that many claim, then a significant moment in the form's elevation to the forefront of modernist fictional practice.

Joyce's often-quoted remark, made to his publisher Grant Richards, that he had composed his stories in a style of 'scrupulous meanness', has generated a great deal of critical comment over the years. Precisely what he meant by the phrase we shall never know, but if one takes it purely as a comment on narrational style, then it probably refers to the way in which, through *Dubliners*, omniscience is curtailed. That is to say, Joyce rarely grants to any one point-of-view in his texts a meta-discursive authority. Rather, he prefers to allow competing and often mutually exclusive interpretations to circulate freely in his narratives. This he achieves by abstemiousness, by a 'scrupulous meanness' about supplying the information that we require if we are to make a determinate reading of the story.

Time and again we find Joyce setting in motion questions and puzzles that his narratives then studiously refuse to resolve. In 'The Sisters', for example, there is the whole matter of the narrator's relationship to the dead priest, about which the text makes a number of insinuations which the narrator neither confirms nor denies. The euphemistic withholdings to which the adults in the story subject him, he in turn inflicts on the reader. Similarly in 'Eveline', there is no meta-narrative voice equipped to mediate between the conflicting versions of the heroine's motives that the story elicits. In 'Ivy Day in the Committee Room', the story in the collection which most conspicuously disavows omni-scient perspective and narratorial metalanguage, characters are not even named as they appear: we do not find out who they are until one of the other characters addresses them. As Colin MacCabe has pointed out,[4] only once is the flow of oblique and tangential dialogue in 'Ivy Day' interrupted by narrative commen-tary, and then only in order to account for a silence. The consequences for the reader of this abstemiousness are most apparent in the difficulties we face ordering and interpreting each character's utterances in relation to a dominant diegesis in the story. It is rather like reading a play script with minimal stage directions in which we are forced to negotiate among a polyphony of voices. The absence of any meta-discursive perspective is intensified by the intertext that appears at the end of the story in the form of Hynes's poem on Charles Stuart. As with the characters' speeches, there is no indication how the poem is to be read, and indeed Joyce renders the responses of those who hear it inscrutable: 'The applause continued for a little time. When it had ceased all the auditors drank from their bottles in silence'. How long exactly is that 'little time', and how does it gauge the men's feelings to what they have heard? And what, furthermore, does Mr Crofton mean when he says, in the story's concluding line, that it was 'a very fine piece of writing'?

Similarly beguiling is the ending to 'The Boarding House'. In that story, which describes the relationship that develops between Polly Mooney, the daughter of a boarding-house keeper, and one of her mother's tenants, Mr Doran, Joyce's strategic reticence comes into force in the final scene when the girl retreats to her room, leaving her mother and Doran to discuss his intentions towards her. We get no access to the crucial deliberations that take place between Mrs Mooney and her lodger; instead, in a scene reminiscent of 'Eveline', Joyce focuses on the enigmatic and inscrutable young woman:

> Polly sat for a little time on the edge of the bed, crying. Then she dried her eyes and went over to the lookingglass. She dipped the end of the towel in the waterjug and refreshed her eyes with the cool water. She looked at herself in profile and readjusted a hairpin above her ear. Then she went back to the bed again and sat at the foot. She regarded the pillows for a long time and the sight of them awoke in her mind secret amiable memories. She rested the nape of her neck against the cool iron bedrail and fell into a revery. There was no longer any perturbation visible on her face.

It is a teasingly unrevealing conclusion. Up to this point, Joyce has permitted access to his characters' thoughts and motives through the use of free indirect discourse. But here, at the decisive moment, he withdraws to an observational position to describe Polly's displacement activities – a narrative gesture that itself is a displacement and deferral of the answers to the questions that the story has prompted us to ask. Once again, Joyce's 'scrupulous meanness' cannot but strike us as a wilful interdiction of our readerly curiosity and need to know.

Artful abstemiousness makes its presence felt in more than just structural lacunae, ellipses and diversions in *Dubliners*, however. It is part of the very texture of Joyce's descriptive prose, which for all its economy of phrasing and modest lexical range is yet highly connotative and suggestive. The inherent instability of signification is frequently played with to set up resonances and equivocations in the narratives. Take, for example, the deceptively brilliant opening paragraph of 'Araby':

> North Richmond Street, being blind, was a quiet street except at the hour when the Christian Brothers' School set the boys free. An uninhabited house of two storeys stood at the blind end, detached from its neighbours in a square ground. The other houses of the street, conscious of decent lives within them, gazed at one another with brown imperturbable faces.

The street is blind in the sense that it is a dead end. That is, of course, a metaphorical use of 'blind', but there is a further metaphor implied in this context – impercipience (ironically, the literal meaning of the word, and suggested synaesthetically by the 'quietness' of the street) in the sense of 'ignorance' or even moral blindness. The 'dead-end' meaning establishes itself, but is then quickly compromised by the return of the 'seeing' metaphor in which the houses are described as 'gazing' at one another. Again, this carries the literal meaning of houses standing opposite each other, but it also suggests lives looking, perhaps censoriously or voyeuristically, in on one another. Later in the story, the narrator watches from behind a blind in one of these houses Mangan's sister, for the love of whom he is blind to his own better judgement. Finally, there is the narrator in his maturity, 'watching' this scene from his former life, seeing seeing.

For an earlier generation of critics, *Dubliners* was 'easy' Joyce – Joyce before the cryptogrammaticism, verbal flightiness and runaway allusiveness of *Ulysses* and *Finnegans Wake*. But as passages like the above suggest, an awareness that it was in the nature of words to express not 'one simple statement but a thousand possibilities', as Virginia Woolf would later excitedly put it,[5] runs through the short stories too. Joyce's 'scrupulous meanness' is such a powerful stylistic instrument precisely because it exploits the inherent polysemy of language, its capacity to mean more than one thing at once. As we saw earlier, Henry James understood that there was a transaction to be made between 'economy' and 'amplitude': the less one says, paradoxically the more interpretative possibilities one releases; in William Empson's phrase, 'ambiguity is a phenomenon of compression'.[6] Joyce's refusal to intervene or mediate in the guise of an omniscient narrator in *Dubliners* is what allows the creative instability of language to come to the fore and thereby disturb the unspoken agreement that readers customarily enter into with texts, namely that they will at some point in their diegeses supply the answers to the questions they themselves have provoked us into asking. Producing such disturbance was Joyce's intention from his very earliest work in the short story form.

As noted above, Joyce's extensive use of free indirect discourse is another defining characteristic of his technique in *Dubliners*. In some ways, free indirect discourse is a kind of 'scrupulous meanness', in that it again involves the suppression of a determinate, mediating point-of-view in the narrative discourse. The play between character and narrational voices in the stories has long been a subject of critical enquiry, at least since Hugh Kenner's famous formulation of his 'Uncle Charles Principle'. Kenner notices how in the opening line of 'The Dead' – 'Lily, the caretaker's daughter, was literally run off her feet' – the word 'literally', while delivered in the words of the narrator, is in fact an emanation of how Lily would speak, of how she would view herself. In other words, the narrative idiom picks up traces of a character's habits of speech and thought, or as Kenner puts it, 'detect[s] the gravitational field of the nearest person'.[7]

In more recent criticism, attention has shifted to how the modulations in point-of-view, fluctuating between the third-person narrator and the characters, is expressive of a fundamentally 'relativist philosophy' in Joyce's work because of the way in which it produces 'epistemological confusion' at crucial moments in the stories.[8] In particular, the effect of free indirect discourse on the reliability of the so-called epiphanies in *Dubliners* has been the focus of a great deal of critical debate. According to Dominic Head, for example, the idea that the epiphany functions as a unifying centre, a kind of structural equivalent for the resolution of plot, is undermined by Joyce's use of free indirect discourse. Many of the epiphanies, Head asserts, are falsified. Rather than revealing a momentary, essential truth about a character, they convey a decided '*lack* of illumination' and even a disruptive contradictoriness.[9]

The sense of reading the epiphanies in this way, as disturbing expectations of closure and resolution rather than fulfilling them, is that it takes us closer to Joyce's initial conception of the epiphany. Here is the account he gives of it in the *Stephen Hero* manuscript:

> He was passing through Eccles Street one evening, one misty evening, with all these thoughts dancing the dance of unrest in his brain when a trivial incident set him composing some ardent verses which he entitled a 'Vilanelle of the Temptress'. A young lady was standing on the steps of one of those brown brick houses which seem the very incarnation of Irish paralysis. A young gentleman was leaning on the rusty railings of the area. Stephen as he passed on his quest heard the following fragment of colloquy out of which he received an impression keen enough to afflict his sensitiveness very severely.

> The Young Lady – (drawling discreetly) . . . O, Yes . . . I was . . . at
> the . . . cha . . . pel. . . .
> The Young Gentleman – (inaudibly) . . . I . . . (again inaudibly) . . . I . . .
> The Young Lady – (softly) . . . O . . . but you're . . . ve . . . ry . . . wick . . .
> ed. . . .
> This triviality made him think of collecting many such moments
> together in a book of epiphanies. By an epiphany he meant sudden
> spiritual manifestation, whether in the vulgarity of speech or gesture or
> in a memorable phase of the mind itself.

The important thing to notice here is that the epiphany itself, that 'sudden spiritual manifestation', is composed around a fragmentary colloquy, the overheard conversation between the young lady and gentleman. It is a pattern found throughout the series of sketches to which he gave the title 'Epiphanies':

> High up in the old, dark-windowed house: firelight in the narrow room:
> dusk outside. An old woman bustles about, making tea; she tells of the
> changes, her odd ways, and what the priest and the doctor said. I
> hear her words in the distance. I wander among the coals, among the
> ways of adventure. . . . . . . Christ! What is in the doorway? . . . . . A skull – a
> monkey; a creature drawn hither to the fire, to the voices: a silly creature.
> – Is that Mary Ellen? –
> – No, Eliza, it's Jim –
> – O. . . . . . O, goodnight, Jim –
> – D'ye want anything, Eliza? –
> – I thought it was Mary Ellen. . . . . . I thought you were Mar
> Ellen, Jim –

There is no attempt here to contain these interlocuting voices within the dominant discourse of the narrator, no attempt to 'explain' them as object-languages. The epiphanies do not function as unifying, determinate moments of insight or closure but rather as spaces in which a variety of voices blend and in which every utterance enters into what M. M. Bakhtin elsewhere characterizes as a 'tension-filled environment of alien words, value judgements and accents'.[10]

That 'tension-filled environment' is in evidence throughout *Dubliners*, particularly at climactic, epiphanic moments in the narratives where the pressure of other discourses acts to qualify the authority and even question the authenticity of the revelations being made. In 'Eveline', as we have seen, it is the phraseology of cheap romantic fiction that infiltrates the heroine's thoughts. In 'A Little Cloud', similarly, the tears that the central character, Chandler, cries at the end of the story as he struggles with his restive child and contemplates his failures as a father, a husband and a writer are similarly difficult to take at face value, owing to Chandler's tendency, evident throughout the story, to construct such scenarios of heightened emotion in his literary imagination. As his wife intervenes to calm the sobbing child, he steps back into the lamplight, 'his cheeks suffused with shame' and 'tears of remorse start[ing] to his eyes', but for the reader this is not the first time of witnessing an impotent surge of sentiment in Chandler. Indeed, the final scene of the story begins with his reading by his sleeping child's bedside some uncharacteristically cloying lines of verse by Byron, determined to experience a frisson of intense feeling:

> He felt the rhythm of the verse about him in the room. How melancholy it was! Could he, too, write like that, express the melancholy of his soul in verse? There were so many things he wanted to describe: his sensation of a few hours before on Grattan bridge, for example. If he could get back again to that mood. . . .

That mood, we might recall, was a quite repugnantly insensitive self-absorption: as he viewed the suffering poor huddled and begging along the river-banks beneath the bridge Chandler wondered only 'whether he could write a poem' about the experience that his friend Gallaher 'might be able to get into some London paper for him'. Then, as at the conclusion to the story, we are drawn to question how much pity or remorse Chandler genuinely feels, and how much he desperately needs to believe that a 'poetic moment' has touched him.

Rarely in *Dubliners* do we find any passage of third-person narration that is not distorted in this way by the 'gravitational field' of the character it describes. The effect of this is that very little of we are told about character thoughts or feelings strikes us as reliable or determinate. Indeed, the relentless use of free indirect discourse makes it difficult even to know to whom we should attribute particular words or phrases, the narrator or the characters. This is what makes 'Clay', for example, such a problematic story to interpret, for so extensively do the vocabulary and expressive mannerisms of the central character, Maria, pervade the narration that it is impossible to work out the extent of her self-awareness. As Margot Norris puts it, Joyce narrates Maria 'as she would like to catch someone speaking about her to someone else'.[11] Accordingly, one can compose equally valid readings of Maria that portray her as intensely knowing and self-aware, and at the same time as quite ignorant and oblivious to her own embarrassment: it depends whether one attributes various statements in the narrative to Maria or the narrational voice – whether, that is, one regards them as objective commentary or self-constructions. The consequences of this epistemological confusion are felt most acutely in the final pages during the Hallow Eve game Maria plays with the Donnelly family. There Joyce has Maria touch the clay, which everyone of course recognizes as symbolic of impending death. But audaciously, he grants no access to Maria's thoughts or feelings at this crucial juncture: on the contrary, the narration draws a blank on the content of Maria's mind. We have no way of reckoning if Maria understands the significance of having touched the clay. For that reason we cannot know if she is simply unconscious of the reality of her own situation, which the touching of the clay signifies for everyone else in the room, or whether she chooses not to acknowledge it as part of an elaborate strategy of self-defence. These are the questions about Maria that we find ourselves asking from the very outset of the story, and we continue to ask them after it has concluded.

Similarly elusive is Duffy, the central consciousness of 'A Painful Case'. More conspicuously than in any other story, Joyce stresses the extent to which subjectivity and identity are fabrications of language. Duffy is a voracious and, to judge by his habit of annotating his books, a critical reader. The Platonic relationship he forms with a married woman, Mrs Sinico, largely centres around reading and knowledge as he lends her books from his own shelves and informs her about the ideas contained in them. As this suggests, the relationship is a somewhat solipsistic affair for Duffy, who finds himself 'listening to the sound of his own voice' as he converses with Mrs Sinico. On the one occasion when she presents an alternative to his point of view, he is left feeling 'disillusioned' and quickly brings an end to their association.

When later Duffy learns of Mrs Sinico's death, he is apparently struck by powerful sensations of regret and by the consequent anxiety that his 'moral nature [is] falling to pieces'. I say 'apparently' because it is at this point, when we seem to draw closest to Duffy's innermost thoughts and feelings, that the discursive complexity of Joyce's style most troubles our reaction to him. Up until the point of his posthumous reflections on Mrs Sinico, Duffy has been characterized largely through his relationship to the texts he reads. Indeed, the central conviction upon which he bases his decision to break off with Mrs Sinico – namely that the sexual instinct makes Platonic friendship between men and women impossible – is a borrowing from the philosopher Friedrich Nietzsche, whose work we know Duffy has read. His dependence on such high-cultural intertexts, along with his arrogant disdain for the 'inane expressions' of newspaper journalists and advertisement writers, are elements of a heightened awareness and self-consciousness around language that infiltrates every aspect of Duffy's thinking and being. At one point we read that he 'had an odd autobiographical habit which led him to compose in his mind from time to time a short sentence about himself containing a subject in the third person and a predicate in the past tense'. The effect of this statement is to cast doubt on the authenticity of Duffy's regretful thoughts about Mrs Sinico, most of which are conveyed in just the sort of sentence he likes to construct about himself:

He turned back the way he had come, the rhythm of the engine pounding in his ears. He began to doubt the reality of what memory told him. He halted under a tree and allowed the rhythm to die away. He could not feel her near him in the darkness nor her voice touch his ear. He waited for some minutes, listening. He could hear nothing: the night was perfectly silent. He listened again: perfectly silent. He felt that he was alone.

Reading this as a passage of free indirect discourse raises the possibility that what Joyce is giving us here is not the dramatic coming-into-being of Duffy's moral nature, but yet another of his solipsistic self-constructions.

Throughout *Dubliners* one witnesses Joyce's coming to terms with the idea that meaning and identity are ultimately discursive phenomena, which is to say that they are constructed in language. What this suggests is that, instead of separating *Dubliners* off from *Ulysses* and *Finnegans Wake* as earlier critics tended to do, we should regard it as the first instalment in Joyce's career-long project of reconceiving the relationship between language, representation and the world. Certainly, Joyce's modernist peers and successors, including Ezra Pound, Edmund Jaloux and Samuel Beckett, regarded the short stories in these terms, Pound praising them for the way they challenged the conventions of modern fiction and claiming that they set an 'international standard of prose writing'.[12] While *Dubliners* may not be as obviously allusive and referential a text as *Ulysses*, it is important to notice that every story in it contains some reference to another text or texts, and that many of the stories, such as 'An Encounter', 'A Painful Case' and 'The Dead', take writing or the status of writing as their subject, at least in part. Placing the book in the mainstream of literary modernism, rather than on its periphery, alerts us to the central role that the short form played in the formation of modernist fictional aesthetics, an issue I will consider in more depth in the discussion of Katherine Mansfield, Virginia Woolf and Samuel Beckett.

Chapter 5

Virginia Woolf

In a widely cited essay, Mary Louise Pratt argues that the relationship between the short story and the novel is not one of 'contrasting equivalents', but is 'hierarchical', 'with the novel on top and the short story dependent'. Pratt offers both conceptual and historical justifications for this claim. The conceptual case is that 'shortness cannot be an intrinsic property of anything, but occurs only relative to something else'. In other words, the short story is 'short' only by comparison to the novel. The historical argument is that the novel has prevailed because it is self-evidently 'the more powerful and prestigious of the two genres', with the short story functioning as a 'training or practice ground for the apprentice novelist'. The attempts by theorists stretching back to Brander Matthews in the 1890s to identify the unique properties of the short form ought now, Pratt contends, to give way to a recognition of the 'dependent (rather than interdependent) relation between short story and novel'.[1]

Pratt's thesis would appear to be borne out in the careers of many twentieth-century writers for whom, as John Barth describes, a 'pattern of working in the short story, building a reputation, and advancing to the novel' has prevailed.[2] What is more, the publishing industry has continued to treat the short story as a low-capital testing ground for talent that will find its full expression in longer work. It is difficult, in fact, to name very many writers of note whose careers and reputations have rested solely on short fiction. In English the list would not run much beyond Katherine Mansfield, Frank O'Connor, Donald Barthelme, Raymond Carver, Amy Hempel and Alice Munro. And yet it does not follow that the relationship between the novel and short story is one of 'dependence', as Pratt puts it, rather than 'interdependence', or that '[t]he novel has through and through conditioned both the development of the short story and the critical treatment of the short story', rather than the other way around. There are two objections one might raise here, covering both the theoretical and historical aspects of Pratt's argument. The first is to Pratt's asserting a principle of non-contamination of the novel by the short story. That is to say, she sees the novel as self-sufficient, a totality, with the short form dependent or supplementary to it. As Jacques Derrida has pointed out, the notion of a totality based on this kind of expulsion, or 'supplementation', is illogical: the very presence of the supplement (in this case the short story) corrupts the idea that we are dealing with a self-sufficient totality at all. More tangibly, however, one can point to numerous historical instances where the short story has served as the aesthetic model by which novelistic practice was revolutionized, rather than the other way around. Modernism is one such instance. Not only did several landmark novels, such as Joyce's *Ulysses* and Woolf's *Mrs Dalloway*, begin life as short stories, but in the case of Woolf, as I now want to explore, revolutionizing the theory and practice of 'modern fiction' was directly connected to her reading of, and experimenting with, the short story form.

Woolf wrote short fiction throughout her career, from early unpublished experiments with narrative voice and characterization in stories such as 'Phyllis and Rosamund' (1906) and 'The Journal of Mistress Joan Martyn' (1906), to plot-driven, playful and somewhat contrived pieces turned out for mass-circulation American magazines like *Harper's Bazaar* in the 1930s and 40s – stories such as 'The Duchess and the Jeweller' (1938), 'The Shooting Party' (1938) and 'Lappin and Lapinova' (1939). Woolf herself described many of these later works as 'pot boiling stories for America', and took pleasure in recording the significant sums of money she received for them. But it is to the period 1916–23 that Woolf's major work in the short story belongs. These were the years in which, as she put it in a letter, she broke free of the 'exercise in the conventional style' of her early writing; it was also when she began her theorizing in earnest about the future of 'modern fiction'. There is an unignorable simultaneity between the appearance of her landmark essays on writing – 'Tchehov's Questions', 'The Russian View', 'Modern Novels', 'The Russian Background', 'Reading', 'On Re-Reading Novels', 'How it Strikes a Contemporary' and 'Mr Bennett and Mrs Brown' – and the composition of her most important and experimental stories, including 'The Mark on the Wall', 'Kew Gardens', 'The Evening Party', 'Solid Objects', 'Sympathy', 'An Unwritten Novel', 'A Haunted House', 'A Society', 'Monday or Tuesday', 'The String Quartet', 'Blue and Green', 'A Woman's College from Outside', 'In the Orchard' and 'Mrs Dalloway in Bond Street'. What is more, it is notable how frequently she turns her essays to the contemporary short story to illustrate a point or carry an argument. Far from 'dependence' on the novel, the short story was the medium in which Woolf set about transforming narrative fiction and adapting it to the task of conveying the texture of human consciousness.

Before turning to the stories in detail, it is useful to describe some of the main aspects of Woolf's thought in this period. Her central concern was with the relationship between the way the mind experiences reality and the way the writer conveys that experience in narrative form. Criticizing her contemporaries

Arnold Bennett, H. G. Wells and John Galsworthy for their 'materialism', she set out on an ambitious quest for a means of rendering in fictional form the multi-dimensional quality of consciousness. Here is how she put it in her 1925 essay 'Modern Fiction':

> Examine for a moment an ordinary mind on an ordinary day. The mind
> receives a myriad impressions – trivial, fantastic, evanescent, or
> engraved with the sharpness of steel. From all sides they come, an
> incessant shower of innumerable atoms; and as they fall, as they shape
> themselves into the life of Monday or Tuesday, the accent falls differently
> from of old; the moment of importance came not here but there; so that,
> if a writer were a free man and not a slave, if he could write what he
> chose, not what he must, if he could base his work upon his own feeling
> and not upon convention, there would be no plot, no comedy, no
> tragedy, no love interest or catastrophe in the accepted style, and
> perhaps not a single button sewn on as the Bond Street tailors would
> have it. Life is not a series of gig-lamps symmetrically arranged; life is a
> luminous halo, a semi-transparent envelope surrounding us from the
> beginning of consciousness to the end. Is it not the task of the novelist to
> convey this varying, this unknown and uncircumscribed spirit, whatever
> aberration or complexity it may display, with as little mixture of the
> alien and external as possible? We are not pleading merely for courage
> and sincerity; we are suggesting that the proper stuff of fiction is other
> than custom would have us believe it.[3]

This passage does many things at once. Notice the way in which the discussion of the receptive processes of the human mind extend seamlessly for Woolf into considerations of narrative form. Understanding the nature of experience – 'an incessant shower of innumerable atoms' – inevitably leads to the abandonment of structural conventions of plot, genre, and 'accepted style', in the same way that materialism (imaged in the gig-lamps, the Bond Street tailors, and everything 'alien and external' to the self) gives way to the quasi-spiritual roster of 'impression', 'feeling', 'halo' and 'consciousness'. Meanwhile, the break with materialist conventions in narrative technique feeds back into an ideological opposition to materialism in its broader, socio-economic sense. By challenging the 'custom' of fiction, Woolf targets not just the established devices of writing, but the tendency of Bennett and his fellows to think about people in terms of class and money – 'custom' in its social and economic forms. Bennett characterizes, Woolf argues elsewhere, by a kind of materialist shorthand, relying on the 'institutions' of culture – 'factories, prisons, workhouses, law courts . . . congeries of streets and houses'[4] – to establish an individual's status or social standing. He is uninterested in the actual convolutions of human

personality. As Woolf sees it, modern fiction must provide a means of transcending this superficial world-view; it must resist rather than collude with the
dehumanizing processes of commoditization. As one recent critic puts it, she
sees the role of fiction as 'laying bare the counterfeit currency of capitalized
culture'.[5]

Woolf first found a means of giving fictional expression to this cluster of
broadly anti-materialist values in the short story. She began reading the work
of Russian writers such as Anton Chekhov, whose stories were then appearing in
Constance Garnett's multi-volume English translation (1916–22). Woolf was
particularly drawn to what she termed Chekhov's 'note of interrogation'[6] – that
is, his willingness to leave matters puzzlingly unresolved at the end of his stories.
More than a mere formal conceit, she considered this the mark of the 'soul' in
Chekhov's writing, his ability transcend the 'affectation, pose, insincerity'[7] that
so beleaguered the work of his English contemporaries. As in 'Modern Fiction',
Woolf finds a close correlation between the aversion to narrative convention
and the expression of anti-materialist, even spiritual values:

> half the conclusions of fiction fade into thin air; they show like
> transparencies with a light behind them – gaudy, glaring, superficial.
> The general tidying up of the last chapter, the marriage, the death, the
> statement of values so sonorously trumpeted forth, so heavily
> underlined, become of the most rudimentary kind . . . There may be no
> answer to these questions, but at the same time let us never manipulate
> the evidence so as to produce something fitting, decorous, agreeable to
> our vanity.[8]

In stories such as 'The Mark on the Wall', 'Kew Gardens', 'Solid Objects' and
'An Unwritten Novel', the refusal to 'tidy up' expresses an ideological resistance
to authoritative, rational-scientific determinations of the sort made by 'profes-
sors or specialists or house-keepers with the profiles of policemen'. That list of
know-it-alls comes from 'The Mark on the Wall', the first story Woolf published
with the Hogarth Press (the imprint she and her husband Leonard founded in
1917). 'The Mark on the Wall' is a particularly revealing text because it makes
explicit the correlation between the pursuit of 'answers' in narrative fiction and
the materialist pursuit of knowledge as a means of comprehensive control. Put
simply, the story revolves around a question: what is the mark on the wall? This
is the question the narrator asks as she sits in her room. It is also, of course,
the question that motivates the reader's curiosity, and we read on in the hope
and expectation that it will be answered, that the narrative's central enigma
will be resolved. The story advances by repeatedly deferring the answer to the
question – not in itself an unusual gesture since narrative customarily creates

suspense in this way, generating forward momentum by provoking curiosity in the reader. Woolf employs this narrative 'hook', however, only to deconstruct it by rendering the 'solution' to the story irrelevant. We are duped into supposing that the answer to the question will, in the manner of a whodunnit, somehow make sense of the preceding narrative, that the various details of the story will come into order as part of some now-intelligible pattern of meaning, just as the clues in a murder mystery suddenly make sense when the culprit is revealed.

In Woolf's narrative, however, the revelation that the mark on the wall is a snail does not have this effect; rather, the point of the story lies in the *not* knowing. The narrator defers discovering the answer to the question not out of a wish to create suspense, but to sustain indefinitely the condition of uncertainty. She does not want to know what the mark on the wall is because she wishes to preserve the 'intoxicating sense of illegitimate freedom' that comes from crediting 'the mystery of life', 'the inaccuracy of thought', the 'ignorance of humanity'. She wants to resist what she terms 'the masculine point of view', that is, the point of view that codifies, classifies and enumerates, that wants to know exactly what the mark on the wall is:

> the masculine point of view which governs our lives, which sets the standard, which establishes Whitaker's Table of Precedency, which has become, I suppose, since the war, half a phantom to many men and women, which soon, one may hope, will be laughed into the dustbin where the phantoms go, the mahogany sideboards and the Landseer prints, Gods and Devils, Hell and so forth, leaving us all with an intoxicating sense of illegitimate freedom – if freedom exists . . .
> In certain lights that mark on the wall seems actually to project from the wall. Nor is it entirely circular. I cannot be sure, but it seems to cast a perceptible shadow.

Whitaker's Table of Precedency, also known as Whitaker's Almanack, is an annually published book of factual information concerning the various ranks in public life and their role on formal occasions. It is, in other words, a record of tradition and convention analogous, in Woolf's mind at least, to the idealized vision of rural Victorian stability represented in Edwin Landseer's paintings. In the second paragraph of this passage, a contrast is established at the level of grammar and vocabulary to the kind of knowledge dealt with in Whitaker's. 'In certain lights' is, despite the allusion to certainty, distinctly non-specific and evasive; and the mark is not 'entirely circular'. Moreover, the mark 'seems actually' to project from the wall. One might wonder from this whether it actually does or actually doesn't project from the wall, but in fact that slippery uncertainty and lack of distinctness in the language is deliberate. By contrast with Whitaker's four-square certainties stand the narrator's hesitant, sensitive enquiries into her environment, her puzzling over minutiae, the quality of air in the room, and the size of thoughts. The final word, 'shadow', captures the quality of the narration – something perceptible but immaterial, composed of inconclusive utterances, ambiguous meanings, gaps, tailings-off and questions unanswered.

In 'The Mark on the Wall', Woolf sets up a dialogue between opposing kinds of knowledge. On the one hand, she presents the rational-scientific mind that lists and quantifies and regulates, that sets out rules and timeframes and schemes of being. On the other, she presents the attitude that relishes uncertainty, resists closure and plays host to contradiction, puzzlement, aperture. The narrator does not want to know what the mark on the wall is because to know would mean being wrenched out of the delightful condition of *not* knowing, of being free to let one's thoughts meander and fill up with the possibility of what *might* be. For the narrator, there is nothing duller than discovering, or worse still being told, what something is or means:

> And if I were to get up at this very moment and ascertain that the mark on the wall is really – what shall I say? – the head of a gigantic old nail, driven in two hundred years ago, which has now, owing to the patient attrition of many generations of housemaids, revealed its head above the coat of paint, and is taking its first view of modern life in the sight of a white-walled fire-lit room, what should I gain? Knowledge? Matter for further speculation? I can think sitting still as well as standing up. And what is knowledge? What are our learned men save the descendants of witches and hermits who crouched in caves and in woods brewing herbs, interrogative shrew-mice and writing down the language of the stars? . . . Yes, one could imagine a very pleasant world. A quiet spacious world, with the flowers so red and blue in the open fields. A world without professors or specialists or house-keepers with the profiles of policemen.

In defusing the story's plot, so that it does not matter what the solution to the central enigma of the narrative is, Woolf simultaneously challenges the values and procedures of scientific-materialist enquiry which advances by the same sort of ratiocinative, teleological processes as conventional storytelling. Discovering, as she does inadvertently, that the mark on the wall is a snail comes as a disappointment to the narrator, and is marked by the move from a hesitant, provisional present tense into the past tense: 'It was a snail'. The 'note of interrogation' is dispelled. It is not by chance that the person who gives the game away departs at the end of the story to purchase that most prosaically informative and fact-based of documents, a newspaper.

'The Mark on the Wall's' ridiculing of materialist fact-mongers and answer-seekers is recapitulated in various ways throughout Woolf's stories from this period. 'Solid Objects', for example, is the account of an aspiring young politician called John who forsakes a parliamentary career for a life of desultory wandering around urban waste ground in search of worthless bric-à-brac. John's strange obsession raises questions about the concept of value in modern commodity society. Nothing he collects possesses what his culture would recognize as an exchange-value: in fact, it is the very absence of fungibility about the objects that seems to attract him to them. Consequently, his friends and colleagues find it increasingly difficult to *account* for him, to maintain a sense of who and what he is as he divests himself of the usual markers of status and identity. Even his closest friend is unable to pluck out the heart of John's mystery and is forced to admit, at their final meeting, that 'they were talking about different things'. Once again, Woolf carries over this epistemological uncertainty into the narrative discourse itself, which is riddled with uncertainty, provisionality, and contingency. Self-doubting assertions, modal qualifiers, and an under-lexicalized impressionism characterize the narrative voice: '*No doubt* the act of burrowing in the sand had something to do with it'; 'That impulse, too, *may have been* the impulse which leads a child to pick up one pebble on a path strewn with them'; '*Whether this thought or not* was in John's mind, the lump of glass had its place upon the mantelpiece.' As with 'The Mark on the Wall', the story displaces declarative certainty with interrogative hesitancy.

Similarly, in the unpublished 'Sympathy', Woolf goes out of her way to disrupt the conventional sense-making patterns of narrative in order to preserve her character from any determinate summary or appraisal. Composed in the spring of 1919, 'Sympathy' is contemporaneous with 'Modern Novels' (published in the *Times Literary Supplement* for 10 April 1919) and with two of Woolf's review essays on Constance Garnett's Chekhov, 'Tchehov's Questions' and 'The Russian Background'. In many respects, 'Sympathy' embodies in fictional form what Woolf gleaned from Chekhov – particularly the need for the writer to resist 'half the conclusions of the world' by working against the teleological impulse: 'Accept endlessly, scrutinize ceaselessly, and see what will happen', as she put it in one essay.[9] 'Sympathy' is a story expressly resistant to conclusions, specifically those which the narrator wishes to draw about the characters she describes. The story dramatizes the moment when the narrator, reading the death notice of her friend Humphrey Hammond in *The Times*, reflects on how the unexpected loss leaves her bereft of the chance ever properly to get to know Humphrey or settle particular questions about him. She straight away attempts to compensate for this loss of narrative purchase on her friend's life by making him significant of a larger philosophical reflection on the imminence of death in all living things: 'Death has done it; death lies behind leaves and houses and the smoke wavering up [. . .] This simple young man whom I hardly knew had, then, concealed in him the immense power of death'. Something similar she attempts with Humphrey's widow, Celia, by forming an impression of her solitary grieving life; but this imaginative depiction quickly runs aground on the realization that Celia will always elude comprehension of this sort, that the familiar anatomy of widowhood will never capture the sense of her: 'The outward sign I see and shall see for ever; but at the meaning of it I shall only guess'. It's all 'fancy', the narrator admits: 'I'm not in the room with her, nor out in the wood'. In such a way does the story systematically disprove its own assertions concerning Humphrey and Celia. The narrator wishes to take knowing possession of these people by assigning them to established representations of grief and death; but they both slip from her narrative grasp, Humphrey most spectacularly when, at the end of the story, it becomes clear that the death notice in fact referred to his father, with whom he shared his name. 'O why do you deceive me?' the narrator asks in the final sentence. Humphrey Hammond, in whose ending she had proposed to find his meaning, remains as intricately evasive as any living person. Even his name does not name him.

Woolf's technique of divesting her narrators of certain kinds of possessive authority in these stories is really a creative manifestation of the change she was striving to effect in her own writing, as she sought a way to release herself from the conventionalism that had, she felt, ensnared her early work. As she would later tell her friend Ethel Smyth, it was experiments in short fiction that provided her with the means of dismantling her own practices. She said of her story 'An Unwritten Novel' that it

> was the great discovery . . . That – again in one second – showed me how I could embody all my deposit of experience in a shape that fitted it – not that I have ever reached that end; but anyhow I saw, branching out of the tunnel I made, when I discovered that method of approach, Jacobs Room, Mrs Dalloway etc – How I trembled with excitement; and then Leonard came in, and I drank my milk, and concealed my excitement, and wrote I suppose another page of that interminable Night and Day (which some say is my best book).

As these comments suggest, 'An Unwritten Novel' can be read as a meta-narrative of the decisive turn in Woolf's own career. The story presents an encounter between an unnamed narrator and a woman on a train during which the narrator composes an imaginary identity and set of relationship entanglements for the stranger, as though she were a character in a novel the narrator is writing. The narrator initially conjures up novelistic scenarios for the woman, whom she names Minnie Marsh, in keeping with established story-telling conventions. Studying Minnie's dress and manner, her face, her slippers, her hat-pins, the narrator confidently concludes that she has 'deciphered her secret', and invokes a range of novelistic scenarios in which she supposes that Minnie must have 'committed some crime!', for example, and that she is susceptible to psychoanalytic explication: 'They would say she kept her sorrow, suppressed her secret – her sex, they'd say – the scientific people'. And this being a realistic fiction, with each detail comes the revelation of its significance to the narrative as a whole:

> But what I cannot thus eliminate, what I must, head down, eyes shut, with the courage of a battalion and the blindness of a bull, charge and disperse are, indubitably, the figures behind the ferns, commercial travellers. There I've hidden them all this time in the hope that somehow they'd disappear, or better still emerge, as indeed they must, if the story's to go on gathering richness and rotundity, destiny and tragedy, as stories should.

The contract binding on any act of storytelling is that causal expectations will be fulfilled, that anything which gains admittance to the narrative – even the figures behind the ferns – will finally be made to count in accountable ways. But of course, in Woolf's text, such rules do not pertain, and Minnie's story ultimately refuses to come to order. 'Have I read you right?' the narrator begins to wonder, pressing on nevertheless in the belief that Minnie's life can be known, that there 'must be Jimmy', there 'must be Moggridge' in it. When Minnie alights from the train to be met by her son, the narrator's version begins to fall apart. The story ends with the narrator acknowledging the failure of conventional narrative aspirations, but descrying a new set of compositional possibilities:

> And yet the last look of them – he stepping from the kerb and she following him round the edge of the big building brims me with wonder – floods me anew. Mysterious figures! Mother and son. Who are you? Why do you walk down the street? Where tonight will you sleep, and then, to-morrow? Oh, how it whirls and surges – floats me afresh! I start after them. People drive this way and that. The white light splutters and pours. Plate-glass windows. Carnations; chrysanthemums. Ivy in dark gardens. Milk carts at the door. Wherever I go, mysterious figures, I see you, turning the corner, mothers and sons; you, you, you. I hasten, I follow. This, I fancy, must be the sea. Grey is the landscape; dim as ashes; the water murmurs and moves. If I fall on my knees, if I go through the ritual, the ancient antics, it's you, unknown figures, you I adore; if I open my arms, it's you I embrace, you I draw to me – adorable world!

Once again, it is the 'note of interrogation' that prevails: 'Who are you? Why do you walk down the street? Where tonight will you sleep, and then, to-morrow?' Minnie Marsh evades capture: she remains singular, 'mysterious', as averse to the narrative fixtures of psychoanalysis, social realism or sensational fiction as the text she inhabits.

For many readers, Woolf's fondness for open-ended questioning and her aversion to omniscient or determinate perspectives in her stories are evidence of an essentially anti-authoritarian, anti-hierarchical impulse running through her major work. Yet one must be careful not to carry too far this idea of an egalitarian, democratic social vision in Woolf. She was, after all, a prominent member of the Bloomsbury circle, that unapologetically exclusive literary and artistic coterie that included her sister Vanessa, the art critic Clive Bell and painter Roger Fry, the economist John Maynard Keynes and the historian Lytton Strachey. It is important therefore to retain a sense of Woolf as embedded in the cultural politics, as well as the aesthetic project, of high-modernism. Her enthusiasm for the short story takes on an additional significance when placed in this context too, for it is clear that she was drawn to the 'note of interrogation' as a deliberate provocation to the sort of unimaginative reader who, wedded to convention, looks for 'some unmistakable sign that now the story is going to pull itself together and make straight as an arrow for its destination'. Such a reader, as she described in 'Tchehov's Questions', is left by the interrogative story feeling 'giddy, uncomfortable' and 'looking rather more blankly when the end comes'.[10] Inherently baffling to the docile consumer of fiction, Woolf saw the short story as a form through which the practice of reading could be reformed; and that reformation was, as she knew, necessary to her own developing aesthetic project. Through the theory and practice of the short story, Woolf cleared a space for herself by constructing an audience responsive to the kind of fiction she was herself wished to produce. By sounding the 'note of interrogation', and by forging a critical discourse that was not, as she put it in 'The Russian Point of View', 'based upon the assumption that stories ought to conclude in a way that we recognise', she put the short form at the very heart of the modernist ambition to 'raise the question of our own fitness as readers'.[11]

Chapter 6

Katherine Mansfield

There are two distinct periods in Katherine Mansfield's short writing life. The first covers the years from 1908 until 1917, during which time she moved from her native New Zealand to take up the bohemian life in London, got married, divorced, contracted gonorrhoea, got married again, published her first volume of short stories, the curiously satirical and commercially unsuccessful *In A German Pension* (1911) and suffered the loss of her beloved brother in the First World War. The second period runs from 1917 until her untimely death from tuberculosis in 1923, and although much the shorter, saw her compose all of the stories for which she is now revered and remembered. Within that period there are two events in particular that represent turning points in Mansfield's life and career: the first is her engagement with Anton Chekhov's short stories; the second is her accepting an invitation from Virginia Woolf to write a story for the newly established Hogarth Press.

The question of Mansfield's indebtedness to Chekhov has had a long and at times controversial history, not least because of the accusation, first levelled in 1935, that her story 'The Child-Who-Was-Tired' plagiarized Chekhov's 'Sleepyhead'.[1] Whatever the extent and nature of the debt in that particular story, Mansfield's critical observations, like Woolf's, reveal the importance of Chekhov's interrogative style to her developing sense of the form the short story might take. 'What the writer does is not so much to *solve* the question but to *put* the question,' she wrote to Woolf in May 1919. 'There must be the question put. That seems to me a very nice dividing line between the true and the false writer'.[2] The following month she told S. S. Koteliansky (with whom she translated some of Chekhov's correspondence) that this refusal to 'solve' was 'one of the most valuable things I have ever read. It opens – it discovers rather, a new world'.[3] Reading Constance Garnett's multi-volume translation, she was struck by the stories' irresolute quality, and particularly the way in which consequential relationships between elements in the Chekhovian narrative were suppressed. She wrote, again to Koteliansky, of Garnett's translation of 'The Steppe' (from *The Bishop and Other Stories*) that it had apparently 'no beginning or end', and marvelled at the compositional method by which Chekhov 'touched one point with his pen – and then another point – *enclosed* something which had, as it were, been there forever'.[4]

Like Woolf, Mansfield regarded Chekhov as a potentially liberating force in English letters. Reading him, as she reflected to Dorothy Brett, she came to disdain the routine contrivances of fiction, such as the motivating 'problem' in a story's plot:

> Tchehov *said* over and over again, he protested, he begged, that he had no problem. [. . .] It worried him but he always said the same. No problem. [. . .] The 'problem' is the invention of the 19th-century. The artist takes a *long look* at Life. He says softly, 'So this is what Life is, is it?' And he proceeds to express that. All the rest he leaves.[5]

Chekhov's example also conditioned Mansfield's view of her English contemporaries, who, she claimed, lacked any sense of what the short story form could do or be. In a review of Elizabeth Robins's collection *The Mills of the Gods*, for example, she questioned whether Chekhov's 'The Lady with the Dog' was a 'short story' at all, so wholly different was it from what English readers and writers evidently understood by the term. Robins she berated for writing the kind of 'wholesome, sentimental' stories 'that might have appeared in any successful high-class magazine' – fiction that exuded a certain '[e]xperience, confidence, and a workmanlike style', but that was ultimately 'hollow' and dismally dependent on 'false situations'.[6]

Again like Woolf, Mansfield saw such conventionalism as symptomatic of an essentially 'materialist' mind-set and failure to engage with the deeper mysteries (a favourite term in her criticism) of the human economy. 'Here is a world of objects accurately recorded,' she noted of George Moore's *Esther Waters*, 'here are states of mind set down, and here, above all, is that good Esther whose faith in her Lord is never shaken, whose love for her child is never overpowered – and who cares?'.[7] John Galsworthy's *In Chancery*, meanwhile, she criticized for presenting 'a brilliant display of analysis and dissection, but without any "mystery", any unplumbed depth to feed our imagination upon'.[8] Technical excellence married to emotional timidity she saw even in the work of her more highbrow English contemporaries. E. M. Forster, she declared, 'never gets any further than warming the teapot. He's a rare fine hand at that. Feel this teapot. Is it not beautifully warm? Yes, but there ain't going to be no tea';[9] while George Bernard Shaw she accused of being 'uninspired': 'a kind of concierge in the house of literature – sits in a glass case – sees everything, knows everything, examines the letters, *cleans the stairs*, but has no part in the life that is going on'.[10]

The writers who occupied the rooms in the 'house of literature' were, by contrast, all Russian: Dostoyevsky, Tolstoy and, of course, Chekhov. If the impact of translated Russian literature on Virginia Woolf's work became apparent when combined with the new publishing freedoms offered by the advent of the Hogarth Press, something of the same is true of Mansfield, whose transformation of her unfinished novel *The Aloe* into the story *Prelude* was made in response to Woolf's request, in April 1917, for a contribution to the new imprint. Eventually published by the Woolfs in July 1918, *Prelude* began 'the phase on which [Mansfield's] reputation as a writer rests'.[11]

Mansfield recognized that *Prelude* was a major breakthrough in her artistic development. It was the story in which, as she put it in a letter to Dorothy Brett, she discovered a narrative form adequate to the representation of memory and experience:

> What form is it? you ask. Ah, Brett, it's so difficult to say. As far as I know it's more or less my own invention. And how have I shaped it? This is about as much as I can say about it. You know, if the truth were known I have a perfect passion for the island where I was born . . . Well, in the early morning there I always remember feeling that this little island has dipped back into the dark blue sea during the night only to rise again at beam of day . . . I tried to catch that moment – with something of its sparkle and its flavour. And just as on those mornings white milky mists rise and uncover some beauty, then smother it again and then again disclose it. I tried to lift that mist from my people and let them be seen and then to hide them again.[12]

The pattern of revealing and hiding that Mansfield pinpoints here captures the substance of the revision that she made to *The Aloe* as she shaped it into *Prelude*, for in taking a 'giant bite'[13] out of her manuscript, she did away with many of the supporting narrative continuities and conventions of the original novel project. Specifically, she divided the four long chapters of *The Aloe* into twelve sections held together less by any discursive logic than by spatial juxtaposition and contiguity. In addition, she cut several lengthy sections that provided psychological elaboration of her female characters. Comparing the two texts, one notices that while most of the material concerning the central male character, Stanley Burnell, is carried over intact, the sections dealing with his wife, Linda, her mother, Mrs Fairfield, and her sister Beryl are severely curtailed. The effect of this is to imbue the female characters, as Mansfield put it in her journal at the time, with a 'sense of mystery, a radiance, an afterglow'. Like Woolf, her vision of a new kind of fiction – 'No novels, no problem stories, nothing that is not simple, open' – would be more than a matter of transcending the limitations of her own earlier work, but the means of reaching beneath the 'appearance of things'.[14]

It has been said of *The Aloe*'s redaction into *Prelude* that Mansfield set out to 'eliminate the personal intrusion' in the narrative, to remove traces of the author's voice, in effect, by 'bring[ing] the narration closer to a specific character's consciousness and away from interpretation by an omniscient narrator'.[15] This is true up to a point. Much of what was omitted in the transition *was* material of this sort – novelistic embellishments such as the satirical characterization of the Samuel Josephs' 'swarm' of children, and of Mrs Samuel Joseph surveying them from afar with 'pride . . . like a fat General watching through field glasses his troops in violent action'. Yet it is clear from comparison of the two texts that Mansfield was just as concerned to curtail passages of interior monologue and character-focalized observation where these restricted or simplified the motives of her characters, and that elsewhere the omniscient point-of-view was retained, as for instance in the description of Mrs Fairfield that commences section six of *Prelude*.

But it is in the material concerning Linda's reflections on her mother and domesticity that we see the most profound effects of Mansfield's revisions, and can begin to descry the outlines of her mature story aesthetic. In *The Aloe*, Linda repeatedly considers her lack of interest in her new home: 'The house can bulge cupboards and pantries, but other people will explore them. Not me,' she thinks at one point, and witnesses by contrast her mother's effortless command of the domestic space: 'There was a charm and a grace in all her movements. It was not that she merely "set in order"; there seemed to be almost a positive quality in the obedience of things to her fine old hands. They found not only their proper but their perfect place.' Linda's aversion to the duties of the home creates an antagonism towards her mother that finds direct expression in *The Aloe*:

> 'If I were to *jump* out of bed now, *fling* on my clothes, *rush* downstairs, *tear* up a ladder, hang pictures, eat an enormous lunch, romp with the children in the garden this [afternoon] and swinging on the gate, waving, when Stanley hove in sight this evening I believe you'd be delighted – A normal, healthy day for a young wife and mother – '

All of this material is absent from the *Prelude*. Section five of the story, where this passage would initially have stood, moves from Linda's waking dream of her father and the bird that is transformed into a baby, through her conversation with Stanley, to her anthropomorphic imaginings about the objects in the room. Mrs Fairfield appears in section six, but when Linda briefly contemplates her then, it is without any trace of the antagonism or threat that was so prominent in *The Aloe*. Instead, the stress falls on Linda's complicated and conflictual need for her mother:

> Linda leaned her cheek on her fingers and watched her mother. She thought her mother looked wonderfully beautiful with her back to the leafy window. There was something comforting in the sight of her that Linda felt she could never do without. She needed the sweet smell of her flesh, and the soft feel of her cheeks and her arms and shoulders still softer. She loved the way her hair curled, silver at her forehead, lighter at her neck, and bright brown still in the big coil under the muslin cap. Exquisite were her mother's hands, and the two rings she wore seemed to melt into her creamy skin. And she was always so fresh, so delicious. The old woman could bear nothing but fresh linen next to her body and she bathed in cold water winter and summer.

Where in *The Aloe* these observations are dominated, and therefore disintricated, by the association of Mrs Fairfield with an oppressively domesticated femininity, Linda's response to her mother becomes a less determinate matter in *Prelude*. Irritation at Mrs Fairfield's 'simply maddening' manner of doing things is reserved to Linda's unmarried sister Beryl, who feels herself to be 'rotting' in the matrifocal environment. Mansfield makes Linda's feelings much more problematic to untangle, and indeed it becomes possible to argue that Linda sees in her mother a version of feminine self-containment that she envies as much as abhors. Linda does not simplify her mother as Beryl does – in fact, it is precisely those passages in *The Aloe* where she does reflect on her mother's limitations that Mansfield removes in the revision.

Those omissions, so characteristic of the interrogative modernist short story, open up further dimensions in the relationship between Linda and Mrs Fairfield, including the possibility that Linda recognizes and even envies the curious power and liberty her mother's competence, modesty and contentment seem to bring. Feminist readings of the story frequently assert that Linda sees in her mother's life an oppressive destiny. The scene in section eleven when the two women go into the garden at night is taken as evidence of this tension and difference between them: while Linda contemplates the 'hate' she feels for Stanley, her mother thinks about harvesting the fruit trees and currant bushes to make jam, thereby revealing an 'ideological commitment to marriage and motherhood' that Linda does not share.[16] But this is to reckon without Mansfield's interrogative narration, which renders Linda's feelings about her mother one of the 'questions put' in the story, as it does Mrs Fairfield's comprehension of her daughter's unhappiness. It is equally valid to infer, for example, that Mrs Fairfield embodies an alternative kind of independence and self-containment that Linda feels herself falling short of, yet which she needs and craves. In the passage quoted above, it is her mother who successfully counters Stanley's 'firm, obedient body', not with Linda's sort of late-sleeping languidness, but with an orderly and eloquent physicality of her own. When they enter the garden together in section eleven, Linda wishes to communicate using 'the special voice that women use at night to each other as though they spoke in their sleep or from some hollow cave'. That Mrs Fairfield responds with thoughts of harvesting the fruit trees and of 'pantry shelves thoroughly well stocked with our own jam' is neither demeaned by Linda nor invalidated by the narration – it is not, as Linda has it in *The Aloe*, a symptom of her mother's confinement. Rather, Mrs Fairfield represents one of several possible fulfilments of feminine identity that her young granddaughter Kezia encounters in the course of the story and that she must negotiate as part of her own journey into womanhood.

The transformation of *The Aloe* into *Prelude* marks the moment when Mansfield began to reckon creatively with the 'note of interrogation' in her short stories. Everything about the revisionary process is aimed at preserving multiplicity and heterogeneity in characterization and meaning. As with Woolf, however, it is necessary to locate the development of that fictional aesthetic within the larger cluster of modernist cultural values. And for this, it is necessary to look at some of the critical material Mansfield collaborated on with her husband John Middleton Murry.

Although Mansfield and Murry always regarded themselves as outsiders among the so-called Bloomsbury set, of which Woolf and her husband Leonard were part, they were nevertheless deeply attracted to the idea of the exclusive avant-garde coterie. In particular, they shared the contempt that many in the Woolfs' circle harboured towards commercialism and the spread of mass popular culture. Early in her career, Mansfield had become associated with the Fauvist group of artists, for whom the function of art was to uncover the strange and barbaric impulses that fester below the surface of civilization. She had formed a particularly close relationship with the painter J. D. Fergusson, who together with Murry launched the magazine *Rhythm* to publicize Fauvist work and thinking and to pass comment on the state of contemporary art and culture. Much Fauvist thinking was explicitly elitist and anti-materialist in nature, taking its lead from Arthur Symons, whose *Symbolist Movement in Literature* envisaged a modern art in 'revolt against exteriority, against rhetoric, against a materialistic tradition'.[17] In the essays she co-authored with Murry for *Rhythm*, Mansfield harnessed Symons' aesthetic credo to an unabashedly elitist sociocultural agenda. 'The History of Art has been the history of a misunderstanding of a minority by a majority', the couple asserted in 'The Meaning of Rhythm', for example, going on to argue that the quasi-divine capacities of 'inspiration' and 'intuition' on which the artist depends had themselves become degraded by use in the common parlance.[18] Against the 'arch-democrat' of popular taste, and against the 'incursion of machine-made realism into modern liteature', the patrician freedoms of the creator must be defended:

> Individuality in the work of art is the creation of reality by freedom. It is the triumphant weapon of aristocracy. It is that daring and splendid thing which the mob hates because it cannot understand and by which it is finally subdued. Only by realizing the unity and the strength of the individual in the work of art is the mob brought to the knowledge of its own infinite weakness, and it loathes and is terrified by it.[19]

In 'Seriousness in Art', similarly, the focus fell on those commercially orientated writers who pander to the mob and who are responsible for turning the 'craft of letters' into a 'trade instead of an art'. Again, it is a symbolist aesthetic derived from Symons that provides the conceptual basis for the social criticism. Art, which should be motivated by 'a perpetual striving towards an ever more adequate symbolic expression of the living realities of the world', languishes instead in dismal compliance with the culture that sustains it, replicating the 'comfortable competence' and 'absolute conformity' upon which 'financial success' and the very 'life of democracy' depend. In that superficial and materialistic world of 'trademarks', 'bagmen' and 'book financiers', where everything has 'a purely external value', the true artist is known by his 'enthusiasm and . . . seriousness', which qualities 'wedded together are the hall-mark of aristocracy, the essentials of the leader'.[20]

That the question of art's place and significance in a money society had long been a concern of Mansfield's is evident from 'Juliet', the unfinished manuscript of a novel composed around 1907. There she depicts her young heroine caught between, on the one hand, a bourgeois colonial existence dominated by her 'commonplace and commercial' father with his 'undeniable *trade* atmosphere', and on the other, life in a dismal London flat: 'This struggle for bread, this starvation of Art. How could she expect to keep art with her in the ugliness of her rooms, in the sordidness of her surroundings'. A journal entry from the same period records Mansfield's growing estrangement from her family and their materialist values. 'Damn my family!' she declares at one point, 'O Heavens, what bores they are! . . . Even when I am alone in my room, they come outside and call to each other, discuss the butcher's orders or the soiled linen and – I feel – wreck my life.'[21] In the signature stories of her major period, Mansfield would return again and again to the image of a bourgeois world whose values and identity are inscribed in the commodities it fashions and exchanges, and like Woolf, she used interrogative, open-ended narrative forms in an effort to convey the ungraspable, unaccountable qualities of singular personhood that such materialism neglects.

Mansfield's most frequently anthologized story, 'The Garden Party', provides a particularly good example of how these formal and ideological considerations came together in the mature work. The story tells of a young middle-class New Zealand girl called Laura and her encounter, on the day of her mother's garden party, with the dead body of young man from a poor neighbouring family. In Laura's tentative embrace of a more emotionally 'strenuous life' than is thought healthy or appropriate for a girl of her class, she comes not only to recognize the density and human familiarity of lives purportedly different from her own, but to question the materialist values and habits of perception that organize that sense of class difference in the first place.

The questioning begins early in the story when Laura finds herself contemplating the 'absurd class distinctions' that quarantine her life from those of the workmen erecting the marquee in her garden. But it is when she is upbraided for her 'extravagant' suggestion that the party be cancelled on account of the dead man and mourning family nearby that the mechanisms by which her family and her class justify and console themselves come into focus:

> 'I don't understand,' said Laura, and she walked quickly out of the room into her own bedroom. There, quite by chance, the first thing she saw was this charming girl in the mirror, in her black hat trimmed with gold daisies and a long black velvet ribbon. Never had she imagined she could look like that. Is mother right? she thought. And now she hoped her mother was right. Am I being extravagant? Perhaps it was extravagant. Just for a moment she had another glimpse of that poor woman and those little children and the body being carried into the house. But it all seemed blurred, unreal, like a picture in the newspaper. I'll remember it again after the party's over, she decided. And somehow that seemed the best plan.

The transformational power of the hat allows Laura escape into an impression of herself, relieving her, for as long as she admires the image, from the tangled burdens of subjectivity and conscience. The hat objectifies her, in short; and it induces self-forgetfulness again a moment later when she passes her brother Laurie on the stairs: intending to tell him of the dead man and solicit his agreement to cancel the party, her resolve is 'blurred' by his mentioning her 'absolutely topping hat': 'Laura said faintly "Is it?" and smiled up at Laurie and didn't tell him after all'. During the party, her costume brings further distracting compliments: 'Laura, you look quite Spanish. I've never seen you look so striking,' one guest declares. Only afterwards, when her mother proposes that she take a basket of leftovers to their stricken neighbours, is she forced to grapple again with the question of her own moral identity.

As she sets off down the road with her gifts, she is still in thrall to the fetishized object-world of her mother and the party:

> Here she was going down the hill to somewhere where a man lay dead, and she couldn't realize it. Why couldn't she? She stopped a minute. And it seemed to her that kisses, voices, tinkling spoons, laughter, the smell of crushed grass were somehow inside her. She had no room for anything else. How strange! She looked up at the pale sky, and all she thought was, 'Yes, it was the most successful party'.

What ensues is Laura's discovery that the commodities that are the outward show of class and privilege are not, as she has been led to suppose, coterminous with identity. Her sudden awareness that her flamboyant hat and dress are inappropriate to the errand on which she is embarked marks the moment when her sense of her true self clashes with her public image. From that point forward in the story every human encounter becomes unsettling and mysterious to her. She gains admittance to the dead man's house 'as though she were expected', and is greeted with a disconcerting familiarity and foreknowlege by the widow's 'fond and sly' sister, whose literal opening of doors and ushering over thresholds has its spiritual corollary in the access she instinctively enjoys to Laura's deeper needs and longings. She it is who uncovers the dead man for Laura to gaze upon, an encounter that completes the separation between what she thinks of as her 'self' and the counterfeit reality of fungible goods she inhabits: 'What did garden-parties and baskets and lace frocks matter to him? He was far from all those things.' When, at the very end of the story, Laura comes upon Laurie for the second time, it is not to seek words of consolation from her older sibling, but to sound the note of interrogation with him: '"Isn't life," she stammered, "Isn't life – " But what life was she couldn't explain . . . "*Isn't* it, darling?" said Laurie.'

Mansfield said of 'The Garden Party' that she had tried to convey in it the 'diversity of life and how we try to fit in everything, Death included . . . But life isn't like that. We haven't the ordering of it.' Her mature stories are littered with moments when those who aspire to comprehension and order are confronted with the inadequacy of their systems of belief, from Monica Tyrell's encounter, in 'Revelations', with the image of her hairdresser's dead child, to Constantia's ineffectual and inarticulate apprehension, in 'The Daughters of the Late Colonel', that her life of enforced 'running out, bringing things home in bags, getting things on approval, discussing them with Jug, and taking them back to get more things on approval, and arranging father's trays and trying not to annoy father', is really no life at all. And, as in 'The Garden Party', such moments of insight yield not new or alternative certainties in Mansfield's narratives, but perpetual equivocations: 'What did it mean? What was it she was always wanting? What did it all lead to? Now? Now?'

That the answers to such questions are permanently deferred in Mansfield's stories (as they are in Woolf's) reflects her impatience with the superficiality of popular fiction and its hackneyed conventions; but it also reveals her attitude towards the broader middle-class culture and its infatuation with what she and Murry in one essay termed 'purely external value'. More than a formal device, the 'question put' creates an interrogative space in a Mansfield narrative that is insusceptible to the rational-materialist world-view – a space in which the self can be preserved against the inauthentic, mass-mediated representations that threaten to swamp it. Characters in her stories can be separated into those, like Laura, who learn to resist such representations, and those, like Laura's mother, who capitulate to them. Growing up in a Mansfield narrative is invariably about discovering whether one has the stomach for the fight, as Kezia must in 'The Doll's House', for example, when her familiy's class-conscious prohibitions debar her from knowledge of the outcast Kelvey children. For those already grown, the struggle is to retain a sense of authentic selfhood in a culture replete with fake identities. When, in 'The Escape', a man retreats from his complaining wife into fantasy and silence, he retreats too from the world that she represents – a snobbish world of appearances, conspicuous consumption, fetishized commodities and (for others, of course) dehumanizing labour. In the only direct observation he makes of her in the story, it is the things she carries that spur his resentment:

> The little bag, with its shiny, silvery jaws open, lay on her lap. He could see her powder-puff, her rouge stick, a bundle of letters, a phial of tiny black pills like seeds, a broken cigarette, a mirror, white ivory tablets with lists on them that had been heavily scored through. He thought: 'In Egypt she would be buried with those things'.

Her need for objects (she prizes her parasol more than she can say) is matched by her need to objectify those around her, denying the 'idiotic hotel people', 'hideous children' and 'Horrid little monkeys' she encounters any semblance of inner life while complaining about their insensitivity to her own. Her greatest fear, unsurprisingly, is loss of face: 'Had he expected her to go outside, to stand under the awning in the heat and point with her parasol? Very amusing picture of English domestic life.' At the end of the story, as the couple travel by train through a darkened landscape, she continues to number him among her possessions – 'My husband . . . My husband' – registering the fact but not understanding the reasons why he is so introverted with her.

A similar estrangement exists between Bertha and Harry Young in 'Bliss', though with the gender roles reversed. Most readings of this story concentrate on the theme of lesbian desire encoded within it, but it is important to note how the subtle and indirect expression of Bertha's feelings towards Pearl Fulton contrast with the acquisitive materialism of the society in which she lives and moves. As in 'The Escape', an opposition emerges between 'self' and 'culture', but unlike that story the conflict that exists between the married couple is played out too in the mind of the protagonist, Bertha. We see it early on when she buys fruit to decorate her home:

> There were tangerines and apples stained with stawberry pink. Some yellow pears, smooth as silk, some white grapes covered with a silver bloom and a big cluster of purple ones. These last she had bought to tone in with the new dining-room carpet. Yes, that did sound rather far-fetched and absurd, but it was really why she had bought them. She had thought in the shop: 'I must have some purple ones to bring the carpet up to the table'. And it had seemed quite sense at the time.
> When she had finished with them and had made two pyramids of these bright round shapes, she stood away from the table to get the effect – and it really was most curious. For the dark table seemed to melt into the dusky light and the glass dish and the blue bowl to float in the air. This, of course, in her present mood, was so incredibly beautiful. . . . She began to laugh.

The fruit, once Bertha arranges it, becomes more than the sum of its parts – indeed, it seems to be a further expression of that imperishable bliss she feels on several occasions during the day. It certainly exceeds Bertha's original intention in buying it, which was to complement her home's interior decoration. A few moments later, she experiences something similar with her baby, Little B, who is transformed from a charming object whom Bertha looks upon 'like the poor little girl in front of the rich little girl with the doll', to a breathing, masticating infant, the loving, needy reality of whom triggers in Bertha another 'feeling of bliss'. She may have lost the keys to her own front door, but she has gained access to something beyond the 'absolutely satisfactory house and garden' that is her public life with Harry.

In that public life, it is objects and commodities – the 'books', the 'music', the 'superb omelettes', the 'money' – that provide the lingua franca of culture and class. From Mrs Norman Knight's 'amusing orange coat with a procession of black monkeys round the hem and up the fronts', to her husband's 'tortoiseshell-rimmed monocle', to Eddie Warren's 'immense white silk scarf' and matching socks, to Harry's box of Egyptian, Turkish, and Virginian cigars, this is a world where personality and status are mediated through possessions. Bertha is part of that world, of course, and she trades in its currency when she invites Pearl and the others to inspect her new coffee machine after dinner. But as before, the *matériel* of Bertha's domestic existence is transformed, this time when the drawing-room curtains are opened to expose the pear tree that stands as the multivalent symbol of her longing for Pearl. That the pear tree, in its various manifestations, is a vividly sexual metaphor should not blind us to its function as an image of Bertha's longing for 'another world', a world of authentic relationships and unmediated intimacy. It is that longing that makes her wish to be alone with Harry, to withdraw from the sham of hospitality and have the Norman Knights and the other guests gone. The 'best of being modern', she reflects, is that she and her husband can be 'such good pals' despite the absence of sex. But in the final pages of the story, it is not just Harry's infidelity but modernity itself in its capitalized, commoditized forms that crowds out togetherness. 'We are the victims of time and train,' the Norman Knights declare, taking their leave, while the image-conscious Eddie seeks refuge from the trials of intimate conversation in what for him is an '*incredibly* beautiful' line of (someone else's) poetry, but which fails to transcend the counterfeit culture it presumes to mock: 'Why Must it Always be Tomato Soup?'. It is left to Harry to state, quite carelessly on his part, the truth of what their life and home have become: 'I'll shut up shop'.

As I have described them, both Woolf's and Mansfield's stories attempt, in various ways, to transcend the forces of commodification; and in both writers' critical statements, we see evidence of what Nicholas Daly considers modernism's concerted effort to 'theorize . . . writing practice as something outside the wasteland of commercial culture'.[22] Of course, it is important to remember that the notion of standing outside of the market and contemporary capitalist culture was one of the central delusions to which the modernists clung. It is more accurate to see modernism as occurring within its own specialist segment of a fragmented literary marketplace, than operating independently of it. Nevertheless, in the way they were able to utilize the short story to reflect the values and ambitions of the cultural elite, Woolf and Mansfield elevated it from its modest origins in oral and popular print culture to a central form of British literary modernism.

Chapter 7
Samuel Beckett

Throughout his career, Samuel Beckett wrote short fiction, and from the publication of *The Unnamable*, in 1952, until his death in 1989 it was his favoured
prose form. Yet Beckett's work is rarely, if ever, considered in the context of
short fiction writing in the twentieth century. This neglect is surprising because,
early on, Beckett explicitly took up with the aesthetic of the modernist story
as he had inherited it from Joyce. Later, after the publication of the Trilogy
(completed 1953), he turned again to short fiction in an effort to find a way
to 'go on' from modernism, and over the next thirty years worked at the very
limits of the genre.

Beckett started writing short fiction in 1932 as work on his first novel, *Dream
of Fair to Middling Women*, began to falter. Salvaging two sections from that
project, he composed a further eight stories featuring the novel's central character, Belacqua Shuah, and published the sequence under the title *More Pricks
Than Kicks* in 1934. In the same year he published another story, 'A Case in
a Thousand', in the *Bookman* magazine, only to then turn his back on short
fiction until the mid-1940s, at which point he began writing in French. From
then on Beckett's career was punctuated by periods of intense experimentation
with short narrative forms and explorations of the limits of expression at the
border with silence. It is in the early work, however, that we find the clearest
evidence of Joyce's influence and of the central role that *Dubliners* would play
in the formation of Beckett's thinking about modernism and how to 'go on'
from it.

'A Case in a Thousand' has been described by John Harrington as Beckett's
'most apparent adoption ... of the style of Joyce's own early work';[1] but perhaps
more telling of the relationship between the two writers are the deliberate
*dis*simulations Beckett makes from Joyce's practice. 'A Case in a Thousand'
centres on a young physician, Dr Nye, who finds himself having to treat his
former nanny's gravely ill son. The young boy dies during surgery, but weeks
later the mother is still to be seen every day lingering in the hospital grounds.
The final scene of the story involves an enigmatic encounter between the mother
and her former ward, Dr Nye:

'There's something I've been wanting to ask you,' he said, looking at the
water where it flowed out of the shadow of the bridge.

She replied, also looking down at the water:

'I wonder would that be the same thing I've been wanting to tell you
ever since that time you stretched out on his bed.'

There was a silence, she waiting for him to ask, he for her to tell.

'Can't you go on?' he said.

*Thereupon she related a matter connected with his earliest years, so
trivial and intimate that it need not be enlarged on here, but from the
elucidation of which Dr. Nye, that sad man, expected great things.*

'Thank you very much,' he said, 'that was what I was wondering.'
(My italics.)

Gaps in Joyce are precisely that – apertures, silences that do not threaten the
illusion of objectivity in the presentation. In Beckett's story, however, the narrating voice is explicit about its act of omission, advertising what it leaves
unsaid. There is no effort here to maintain the objective stance, to disguise the
authorial sleight of hand. Beckett's candour of procedure here demonstrates
his divergence from what is perhaps the defining mannerism of Joyce's short
fiction. The narrator's refusal to tell all is revealed at the same time as it is
enacted; Beckett is not willing to adopt uncritically the Joycean persona of the
artist 'refined out of existence'.

Throughout *More Pricks Than Kicks*, Beckett picks up on aspects of
Dubliners, making explicit that which is normally implicit in the Joycean story.
Linda Hutcheon's description of post-modernist parody as 'repetition with
critical distance', an 'ironic signalling of difference at the very heart of simi-
larity' which allows the writer to 'speak *to* a discourse from *within*', usefully
indicates how Beckett's irony functions.[2] As Hutcheon implies, the parody
here acts not to diminish, or reveal the fallibility of, the text to which it refers.
Rather, it infiltrates the language of its predecessor in order to conduct an ironic
rearticulation of it. When we read the following passage in 'Draff', for example,
we are struck not by the sense that it ridicules the kind of epiphanic moment
experienced by, say, Chandler in 'A Little Cloud', but by the way in which
Beckett gives playful voice to the agonized suppressions of the Joycean story as a
whole:

Hairy, anxious though he was to join the Smeraldina while his face was
at its best, before it relapsed into the workaday dumpling, steak and
kidney pudding, had his work cut out to tear himself away. For he could
not throw off the impression that he was letting slip a rare occasion to
feel something really stupendous, something that nobody had ever felt
before. But time pressed. The Smeraldina was pawing the ground, his

own personal features were waning (or perhaps better, waxing). In the end he took his leave without kneeling, without a prayer, but his brain quite prostrate and suppliant before this first fact of its experience. That was at least something. He would have welcomed a long Largo, on the black notes for preference.

The irony directed at Hairy and his lusting after a certain melancholy depth of feeling is also an illustration of the structural device of the epiphany and the way in which it sets itself up as a moment of illumination. Hairy's appearance is actually 'waning', but the scene demands a dilation of feeling, a 'waxing' – lyrical and lachrymose. Where Joyce's epiphanies are insidiously qualified, if not undermined, by suggestions that they may be fabricated or delusory, Beckett is blatant about the constructed nature of the epiphanic moment: 'Hairy,' we are told, 'felt it was up to him now to feel something'. Beckett's irony works not by supplying a superior rendering of the epiphany, but by exposing the implicatory sleight of hand by which the Joycean story achieves its complexity of effect.

'Draff' ends in a spirit of mild suspensefulness as Hairy and the Smeraldina try to think of an inscription for Belacqua's headstone: 'He did mention one to me once,' Hairy says, 'that he would have endorsed, but I can't recall it'. In typically Joycean fashion, no effort is made to recall it: instead the narrative shifts its focus, in a manner similar to 'Clay' and 'The Boarding House', to a deliberately unrevealing figure – that of the groundsman. 'So it goes in the world' is the final line of the story, but it is not made clear whether this sentiment emanates from the groundsman (perhaps in relation to his own emotion at the 'little song' he is humming to himself), or whether it is meant by the narrator to be the missing epitaph for Belacqua. It might also be read as an oblique acknowledgement of the story's own failure to provide the inscription for Belacqua's headstone. Like Joe's comments on Maria's singing at the end of 'Clay', and like Crofton's opinion of Hynes's poem in 'Ivy Day in the Committee Room', and like the inscrutable thoughts of Polly which conclude 'The Boarding House', the statement hovers interrogatively. Beckett's ending, however, openly signals its ironic self-consciousness about its method:

> The groundsman stood deep in thought. What with the company of headstones sighing and gleaming like bones, the moon on the job, the sea tossing in her dreams and panting, and the hills observing their Attic vigil in the background, he was at a loss to determine off-hand whether the scene was of the kind that is termed romantic or whether it should not with more justice be deemed classical. Both elements were present,

that was indisputable. Perhaps classico-romantic would be the fairest estimate.

Personally he felt calm and wistful. A classico-romantic working-man therefore.

Again, Beckett is simultaneously presenting an epiphany and exposing its inner workings as a device. The groundsman is a figure from the margins, a representative of that 'submerged population group' in which Frank O'Connor says the short story specializes. As with Joyce's endings, there is a refusal to synthesize the various elements of the plot here; instead the narrative shifts to an impressionistic soft-focus. But Beckett applies one more twist by ironically signalling his own contrivance in the scene – its 'classico-romanticism'.

Beckett draws attention in this way to the act of narration itself throughout his early stories, particularly at structural points. In 'A Wet Night', the broad parody of the end of Joyce's 'The Dead' climaxes in this passage:

> But the wind had dropped, as it so often does in Dublin when all the respectable men and women whom it delights to annoy have gone to bed, and the rain fell in a uniform and untroubled manner. It fell upon the bay, the littoral, the mountains and the plains, and notably upon the Central Bog it fell with a rather desolate uniformity.

The parody here functions on many levels. The second sentence ostentatiously fails to follow Joyce's famous original where it leads – from 'treeless hills' and the Bog of Allen, through images of Calvary, to the 'universe', with all its living and its dead. On the Central Bog it's only raining, not snowing. Hugh Kenner has written of how in Joyce's original snow 'rhymes with the uniform inevitability of human stasis', of how it 'levels and unifies all phenomena' in Gabriel's sight.[3] In Beckett's parody, this effect of uniformity, of the levelling of the gravestone, the mountains, Dublin, is toyed with, but the rain's uniformity is grey and mundane and transfigures nothing. Beckett's reiterative use of rain throughout the ruminative last parts of the story imitates Joyce's technique of narrow semantic repetition ('falling softly', 'softly falling', 'falling faintly', 'faintly falling'). Beckett's reiteration, however, plays on a word that has been explicitly depoeticized: 'Now it began to rain upon the earth beneath and greatly incommoded Christmas traffic of every kind by continuing to do so without remission for a matter of thirty six hours'. Furthermore, he does not allow the parodic epiphany to conclude his story. Belacqua leaves his girlfriend's house (having enjoyed the kind of passionate intimacy denied to Gabriel Conroy) in the pitch-dark small hours. The street lamps, which in Joyce's story provide the 'ghostly' twilight shrouding Gretta and also prompt Gabriel's vision of Michael Furey, are extinguished.

In 'Love and Lethe' the crucial scene is again exposed, though in a somewhat different way:

> Who shall judge of his conduct at this crux? Is it to be condemned as wholly despicable? Is it not possible that he was gallantly trying to spare the young woman embarrassment? Was it tact or concupiscence or the white feather or an accident or what? We state the facts. We do not presume to determine their significance.
> 'Digitus Dei' he said 'for once.'
> That remark rather gives him away, does it not?

Beckett's narrator makes explicit the uncertainties which the narrative itself has prompted concerning the motives of the central character – the kinds of questions that Joyce's stories by their reticence cause us to ask. The comment 'That remark rather gives him away, does it not?' makes explicit the relationship the reader typically finds in Joyce: in the absence of a superintending, directive presence we are obliged to supply our own provisional confirmation of the meaning of the various textual details. Earlier in 'Love and Lethe' the narrator was similarly benighted concerning the recurring question in the book, why Belacqua wishes to kill himself:

> How he formed this resolution to destroy himself we are quite unable to discover. The simplest course, when the motives of any deed are found subliminal to the point of defying expression, is to call that deed ex nihilo and have done. Which we beg leave to follow in the present instance.

More than comically disingenuous, this disclaimer again parodies the kind of narratorial withholding which we find repeatedly in Joyce's short fiction. But it does so not by revealing Joyce's blind spots or expediencies but by uncovering the full complexity of his practice. All Beckett's early stories, in fact, can be read as counterpoints to Joyce's. In the treachery of apprenticeship, Beckett voiced the Joycean story's scrupulously unarticulated knowingness. As the narrator says at one point of Belacqua, 'Notice the literary man'. Indeed we do.

Beckett's sensitivity to the devices of *Dubliners* is perhaps best borne out by the opening story from *More Pricks Than Kicks*, 'Dante and the Lobster'. The story begins with Belacqua worrying over an 'impenetrable passage' in Dante – Beatrice's explanation, in the *Paradiso* (ii, 52–148), of why the moon has dark patches. He can follow her 'refutation', but is bemused by the 'proof' because it is delivered as 'a rapid shorthand of the real facts'. Still, he 'pore[s] over the enigma' of the passage, endeavouring to understand 'at least the meanings of the words' – as monads, one presumes, rather than as a connected sequence delivering a singular 'meaning'. Later in the day, at his Italian lesson, Belacqua asks the Ottolenghi about the passage, but she defers an explanation of its sense: 'It is a famous teaser. Off-hand I cannot tell you, but I will look it up when I get home'.

To these puzzles and textual enigmas is added, finally, Dante's pun, 'qui vive la pieta quando e ben morta'. In English the pun on 'pieta' (meaning both 'pity' and 'piety') is lost, which leads Belacqua to wonder if the line is really translatable at all. At any rate this textual enigma patterns his subsequent thoughts: 'Why not piety and pity together both, even down below? Why not mercy and Godliness together? A little mercy in the stress of sacrifice, a little mercy to rejoice against judgement.' As he approaches his aunt's house at the end of the story Beckett conspicuously shifts the scene, preparing us for the epiphanic moment and the emergence of the story's deep-laid significance: 'Let us call it Winter, that dusk may fall now and a moon rise'. Once at his aunt's house, Belacqua is horrified by the realization that the lobster she is about to cook will be boiled alive. There it lies, 'cruciform on the oilcloth', having 'about thirty seconds to live':

> Well, thought Belacqua, it's a quick death, God help us all.
> It is not.

That final line – sounding as an 'impersonal voice out of the heavens'[4] – strikes many readers as a false note, an unnecessary and heavy-handed narratorial intervention. Indeed, the critic John Fletcher takes the presence of this and other 'Beckettian asides' as evidence that the author was unsuited to the short story – a genre, Fletcher explains, in which writers must 'work their effects by understatement and humour rather than explicit comment'.[5] This is to miss the point of Beckett's irony. His story proceeds as though about to reach a highly inferential and impressionistic ending which will bring together, at some deep-laid metaphorical level, the 'meanings' of all its enigmatic details. The last line seems incongruous because instead of the characteristic short story withdrawal at the point of closure, Beckett allows the blatant intrusion of a voice signalling over the characters' heads. He blows the cover under which the story operates, exposing the narrator's presence by making it explicit. It is as though he wishes to terminate the kind of 'lost' or indeterminate endings which characterize the Joycean story. As with 'A Case in a Thousand' and 'A Wet Night' he is unwilling to allow the naturalistic illusion of the inconspicuous or objective narrator to predominate, signalling instead an ironic awareness of how Joyce defers meaning and creates an enigmatic openness in his texts by suppressing the personality of the narrator. As Hugh Kenner put it in his 'Progress Report' some years later, 'To play one more game by the old rules would merely be competence.'[6]

Throughout his career, Beckett was fascinated by the idea of writing 'short' and with taking economy and impoverishment of expression to its limits. He even toyed with the question of how to incorporate silence within the body of a text. In the so-called 'German Letter of 1937' to Axel Kaun, he observes how the 'sound surface' of Beethoven's Seventh Symphony is 'torn by enormous pauses . . . so that through whole pages we can perceive nothing but a path of sounds suspended in giddy heights, linking unfathomable abysses of silence'. Why, he asks, shouldn't writing try to do something similar? Must language be always confined within 'the forest of symbols' and pestered by 'the little birds of interpretation'?[7]

From the 1940s onward, in pieces like 'The End', 'The Expelled' and 'The Calmative', and in *Stories and Texts for Nothing* (1954), Beckett explored these questions in earnest. An early indication of where this journey would take him can be seen in 'The Expelled', which does not simply expose the inner workings of the modernist short story, but questions the validity of the narrating act itself. 'The Expelled' is constructed along the lines of an excursion narrative, a kind of stumbling picaresque in which the narrator, expelled from some undetermined abode, takes his way about a city, eventually bedding down for the night in a cabman's stable. The crux of the narrative is reached as he ponders the potential energy in a box of matches:

> I held the box of matches in my hand, a big box of safety matches. I got up during the night and struck one. Its brief flame enabled me to locate the cab. I was seized, then abandoned, by the desire to set fire to the stable.

We are familiar with such moments of decisive intersection in the modernist short story, possible points of closure and resolution that are summoned up and then dismissed, and Beckett's narrative appears to act in precisely the same way: instead of lighting the fire the narrator leaves the stable and walks towards the dawn light. However, Beckett is not content just to give us a cancelled ending. Instead, he begins to question the arbitrariness of the act of telling the story at all. 'I don't know why I told this story,' the narrator says. 'I could just as well have told another. Perhaps some other time I'll be able to tell another. Living souls, you will see how alike they are'. The critic Linda Hutcheon has said that narrative is the translation of 'knowing into telling';[8] Beckett here questions that intuition, suggesting that what is 'known' is intimately dependent upon what is 'told'.

By the time of the so-called 'residua' of the 1960s, which include pieces such as 'Imagination Dead Imagine', 'Ping' and 'Lessness', Beckett had taken his aesthetic of reduction to new limits. In the modernist short fictions we have been looking at, there is a clear connection between brevity and plurality – the trick of writing less and implying more. Joyce, Woolf and Mansfield were all able to utilize techniques of reduction – ellipsis, occlusion, the suppression of the omniscient narrator – in order to generate open-endedness in their texts. Beckett's abstemiousness goes much further, destabilizing language and its relationship to the world:

> No trace anywhere of life, you say, pah, no difficulty there, imagination not dead yet, yes, dead, good, imagination dead imagine. Islands, waters, azure, verdure, one glimpse and vanished endlessly, omit. Till all white in the whiteness the rotunda. No way in, go in, measure.

This passage (from the beginning of 'Imagination Dead Imagine') achieves its remarkable fluidity of meaning by suppressing deictic elements in its structure. Deictic elements in a statement orientate the various propositions spatially, temporally and in relation to the speaker and his implied listener or reader. Normally texts work to stabilize the relationships between these various parts through the use of deixis. Here, however, we are uncertain about the coordinates of the scene being described, and about the interaction between the narrator and his supposed interlocutor. How are we to understand that first sentence? The opening phrase seems to imply that the narrator and his implied addressee are located in relation to some reality in which there is no trace of life. But this would depend on who speaks that first phrase. If it is the narrator, and the tag 'you say' refers to what follows rather than to what has just been said, then the deictic element in 'no difficulty *there*' directs the interlocutor's reply to that first statement made by the narrator. Hence we might read the sentence along these lines:

NARRATOR: No trace anywhere of life
OTHER: Pah, no difficulty there, imagination not dead yet
NARRATOR: Yes, dead, good, imagination dead imagine

In this case, the sentence appears to operate as an instruction from the narrator first of all to imagine no trace of life, then, when the other objects that that is easy and does not signify the limit of imagination, the narrator instructs him to imagine the death of imagination.

Alternatively, that first phrase can be read as the narrator's report of the interlocutor's speech act. In that case we attach the tag 'you say' to the opening statement. What follows can be read as a continuation of the reported speech act, or alternatively it can be taken as the narrator's reply to the assertion by the interlocutor that there is no trace of life anywhere. In the latter case, we might understand the narrator as saying that just because no trace of life can be seen it does not follow that there is nothing: imagination is not dead yet, and to imagine it dead is still to imagine.

Other equally valid readings might understand the narrator's reply as asserting that only when imagination is dead will it be possible to detect a trace of life. 'Islands, waters, azure, verdure . . .': all these 'baseless fabrics' of conventional imagining need to be eradicated if one is to catch truly a glimpse of life. Alternatively, the narrator may simply be imploring his interlocutor to imagine the death of imagination, and then proceeding, paradoxically, to envisage that.

The impossibility of determining the meaning of this passage arises because guiding material has largely been removed. As we have seen throughout this section, such occlusiveness causes individual sense units to become dirigible. What punctuation there is has the effect not of assisting interpretation but of further breaking down any chain of meaning in the language. A simple orientational phrase like 'you say' hovers uncertainly between its commas; instead of securing the speech acts that surround it, it operates as a kind of revolving door by which one both exits and enters the various semantic fields in the passage. Rather than assisting in an essentially teleological, cumulative refinement of meaning, the repeated commas emphasize the way in which these individual units create apertures and loops in the narrative logic – words as pure ratio.

The principle of reduction, then, involves removing differential elements in the language, the markers that separate one possible meaning from another. Throughout the 'residua' Beckett undermines the idea that writing refers us to a 'real', experiential world. In the quoted passage from 'Imagination Dead Imagine' the reduction of differential elements in the language leaves us a world bereft of differentiation: 'all white in the whiteness . . . The light that makes all so white no visible source, all shines with the same white shine, ground, wall, vault, bodies, no shadow'. The rotunda cannot be 'seen' in any naturalistic sense of the word. In fact, the point is that we are not supposed to 'picture' it, refer it to reality – it is imaginable only.

Another way in which Beckett toys with reduction is through the use of repetition. Now usually, repetition helps to creates semantic or sound patterns which in turn assists in our comprehension of a text. In Beckett's case, however, repetition is used to break up any linear movement or narrative, to impede the reading process and undermine our effort to construe meaning from what is said. Along with the other paraphernalia of reduction, in syntax, vocabulary and punctuation, repetition acts against sense-making. Again, we find Beckett striving to free language from the task of representing the world to us. Here is a passage from 'Ping':

> All known all white bare white body fixed one yard legs joined like sewn. Light heat white floor one square yard never seen. White walls one yard by two white ceiling one square yard never seen. Bare white body fixed only the eyes only just. Traces blurs light grey almost white on white . . . Traces blurs signs no meaning light grey almost white.

We are given here the 'traces blurs signs' but 'no meaning'; the words of the text will act not as units in some gathering continuity, but as impediments to our progress as readers in search of meaning. The repetition is no help because it actually reduces differentiation and therefore sense. Beckett has cut away the very orientational material we need to make meaning; he has undone the apparatus of representation, taking his text as close to silence as he can.

Beckett takes to its logical limit the modernist interest in the effects of writing 'short'. In that sense his work answers to those many commentators who, from the 1890s onwards, have probed at the idea that 'shortness' is other than simply a matter of physical extent, and that there is a relationship between what Henry James called 'brevity' and 'multiplicity'. It is for that reason that I have given to this section on modernism a subtitle drawn from Beckett, in one of his imaginary dialogues with George Duthuit. There, Beckett makes a distinction between, on the one hand, the 'incomplete object', and on the other, the '[t]otal object, complete with missing parts'.[9] The distinction may seem a fine one, but it narrates as well as any how modernist writers came to understand the shortness of the short story.

Part III

Post-modernist stories

Introduction: theories of form

In this section we turn to what might broadly be called the 'afterlife' of the modernist short story. It should be clear from the title that interest here lies in the ways in which the theory and practice of the modernist short story were variously sustained, transfigured, attenuated, challenged and amplified after the high-tide of modernism proper had passed. What this presupposes, of course, is that the short story in its modernist guise remained vital and valid in the minds of writers in this period; that it did so is a central assumption of this section, but one that we should feel justified in making when we look at what writers in the inter-war and post-war years did in the form, and what, in their critical work, they said about it.

The period from around 1930 until approximately 1980, roughly the time span covered in this section, sees the publication of four major critical works on the short story, all of them by practising writers. These are Elizabeth Bowen's introduction to the *Faber Book of Modern Short Stories* (1936), H. E. Bates's *The Modern Short Story* (1941), Sean O'Faolain's *The Short Story* (1948) and, most renowned of all, Frank O'Connor's *The Lonely Voice* (1962). One thing that will be immediately noticed about this quartet is that three of them are Irish born. This reflects the fact that in the period following modernism – or more accurately, perhaps, the period after Joyce – Irish writers excelled in the short story, to the point that many wished to claim it as the national art form.

To a great extent, the work of Sean O'Faolain and Frank O'Connor, the subjects of chapter 8, can be read as a reaction against the internationalism of modernism, and of Joyce. Both men desired to forge, or perhaps re-establish, a sense of connection between the short story and traditions of regional and national writing. Their reaction to Joyce was not Beckett's; it was, rather, to turn away from the abstruse, elliptical or experimental modernist text and re-engage with the popular oral culture that had given rise to storytelling in the first place. Which is not to say that either O'Faolain or O'Connor was straight-forwardly or reductively *anti*-modernist, only that they did not choose to follow Joyce into what they regarded as an insular and rebarbative preoccupation with language for its own sake. Both men were too much animated by the notion of the short story writer functioning in, and as part of, his or her community for that.

O'Faolain's and O'Connor's views on writing were undoubtedly a reflection of their active engagement as young men with Irish republican politics in the 1910s and early 1920s. Both saw military action during the revolutionary and Civil War years, and both made this the subject of some of their most memorable fiction. But, as with their complex and at times conflicted reaction to modernism, neither O'Connor nor O'Faolain is in any sense unquestioningly nationalist in his work. In fact, both probe critically at the ideological structures of the Irish conflict and Irish national identity by revealing the moral duplicities and political expediencies that underpin them. In that sense, their work has a good deal in common with that of Joyce and other modernists, who utilized enigmatic and interrogative narrative techniques to challenge the oppressive meta-narratives that circulate in any culture.

Like her countrymen, Elizabeth Bowen was a critic and theorist of the short story as well as being one of the pre-eminent practitioners of it in the twentieth century. Her 1936 introduction to the *Faber Book of Modern Short Stories* stands as perhaps the first masterpiece in criticism of the form. It is there that Bowen describes the necessity of treating the 'shortness' of the short story as a 'positive' quality, rather than a matter merely of 'non-extension'. Bowen's essay also establishes her affinities with her modernist predecessors, particularly in its devoted admiration, and sensitivity to the achievements, of Anton Chekhov and Henry James. Bowen's relationship to modernism is not an easy one, however, and she was frequently dismissed as a 'middlebrow' or 'practical' writer who was committed to the popularization, which is to say vulgarization, of high-modernist aesthetic and cultural values. In fact, as chapter 9 shows, Bowen's fiction takes up with modernist fictional practice in a number of critical and surprising ways. Like Woolf and Mansfield, she was drawn to the 'note of interrogation' she heard in Chekhov, but she used that to give a quite different, and radically new, account of human personality and the dynamics of inter-subjectivity.

The tag of 'middlebrow' has also frequently been applied to V. S. Pritchett, who is commonly (and unfairly) considered a minor figure in the minor movement of post-war English comic writing. In fact, Pritchett was an astutely formalist writer who, in his stories and in his criticism, showed that he had absorbed, and moreover thought how to transform, the impact of modernism on contemporary fiction. Like O'Connor and O'Faolain, he was determined to mediate modernism in such a way as to permit writing of a distinctively regional sort. As one critic has put it, he attempted an audacious blending of Dickens and

Chekhov in his stories. Unlikely as that sounds, at his best Pritchett was able to author stories that draw us in with their homely familiarity of voice and gentle portraiture only then to enact disturbing and often morbid ratios upon the scenarios they present. Pritchett was not interested in performing prodigies of introspection of the order of Woolf and Mansfield. Rather, his subject was what Elizabeth Bowen called that 'human unknowableness'[1] nestling at the heart of the familiar. In that respect, Pritchett's stories match his stated ambition to produce a writing capable of embodying 'the nervousness and restlessness of contemporary life'.[2]

The final chapter in this section moves ahead to the 1970s and the work of Angela Carter and Ian McEwan. At first sight, it might appear odd to include these writers alongside the likes of O'Connor, Bowen and Pritchett. And yet they are both authors whose short stories take up with, take off from, or take against aspects of the modernist inheritance. In situating them thus, I am suggesting that it is helpful to get away from definitions of post-modernist fiction as representing some sort of emphatic 'breakthrough' against the values and practices of modernism. One might point, as Brian McHale for instance does, to Carter's redactions of popular fairy tales as marking a shift from modernist questions of meaning, or epistemology, to post-modernist questions of being, or ontology. But that line, between meaning and being, is, as McHale is repeatedly forced to concede, impossible to maintain. In Carter's case, as in McEwan's, it is both legitimate and desirable to view the use of established story types and patterns as analogous to modernist treatments of popular narrative forms and structures in their work, if for no other reason than that it allows us to deal with their stories *as* short stories, rather than as abstracted representations of something called 'post-modernity'.

Chapter 8

Frank O'Connor and Sean O'Faolain

Like most of the writers in this section who came to prominence in the wake of international modernism, Sean O'Faolain distinguished himself not just as a practitioner of the short story form, but as a critic and theorist of it too. He published a full-length book on the subject, *The Short Story* (1948; revised 1972), as well as several essays and introductions in which he explored both the history of the form and the technical business of writing in it. O'Faolain was a peculiarly candid commentator on his own work, and at intervals in his long career revisited his earlier stories with a severely critical eye. For these reasons he is perhaps the writer best placed to help us to begin negotiating the development of the short story in the decades immediately after modernism.

That said, it is likely to strike any reader coming upon *The Short Story* how little O'Faolain appears to be taken with his modernist predecessors, most obviously James Joyce. *Dubliners* is acknowledged in the book, but briefly and grudgingly. While he admits that the early Joyce startled with the 'innocence' and deliberate 'superficiality' of his language, he goes on to complain that there is now, with hindsight, comparatively 'little of this kind of pleasure' to be had from *Dubliners*, and that the stories suffer badly from Joyce's overweening fondness for simile.

Much closer in spirit for O'Faolain is Henry James, who understood (in ways that the relentlessly metaphorical Joyce did not) that the art of the short story is an art of implication or, to use his own term, 'dilation':

> Telling by means of suggestion or implication is one of the most important of all the modern short-story's shorthand conventions. It means that a short-story writer does not directly tells us things so much as let us guess or know them by implying them. The technical advantage is obvious. It takes a long time to tell anything directly and explicitly, it is a rather heavy-handed way of conveying information, and it does not arrest our imagination or hold our attention so firmly as when we get a subtle hint. Telling never dilates the mind with suggestion as implication does.[1]

Such remarks take us back to the 1890s and the efforts of early commentators like James and Brander Matthews to forge an aesthetic of the form that treats its shortness as a 'positive' quality. O'Faolain was strongly drawn to the late nineteenth century in his choice of illustrative material for *The Short Story*. He includes the complete texts of stories by Alphonse Daudet, Anton Chekhov, Guy de Maupassant, Robert Louis Stevenson and of course Henry James. He then leapfrogs the central modernist years (with the exception of Ernest Hemingway) to reprint work by his contemporaries Frank O'Connor and Elizabeth Bowen. According to the critic Clare Hanson, O'Faolain, like O'Connor, 'strongly disapproved of the uses to which the short story had been put by the modernists' and 'rejected the extreme self-reflexiveness of writers such as Joyce'.[2] While it is obvious that O'Faolain looked to take the short story in a different direction from Joyce, it is something of a simplification to say that he did so out of an anxious reaction against the 'extreme self-reflexiveness' of modernism. Joyce may have led fiction down those by-ways in *Ulysses* and *Finnegans Wake*, but not so in *Dubliners*. A more accurate explanation for why O'Faolain wrote and theorized as he did lies, I would suggest, in his wish to identify the short story with particular regional and national literatures – something that the insistent internationalism of the modernist moment did not allow.

The potted history of the form that O'Faolain gives in *The Short Story* stresses the pre-eminence of Irish, American, Russian and French writers; in that respect, the account closely resembles that given by H. E. Bates, which I discussed in the introduction. Like Bates, O'Faolain argues that, in England, affinity with the novel precluded the development of the short form until the very end of the nineteenth century. '[T]he English do not admire the artistic temperament', he argues; 'the English way of looking at life is much more social and much less personal and individual' and therefore works 'more effectively inside the broad frame of the novel, which is in the nature of a sweeping gesture over a large landscape of life'. The reason for this more social or inclusive vision, he suggests, lies in the degree of political and cultural disorder that England experienced in the nineteenth century, which was far less profound than in America, Russia, or elsewhere in Europe. The 'intellectual and emotional break-up' of that period

> is scarcely reflected in Dickens or Thackeray or George Eliot. The
> implications of *Madame Bovary*, for example, did not even remotely
> touch Dickens who was at the date of its publication writing *Little
> Dorrit*. Life in Britain was too stable. English novelists . . . were either
> unaware of or indifferent to the rise of the worker, the decay of the

Church, the increase in scepticism, the evil social effects of the industrial revolution, the growing influence of science on education, the crumbling away of the old traditional moral values.[3]

Whatever one makes of these remarks (and there is much to quarrel with in them!) it is important to notice the alignment O'Faolain is striving to make here between the short story form and particular kinds of social and cultural upheaval. The reason for his making that argument becomes clearer when we turn to his own stories.

In the Foreword to a 1970 edition of his work, O'Faolain identifies three stages of development in his career. The first, in the shape of his debut collection, *Midsummer Night Madness* (1932), he characterizes as a period in which he was 'very romantic' about Ireland. In the second, culminating in *A Purse of Coppers* (1937), he had a more clear-sighted appreciation of his home as a nation, which he regarded as not 'paralysed by its past', as Joyce had thought, but only 'sleeping'. With his next collection, *The Man Who Invented Sin* (1948), he entered the mature phase of his work which, at the time of writing in 1970, was still in process. As he envisages it, the challenge of his career had been to find a way of writing about Ireland as a place and a people still full of romantic wonder and 'beautiful, palpitating tea-rose souls' that was nevertheless chastened by social and political realities calling for 'hard, coolly calculating heads'.[4]

What is striking about this career-encompassing self-assessment is the extent to which O'Faolain calibrates his writing in terms of its relationship to Irish national politics and history. For the student of literature this poses certain challenges. It may be tempting, for example, to suppose that our task in reading O'Faolain is to uncover 'explanations' for his work in the extra-textual reality of modern Ireland, and to perform some sort of contextual decoding of it thereby. The most obvious shortcoming of such an approach is that it constrains the texts within a deterministic allegorical framework. On the other hand, one would not wish to understate the importance of Ireland both as the dominant subject of O'Faolain's work, and as the principal condition of its production. My own solution to this difficulty, for the purposes of this introduction at least, is to consider how O'Faolain's *representation* of Ireland in fictional form altered over the course of his career. That is to say, rather than exploring the political or cultural realities of Ireland as these may have shaped the work, we can use the subject of the nation as a means of gauging and describing O'Faolain's development as a short story writer. The emphasis falls, then, not on what his work reveals about Ireland, but on what O'Faolain's shifting treatment of Ireland tells us about his work.

When in 1970 O'Faolain made a selection of his stories for a new selected edition, he chose only three pieces from his first book. These were 'Midsummer Night Madness', 'Fugue' and 'The Patriot'. It is an intriguing distillation because all three stories are set during the Irish Revolution (1916–21), in which O'Faolain saw action, and all three record a gathering sense of disillusionment both with the republican cause (which O'Faolain supported) and with the ways in which nationalist discourse represents Ireland. At first glance, the stories give the appearance of being romantic depictions of the revolution in the manner of O'Faolain's sometime friend and mentor Daniel Corkery. All three stage a love story in the context of the struggle for a free Ireland, and in highly descriptive language make appeal to the romantic idea of a nation and people whose identity is rooted in the landscape and customs of rural life. This pastoral setting acts as a constant reminder in the stories both of the crime perpetrated by the colonial English and of all that stands to be won by means of revolution. It performs these functions from the very first page of 'Midsummer Night Madness', to take just one instance, as the narrator, venturing out from the city of Cork into the 'open fields' and 'May-month sweetness' of the Munster countryside, finds himself alienated by the threat of English patrols and raiding parties: 'I kept listening, not to the chorus of the birds, not to the little wind in the bushes by the way, but nervously to every distant, tiny sound'.

Yet even in these early stories we detect a questioning and qualifying of the romantic-nationalist paradigm. It is as though O'Faolain, for all his self-confessed susceptibility to what he calls the 'boss-words' of romance (among which he lists *dawn, dew, onwards, youth, world, adamant,* and *dusk*), is nevertheless pulling in the opposite direction at the same time, towards a destitution of the language of nationalist mythology. In the case of 'Midsummer Night Madness', the narrator, a republican rebel, finds himself drawn into acknowledging the force and authenticity of the Anglo-Irish position through his close encounter with the landowner Henn. The narrator starts out detesting Henn, but comes to identify with him as a fellow victim of Irish history. Not only that, but his antagonism grows towards his fellow revolutionaries and their increasingly haphazard acts of retributive violence, which contrast with Henn's cultural sophistication and (albeit limited and self-serving) wish to encourage the local workers towards economic self-reliance – superstructural complications that disturb the familiar romantic-nationalist base on which the story at first appears to rest.

By the time we reach 'The Patriot', those complications have developed into full-fledged doubt and disillusionment with the republican cause. In this story, which takes place during the Civil War (1922–3), we again have a love story played out against the customary backdrop of a romantic landscape; but as the central character, Bernie, moves around in the Munster mountains to evade capture by the Free State forces, he encounters an increasingly disparate, desperate and divided republican army. Now what disturbs the Irishman's sense of identification and refuge in the rural landscape is not the English but the hopeless disarray and fecklessness of his countrymen. Bernie finds himself longing to return to the city, 'out of these mountains where they did nothing for month after month but eat the substance of the people and lounge over the fire like sleepy dogs'. In the event Bernie is captured and imprisoned by the Free State forces, but after his release he is unable to reconnect with his republican convictions, and finds himself increasingly alienated from the firebrand nationalist rhetoric of his friend Edward Bradley. In the story's final scene Bernie turns symbolically from the sight of the ageing Bradley, 'the old bachelor, the patriot', as he passes in his car, turning instead towards the warm, life-giving body of his sleeping wife.

With O'Faolain's second collection, *A Purse of Coppers*, the breakdown of the romantic ideal begins to permeate the narrative idiom itself. The opening paragraph of the first story, 'A Broken World', signals this shift in its description of a farm landscape viewed from within a moving railway carriage:

> Peering I could barely see . . . through the fog of the storm, a lone chapel and a farmhouse, now a tangle of black and white. Although it was the middle of the day a light shone yellow in a byre. Then the buildings swivelled and were left behind. The land was blinding.

O'Faolain himself described this new writing style as one of 'detachment'. Gone are the poetic consolations of landscape, just as the narrator's view from the carriage window is restricted, then entirely obscured; and the farmer whom the narrator meets en route, and whose mulish indifference so depresses him, is symbolically abandoned at his country station as the train rolls on towards the city. It is as though O'Faolain is signalling the inaccessibility of the old myths of rural Ireland to which his early work, like the revolutionary nationalism it depicts, appeals. Not that the story is in any sense despondent about the future: as O'Faolain said about 'A Broken World', it showed an Ireland 'not dead but sleeping', as against Joyce's feeling that Ireland is paralysed by its past'.[5] What is demanded, however, and enacted in O'Faolain's newly eviscerated narrative style, is a clear-sighted realism that addresses not a mythologized Irish people of the land, but the urban multitude who '[walk] against the wind with huddled backs . . . shrouding something within them' ('A Broken World').

In his later stories, O'Faolain continues to probe at the question of where, and in what, Irish national identity resides in an increasingly urbanized and technologized modernity. At times, as in 'The End of the Record', he deals directly with this vying of the contemporary with the traditional (in that story a commercial recording team visits a poorhouse in order to capture songs and verses and stories from the mouths of the elderly residents). Elsewhere he explores the fate of rural traditionalism in commercialized cosmopolitan Ireland. 'The Silence of the Valley' is perhaps O'Faolain's most profound statement on this theme; it is also a story that marks another stage in the development of his narrative style. While the familiar questions about Irish identity are raised – in discussions about the status of the Gaelic language, for example – the story is far less tendentious than O'Faolain's earlier work. Instead, it discloses a number of contradictions that the narration makes no attempt (or is perhaps powerless) to resolve.

The story concerns the visit made by an international group of tourists to a lakeside fishing hotel in an unspecified district of Ireland. Their visit coincides with the wake and funeral for the local cobbler, who was renowned as the valley storyteller. O'Faolain initially sets up a contrast between the traditional way of life, part of which is passing away with the cobbler, and the moneyed materialism of the tourists. But soon this simple opposition is complicated, for instance through the conversations that take place between two of the visitors, a young Celtic man and a woman from Scotland. He presents himself as the custodian of Ireland's past, there to 'learn the language of our forefathers', and is dismayed when the old tramp providing the evening's entertainment in the hotel sings songs in English rather than Gaelic. The red-haired Scottish woman, sardonic, witty and distinctly modern, teases the young man about his 'primitive' values and draws out the contradictions in his position. Yet at the end of the story, having witnessed the cobbler's funeral, it is she who seems more affected by the experience. Once again, O'Faolain's treatment of landscape provides the key to the scene:

> The red-haired girl leaned to the window and shaded her eyes against the pane. She could see how the moon touched the trees on the island with a ghostly tenderness. One clear star above the mountain wall gleamed. Seeing it her eyebrows floated upward softly for sheer joy.
> 'Yes,' she said quietly, 'it will be another grand day – tomorrow'.
> And her eyebrows sank, very slowly, like a falling curtain.

To the young Celtic man's earlier claim that the Irish were a 'spiritual people', she had responded, 'What enchanting nonsense!' Now, for the first time in the story, she says something affirmative rather than disputatious. But like so much else in the narrative, the moment is heavy with ambiguity: perhaps her eyebrows sink again from disappointment, and how far does she feel that today has really been a 'grand day'? 'The Silence of the Valley' revolves around such unanswered questions. At one moment the custom and ceremony of the traditional life seem to provide a moral centre to the story – a way of showing up the tourists' ignorance ('Let's holiday in Ireland among the peasants!') – yet at other times it figures as itself ignorant, static and dutifully oppressed: 'it was as if they were cycling not through space but through a maw of time that would never move'. O'Faolain's mature style does not offer to disentangle these paradoxes for us, but merely stages them. More provisional and circumspect in many ways, his later work is nevertheless more confident about allowing meaning to be carried, as he proposed in his criticism, by implication and dilation. In that respect at least, he stands squarely in the line of great Irish writers who, as Declan Kiberd puts it, were able to see beyond the 'either-or polarities' of Irish history and achieve 'a more inclusive philosophy of interpenetrating opposites'.[6]

Frank O'Connor is better known today for what he said *about* the short story than for any prodigy he performed in it. Unlike most of the six volumes of stories published in his lifetime – *Guests of the Nation* (1931), *Bones of Contention* (1936), *Crab Apple Jelly* (1944), *The Common Chord* (1947), *Traveller's Samples* (1951) and *Domestic Relations* 1957) – his critical study of the short form, *The Lonely Voice* (1962), has never been out of fashion. For this we have the Creative Writing industry to thank, particularly in the United States, where O'Connor's book has enjoyed a glorious afterlife as the definitive study of the modern short story for aspirant writers and the professionals who teach them. It is a curious acclaim, however, for O'Connor's book hardly reads as a 'how-to' manual. Unlike O'Faolain's *The Short Story*, it contains little on what might be called 'technique'; rather, it stages a polemical history of the form in English (and English translation) beginning in the nineteenth century with Ivan Turgenev and ending with O'Connor's contemporary and compatriot Mary Lavin. About these two writers, as about Chekhov, O'Connor is rhapsodic. Rudyard Kipling, by contrast, is attacked for the insensitivity of his 'oratorical approach' (like O'Faolain, O'Connor considers the English imagination to be out of sympathy with the short form), while Katherine Mansfield is dismissed as a 'clever, spoiled, malicious woman' guilty of 'falsity' and 'sentimentality' on the page.[7] James Joyce, to whom O'Connor was inevitably compared in his early career, enjoys only conditional praise for his achievement in *Dubliners*.

As these remarks suggest, it is difficult to derive any consistent theory of the short story from *The Lonely Voice*, which makes it all the more surprising that it should have been taken so to heart in the Creative Writing classroom. Such general statements as O'Connor advances about the form are hedged about with qualification and apology. Nevertheless, the claim he makes in his introduction, that the short story specializes in the depiction of the outlawed, the lonely, the 'submerged population group', has enjoyed a remarkable longevity in subsequent criticism, where it provides a means of answering (while actually evading) the question of why the form has thrived in American, Irish and Russian, much more than in English, literatures. According to O'Connor, the key to the short story's prevalence in a particular place lies in what he calls 'the national attitude toward society', which in England has been much more concerned with the intricate machinations of 'civilized society', to which the novel is ideally suited, than with the 'romantic, individualistic, and intransigent'[8] – the stuff of short stories. It is a claim that has rung true for subsequent generations of writers and teachers, especially in America and Ireland, eager to lay claim to the short story as *their* national art form.

The idea that pre-eminence in a particular literary form bespeaks a national disposition towards it should strike the modern reader as a step too far; and indeed, recent criticism of the American short story has turned its attention away from the questions O'Connor raises and towards the commercial and material conditions shaping the form's development since the nineteenth century. Nowadays *The Lonely Voice* is best read as a reaction to, or attempted rationalization of, literary modernism. It should be remembered that O'Connor came to notice in the immediate aftermath of high modernism (his first collection appeared in 1931) and that he repeatedly defined his own work in terms of a departure from the excesses of his experimental forebears, including Joyce. In *The Mirror in the Roadway* (1956), he attacked the rebarbativeness of modernist writing as a kind of solipsism designed to exclude the common reader: 'style ceases to be a relationship between author and reader and becomes a relationship of a magical kind between author and object'.[9] The same anxiety about writing losing its communicative function surfaces in *The Lonely Voice*, and it is arguably what drives O'Connor's thinking about the short story as a distinctly 'modern art'. It embodies, he argues, 'our own attitude to life'[10] and to the defining modern experience of social dislocation, or what he calls the 'intense awareness of human loneliness'.[11] In the short story's fascination with 'submerged population groups', O'Connor sees the reflection of a society 'that has no sign posts, a society that offers no goals and no answers'.[12] This sense of alienation is the principal legacy of modernist period, he thinks, where in both choice of subject matter and narrative technique the short story evolved to 'exclude the reader'.[13]

Modernism, then, functions in two ways for O'Connor: it both bears out his thesis that the short story is expressive of a peculiarly modern sense of isolation and social fragmentation, yet also provides the foil for his own writing, in which he stages a return to more traditional and narratologically stable forms of storytelling. Which is not to say that O'Connor's work is anti-modernist in a reactionary sense (his first collection was called *My Oedipus Complex*, after all). Rather, as *The Lonely Voice* stresses, he was more concerned with what he called the 'ideological' than the 'formal' aspects of the short story. With that in mind, I would suggest that a clearer route to understanding O'Connor's own aesthetic of short fiction is through his autobiographical disclosures, in particular his memoir of his youth and young manhood, *An Only Child* (1958). Less tendentious and polemical than *The Lonely Voice*, this volume uncovers the inter-animation of artistic self-fashioning and revolutionary politics that shaped O'Connor's identity as a writer, and that drew him to the short story form.

A turning point in *An Only Child* comes when O'Connor, writing about his involvement with revolutionary republicanism during the Irish Civil War (1922–3), recounts a conversation with his friend and mentor Daniel Corkery, a politician, writer and leading figure in the Irish-language Revival movement.[14] 'You must remember there are more important things in life than literature,' O'Connor recalls Corkery saying, the implication being that, in a state of war, 'men of action had more to give than the mere artist'. For O'Connor, this was the point at which the political ideologue began to subsume the writer in Corkery, and the moment in Irish cultural life when 'the imaginative improvisation of the community' began to 'dominate the imaginative improvisation of the artist'.[15] Though O'Connor took up arms on the republican side, he was never less than chary in his commitment to the revolutionary cause or the actions it demanded. Looking back on his involvement, he realizes that he was guilty of an uncritical, idealistic romanticism in his choice of sides during the war:

> To say that I took the wrong side would promote me to a degree of intelligence I had not reached . . . I still saw life through a veil of literature – the only sort of detachment available to me – though the passion for poetry was merging into a passion for the nineteenth-century novel, and I was tending to see the Bad Girl of the neighbourhood not as 'one more unfortunate' but as Madame Bovary or Natasya Filipovna, and the Western Road – the evening promenade of clerks and shopgirls – as the Nevsky Prospekt.[16]

The self-mockery here masks a more serious reflection, reiterated on several occasions in *An Only Child*, that so much revolutionary thinking was hopelessly distorted by its association with romantic idealism, much of it literary. In the young O'Connor's case, that romance was drawn from the great European literature of the nineteenth century (he is alluding to Gustave Flaubert's *Madame Bovary* and Fyodor Dostoyevsky's *The Idiot* in this passage), but for his fellow countrymen it had its source in the revolutionary Romanticism of the likes of Shelley and in the more recent Irish Revival movement. For O'Connor, there was too much self-deception involved in a political nationalism that saw matters through 'the heavy veil of literature'.[17] In one of the most powerful passages in *An Only Child*, he describes listening to a ballad air being sung when suddenly he is overcome by the memory of a young man he had seen beaten and later executed during the War, and whose hand he had briefly held in prison. 'I shouted . . . that I was sick to death of the worship of martyrdom,' he recalls, 'that the only martyr I had come close to was a poor boy from the lanes like myself, and he hadn't wanted to die any more than I did; that he had merely been trapped by his own ignorance and simplicity into a position which he couldn't escape.'[18] From that moment, O'Connor became deeply suspicious of the kind of idealism, be it political, philosophical or religious, in which 'sentimental high-mindedness' exists 'side by side with an extraordinary inhumanity'.[19] His turning to the short story and away from poetry arose, he claimed at the end of *An Only Child*, out of a desire to testify to another sort of 'immortality', lodged in the values of those ordinary people, like his own mother, who 'represented all I should ever know of God'.[20]

If one was to name a recurrent trope in O'Connor's diverse stories of child-hood, warfare, family, faith, old age and death, it would be the encounter between 'high-mindedness' in its various forms and the contrary incidentals and ironies of human experience. In his stories of the Civil War, for example, he probes at the very ideological structures of the conflict by depicting the moral uncertainties and circumstantial predicaments faced by the individuals who have to prosecute it. In 'Guests of the Nation' (1931), to take the best known of the war stories, a group of republican troops is forced to execute two English soldiers called Belcher and Hawkins whom they have been holding prisoner for some time and whom they have come to know as friends and familiars. The story is narrated by one of the Irishmen, Bonaparte, charged with carrying out the executions, and through his elliptical reflections O'Connor traces the faultline between the ideology and the actuality of conflict. Throughout the story, Bonaparte stresses not the otherness of the enemy soldiers, but their socio-cultural familiarity. He notices, for example, how readily the men are absorbed into the customs and landscape of Ireland: 'it was my belief that you could have planted that pair down anywhere from this to Claregalway and they'd have taken root there like native weed. I never in my short experience saw two men take to the country as they did'. This sense of commonality among the men takes on a deeper resonance still through Hawkins's provocative conversation about politics and religion. He declares himself a communist and non-believer, forging an alliance with his captors on the basis that they are all the subjects of capitalism and victims of its injustices. As he pleads for his life, Hawkins appeals to the Irishmen to see beyond the nationalist ideology that divides them into friend and foe: '[You're] not the sort to make a pal and kill a pal. [You're] not the tools of any capitalist'.

A less direct but emotionally equally compelling case for clemency is made by the other Englishman, Belcher. He accepts his fate calmly, but reveals, for the first time to his captors, details about his own life, such as the loss of his wife and child: 'I like the feeling of a home, as you may have noticed, but I couldn't start another again after that'. To his executioner's remark that he is only doing his duty, Belcher responds with his own, homelier version of Hawkins's socialism: 'I never could make out what duty was myself . . . I think you're all good lads, if that's what you mean.' While Bonaparte's reaction to the killings is communicated tangentially, through his partial recollections of burying the bodies in the 'mad lonely' landscape of the bog, the sense takes hold in the story that he too longs to transcend the subject position offered to him by the war, just as Belcher's candid revelations conspired to release him, momentarily, from the label 'British':

> It is so strange what you feel at times like that that you can't describe it. Noble says he saw everything ten times the size, as though there were nothing in the whole world but that little patch of bog with the two Englishmen stiffening into it, but with me it was as if the patch of bog where the Englishmen were was a million miles away, and even Noble and the old woman, mumbling behind me, and the birds and the bloody stars were all far away, and I was somehow very small and very lost and lonely like a child astray in the snow. And anything that happened to me afterwards, I never felt the same about again.

The force of this passage, which marks the story's conclusion, lies in the way O'Connor renders Bonaparte's experience of transcending his time and place in a markedly untranscendent language. Bonaparte's under-lexicalized vocabulary ('very small and very lost') like his images and metaphors ('stiffening', 'like a child astray in the snow') are rooted in the here and now of circumstance and personality, yet they are charged with philosophical, quasi-spiritual appeal to a notion of impersonal, common humanity. The ideological 'high-mindedness' that justifies killing in the name of principle is set against values that are at once universal and yet intensely personal.

O'Connor's stories are littered with characters who, like Bonaparte, wrestle with the roles and identities foisted upon them by state politics, religious dogma or social convention. And this is as true of the stories set in peacetime as of those dealing with fraught episodes in modern Ireland's constitution. O'Connor's portrayals of provincial life, for example, frequently explore the conflict between a (sometimes eccentric) individualism and those institutions, such as the church, the law and the family, charged with maintaining social order and cohesion. 'The Majesty of the Law' (1936), for example, relates a visit paid by a police sergeant to an old man, Dan Bride, who has been convicted of an act of violence against a neighbour and who must either pay a fine or serve a sentence in prison. It becomes clear, however, that Dan's 'crime' is considered by all the village, and by the sergeant, to have been a just and reasonable action in response to a neighbour's 'unmannerly method of argument'. A gap is thus opened between the spirit and letter of the law, between justice in the true sense and the legalistic expediency of the civil courts. The story proceeds by demonstrating that the very virtues the law is set up to test and preserve – honesty, integrity, fairness – have their proper habitation outside of that establishment. As soon as the sergeant enters Dan's dwelling, he finds himself abandoning the rules and principles he is employed to protect, unbuttoning his tunic, smoking tobacco and not only drinking illegally distilled whiskey but lamenting the law that prohibits it. It is not, however, that Dan's home is the site of any Bacchanal revolt against law and convention. Far from it. If anything, Dan's dissidence and delinquency seem to be the very conditions of a more stable and viable social order. Dan's home represents what the French theorist Michel Foucault calls a 'heterotopia', that is, an 'effectively enacted utopia' that corresponds to an actual, as opposed to an imaginary, place.[21] It is a place where mutually respectful, reciprocal human interaction takes place without the mediating presence of the law.

Given these preoccupations, it makes sense that O'Connor should have been drawn to childhood, or more precisely to the child's-eye point-of-view as a narrative device, in so many of his later stories. In such pieces as 'First Confession' (1951), 'My Oedipus Complex' (1952), 'The Genius' (1957) and 'The Study of History' (1957), he exploits the literalness and naivety of the child's perspective as a means of exposing the complexities and contradictions in two foundational and closely related structures of Irish life, the family and religion. Like the earlier fiction, these stories, which are among O'Connor's best known, stage close encounters with 'high-mindedness', be it familial or ecclesiastical. 'First Confession' deals with both in its account of a young boy's first visit to church to repent for his sins. In preparation for this event he is warned, through accounts of sinners consumed in the flames of hell, of the dire consequences of making a false or 'bad' confession. When the time comes to make his disclosure to the priest he reveals not only his most exaggerated childhood thoughts and misdeeds (his elaborate plan to murder and dismember his grandmother and attempt to kill his sister Nora with a bread knife), but also the sins of others in his family. He tells the priest that his grandmother drinks porter, 'knowing well from the way Mother talked of it that this was a mortal sin, and hoping it would make the priest take a more favourable view of my case'. Clearly amused by what he hears, the priest humours the narrator, admitting that he too would like to take a bread knife to certain people, but doesn't because he lacks 'nerve' and besides, 'hanging is an awful death'. The narrator gets off with three Hail Marys, and reflects that this priest was 'the most entertaining character I'd ever met in the religious line'. But within that remark nestles the deeper, sceptical meaning of O'Connor's story. The suggestion that the priesthood is a 'line' of work like any other reflects a more general intention, evident throughout the stories of childhood, to reveal the constructed, man-made (as opposed to essential or God-given) nature of authority, including the authority of adulthood. The priest emerges favourably from O'Connor's story as a man, but troubling questions persist in the story about the function of confession, whether it can ever be 'true', and the extent to which a confessor can ever be undeceived by himself or herself. It is the sort of question O'Connor asks repeatedly in his stories as he probes at the institutions, conventions and ideologies that we all, for most of the time, agree to live by.

Chapter 9

Elizabeth Bowen and V. S. Pritchett

If you have been reading this book from the beginning, you will be aware that Elizabeth Bowen's is a name to conjure with in the history of short story criticism. She would doubtless have wondered at this, for unlike many of her modernist predecessors she had little truck with the academy, nor did she believe that professional reading furnished one with special purchase over literary work. Indeed, it struck her as 'sad to regard as lecture-room subject books that were meant to be part of life'.[1] And yet, over the course of a long career she amassed a sizeable quantity of reviews, prefaces and essays, and in the case of her 1936 introduction to *The Faber Book of Modern Short Stories* produced arguably the first masterpiece in criticism of the short form. For all that she disdained the institutionalization of literature, Bowen has come to occupy a central place in the academic study of twentieth-century fiction both as a writer and critic.

It was not always so. Only in the last ten years has Bowen's work begun to attract the scholarly attention it demands and deserves. Before that, it suffered the fate of so much of the literature produced in the wake of high-modernism, of being somehow after the fact.[2] Unlike the central modernists – Eliot, Pound, Beckett, Woolf – Bowen never adhered to any manifesto or 'boarded any band-wagons', with the effect that her writing has 'tended to elude the standard taxonomies of modern writing'.[3] This gave rise, in the post-war period, to the widely held opinion that her work was, by comparison with the likes of Woolf's, 'middlebrow', a popularized, intellectually desiccated version of modernism. Only now that the academy has undergone a cultural revolution of its own has a reassessment of Bowen's work become possible. It is now common to find her writing appraised through the lenses of feminism and psychoanalytic theory, as well as in the context of Anglo-Irish culture and history.

And yet, the question of the relationship of Bowen's work to that of her modernist predecessors remains a troubling one, particularly for the historian of literary form. It is worth remembering that, although Bowen's name is principally associated with the late 1930s and 1940s (the period of her two best-known novels, *The Death of the Heart* (1938) and *The Heat of the Day*

(1949), as well as her celebrated wartime stories), she published her first book, a volume of stories called *Encounters*, in 1923, only a year after the *annus mirabilis* of high modernism, which saw into print James Joyce's *Ulysses*, T. S. Eliot's *The Waste Land* and Virginia Woolf's *Jacob's Room*. At the same time, her critical work shows her restlessly turning over the achievement of her predecessors, questioning in particular their anxiety about cultural distinction – the high-, middle- or lowbrows of reading and writing. By comparison with the modernists', Bowen's fiction is generically diverse, freely plundering the resources of psychological realism, pastiche, the ghost story, the Gothic melodrama, the thriller and the comedy of manners. It is strikingly dependent on plot and the attendant melodramatic repertoire of supernaturalism, peripeteia and twisted endings; what is more, it happily reinstates in its discursive machinery a presence that, since Henry James, had been subject to erasure in literary (as distinct from popular) fiction: the omniscient narrator. Situating Bowen vis-à-vis the literary-historical moment of modernism, then, is no simple matter.

As regards the short story, Bowen again both indulges and antagonizes modernist theory and practice. Coming to her stories after Woolf and Mansfield, one is immediately struck, for example, by their quite different treatment of interiority. Where in modernist fiction, material reality is invariably filtered through what Henry James calls (in 'The Art of Fiction') the 'chamber of consciousness', and tends thereby to function as a trigger to introspective voyaging and the dilation of subjectivity, Bowen refurnishes her fictional world with objects and actions enjoying, as it were, a life of their own. Her stories are played out in detailed environments thronging with incident and dramatic complication. What is more, they frequently redeploy an impersonal, omniscient style of narration. Where in Woolf, Mansfield and Dorothy Richardson the disembodied, authoritative omniscient narrator gives way to a highly subjectivized mode of representation, in which knowledge is focalized through character consciousness, Bowen blithely signals over the heads of her characters, embroiling them in predicaments of which the narrator enjoys a superintendent view and comprehension.

A couple of examples will serve to illustrate the quite different direction in which Bowen was taking the short form. 'The Evil That Men Do – ' (1926) opens with the description of the death in London of a 'little man' who is run over by a motor-lorry. The next morning an unnamed married woman at home receives a letter from a man called Charles Simmonds with whom she has previously enjoyed a brief flirtation at a poetry reading in London. In the letter he declares his passion for her (he is an unpublished poet): 'You came slowly out of yourself at that poetry-reading, like a nymph coming out of a wood'. The woman sets about composing a reply in which she confirms Charles's suspicion that she lives an intolerably dull life with a husband who takes no interest in her 'inner' life. At that moment her husband presents her with the gift of a new handbag and make-up compact, causing her to append to the letter a P.P.S. in which she concedes that there are moments when her husband 'touches very closely [her] *exterior* life'. With the final paragraph Bowen reveals the story's conceit: the 'little man' who was killed in London the previous day was none other than Charles Simmonds. The paragraph switches to omniscient mode to point up the irony: 'She wondered for some time what Charles would think when he came to the last postscript, and never knew that Fate had spared him this'.

The intrusive narrator is even more visible in 'Look at All Those Roses' (1941), a story that borrows many of the tropes and conventions of Gothic melodrama:

> There stood the house, waiting. Why should a house wait? Most pretty scenes have something passive about them, but this looked like a trap baited with beauty, set ready to spring. It stood back from the road. Lou put her hand on the gate and, with a touch of bravado, the two filed up the paved path to the door. Each side of the path, hundreds of standard roses bloomed, over-charged with colour, as though this were their one hour. Crimson, coral, blue-pink, lemon and cold white, they disturbed with fragrance the dead air. In this spell-bound afternoon, with no shadows, the roses glared at the strangers, frighteningly bright. The face of the house was plastered with tea-roses: waxy cream when they opened but with vermilion buds.

This paragraph reads like pastiche. It is redolent not just of eighteenth- and nineteenth-century Gothic fiction, particularly in the tropes of the house façade and its anthropomorphized environs, but of Grimm fairy tales and the allegorical romances of Nathaniel Hawthorne. Elsewhere it contains elements of psychological realism and fey domestic comedy. At the same time, the knowingness of the narrator's interventions leads us to suspect that we are reading a parody of these genres. The description of the house as 'like a trap baited with beauty' makes explicit the technique of suspensefulness that the scene is utilizing; likewise, the question 'Why should a house wait?' bears out the device of endowing inanimate objects with conscious life.

We have travelled a long way in these stories from modernist impersonality, 'scrupulous meanness' and the image of the author figure 'refined out of existence'. In restoring these two cynosures of Victorian fiction, plot and omniscient narration, to the short story, Bowen challenges the orthodoxy that had, since the 1890s, associated these devices with the 'popular', as opposed to 'literary', species of the form. As Frederick Wedmore had put it back in 1898, the 'finer art' of short fiction lay in refusing to give 'sops' to the 'gallery': it was an affair of suggestion and implication, 'omission' and 'brevity of allusiveness', an art 'adapted peculiarly to that alert intelligence, on the part of the reader'.[4] Bowen's stories enlarge our sense of the forms and function of the 'literary', but as her landmark 1936 introduction to *The Faber Book of Modern Short Stories* makes clear, this was only one part of an on-going discourse with the aesthetic and cultural values of modernism that lasted throughout her career, and that reveals as many points of affinity as it does difference.

In many respects, the *Faber* introduction is the key to understanding Bowen's complex relationship with modernism. Reading it, one is made aware of what she rejected in the work of her predecessors, and at the same time of what she wished to preserve and even emulate in her own writing. More than once she takes the view that the short story has, in recent years, suffered from its association with 'arty' or 'high-hat' literary values. She laments the fact that Chekhov (whose work she nevertheless reveres) has exerted such a powerful hold over English writers, his 'deceptive looseness' inciting them to any number of technical infelicities and 'outpourings of minor dismay, of mediocre sentiment'.[5] A more useful model for the English, she concludes, would have been Chekhov's contemporary Guy de Maupassant, not just because of the cleansing 'astringency' and 'iron relevance' of his technique, but because he was a 'born popular writer'.[6] In stressing Maupassant's populism, Bowen asserts her belief in the short story as a modern mass art form (she likens it to cinema for the same reason) capable of exceeding the formal, generic and cultural limitations that constrained the work of the high modernists. In that sense at least, the essay can be regarded as a statement of post-modernist intent.

At the same time, however, Bowen's account of the inner workings of the short form is strikingly similar to that of the modernists. 'Free from the *longueurs* of the novel,' she argues, the short story 'is also exempt from the novel's conclusiveness'. It is, in that respect, a form ideally suited to rendering 'the disorientated romanticism of the age':

> an affair of reflexes, of immediate susceptibility, of associations not examined by reason: it does not attempt a synthesis. Narrative of any length involves continuity, sometimes a forced continuity: it is here that the novel too often becomes invalid. But action, which must in the novel be complex and motivated, in the short story regains heroic simplicity.[7]

There is nothing here that would not serve as a description of the short story as practised and described by Woolf or Mansfield, both of whom used the form to explore realms of experience outside of rational synthesis and, in the case of Woolf, to free herself from the novelistic obligation to render action as part of a 'complex and motivated' sequence of events and volition. What this suggests, if we allow that Bowen's essay in part functions as an account of her own aesthetic, is that her stories, far from simply reacting against modernism, explore further the consequences of the break it made in our understanding of human personality. This makes sense when one considers later statements of Bowen, such as the preface she wrote for a 1951 edition of her early collection *Ann Lee's.* There she gave her own version of Woolf's 'note of interrogation': 'The stories are questions posed – some end with a shrug, others with an impatient or dismissing sigh'.[8] For Bowen, these were not 'trick endings' or contrivances, but the expression of what she considered her central subject: 'human unknowableness'.

To return to 'The Evil That Men Do – ' for a moment, we can see how the narrative, for all its contrivances in plot and point-of-view, ultimately confronts us with 'unknowableness'. The woman at the centre of the story is not accessible to us; like Minnie Marsh in Woolf's 'An Unwritten Novel', she eludes the grasp of the narrative that embodies her. The crucial difference between the two stories, however, lies in the reasons for that elusiveness. As Woolf saw it, human personality would always exceed the rational discursive structures devised to contain it, hence her efforts to reform narrative so that it might somehow take account of the 'varying . . . unknown and uncircumscribed spirit', as she called it in 'Modern Fiction'.[9] Bowen, on the other hand, makes no such attempt to access the interior life of her character. On the contrary, she presents the woman as an entirely performative figure. It is not that her core, or 'true' essence or meaning is inaccessible, but rather that her identity resides in the actions she performs. Take, for example, the scene when she rereads the letter she has written to Charles Simmonds:

> It was a stiff little letter.
> 'I know it is,' she sighed, distressfully re-reading it. 'It doesn't sound abandoned, but how can I sound abandoned in this drawing-room?' She stood up, self-consciously. 'The cage that is,' she said aloud, 'the intolerable *cage!*' and began to walk about among the furniture. ' – Those chintzes are pretty, I am glad I chose them. And those sweet ruched satin cushions . . . If he came to tea I would sit over here by the window, with the curtains drawn a little behind me – no, over here by the fireplace, it would be in winter and there would be nothing but firelight. But people of that sort never come to tea; he would come later on in the evening and the curtains would be drawn, and I should be wearing my – Oh, "Like a nymph." How trivial it all seems.'

And Harold [her husband] had wondered what there would be left for her to do if she didn't go down the High Street. She would show him. But if she went through with this to the end Harold must never know, and what would be the good of anything without Harold for an audience?

Identity here is a matter of deliberate orchestration. Where in Woolf the material object, like the social gesture, is merely an outward show beyond which one must penetrate in order to capture the essence of personality, here the self is dispersed across a range of cultural signifiers. Bowen is not concerned to say what or who her character *is*, but to show what she *does*; being, to put it another way, is a matter of being seen, hence the woman's need to retain her husband as an 'audience'. This is an important development to note in Bowen's fiction, because it reflects a deeper apprehension running throughout her work, namely that identity is not something given, but produced.

In her mature stories, particularly those set in London during the Second World War, Bowen explores with ever greater subtlety and variety the question of 'unknowableness'. Contrary to the popular stereotype that the 'war at home' was a period of unprecedented national unity and communality, Bowen dramatizes the deracinating effects of war on private life and the imagination. Stories such as 'In the Square', 'Mysterious Kôr', 'The Demon Lover' and 'Ivy Gripped the Steps' revolve around scenes of arrested intimacy, of human interaction rendered destitute, depthless and ridiculous by the upheaval, disorder, downright boredom and what Adam Piette calls the sheer 'theatricality' of the war.[10] Bowen's war fiction is widely regarded as her finest work, and, thinking about her preoccupation with the performative aspects of personality, it isn't difficult to see why she should have found the environment and experience of blitzed London – emptied out, both literally and figuratively, of human presence and significance – so compelling a subject.

To focus on just one of these masterly stories, 'In the Square' (1941) tells of a visit paid by a man, Rupert, to the London home of a female friend called Magdela whom he has not seen for some time. Magdela, whose husband we learn is up north, is living with her nephew and maid in an affluent precinct of the city largely emptied of its inhabitants, most of whom have decanted to the country. The couple know one another but it is unclear what the precise nature of their relationship was before the war intervened. During the visit, which is largely made up of tense, tangential conversation between the two, she receives a phone call that clearly disturbs her mood, but we do not know from whom the call comes or for what purpose. Meanwhile, the narrative switches downstairs to the maid Gina who, we are told, has been having an affair with Magdela's husband Anthony. Sitting alone, she begins to compose a letter to him ending their relationship. She gives as her reasons the remoteness of the house and the awkwardness of cohabiting with his wife and nephew, but it is revealed to us that she is in fact in love with someone else 'in a big way'. The story concludes with the nephew making his way across the square while his aunt and Rupert converse at the open window. "'But do talk to me," she implores, ". . . Do tell me how things strike you, what you have thought of things – coming back to everything like you have. Do you think we shall see a great change?"'

None of these questions is answered because the narrative breaks off here (in the *Faber* introduction Bowen speaks of how the short story 'permits a break at what in the novel would be the crux of the plot').[11] It is as though a point of confiding intimacy is advanced upon only to be denied. What we are left to work with in the story is not disclosure but dissembling, the *performance* of self. The sense of Magdela and Rupert 'acting out' before the audience they provide for one another permeates the whole narrative. It is there from the moment of Rupert's arrival as he puzzles over Magdela's failure to greet him at the door when he knows she has been expecting him and has doubtless heard his taxi arrive. The suggestion is made that the 'impulsive informality of peacetime' that would have allowed her to advance to the door is impossible now. And herein lies the ironic centre of the story. For in the midst of a conflict that has caused the breakdown of any number of social conventions and behavioural norms (imaged in the disorder of Magdela's home and the infidelity of her husband with the lower-class maid), the couple yet seem hamstrung by a curiously persisting decorum and emotional reticence:

> 'I do hope you will dine with me, one night soon.'
> 'Thank you,' she said evasively. 'Some night that would be very nice.'
> 'I suppose the fact is, you are very busy?'
> 'Yes, I am. I am working, doing things quite a lot.' She told him what she did, then her voice trailed off. He realized that he and she could not be intimate without many other people in the room.

One is reminded here of Philip Larkin's poem 'Talking in Bed', where that most symbolically intimate of human venues, the marital bed, becomes a place of severance and solitude in which it is increasingly difficult to say 'Words at once true and kind, / Or not untrue and not unkind'.[12] In Bowen's stories, war does not liberate a more candid, urgently communicative, communal citizenry; rather it invades and colonizes psychic life, robbing the individual of the power to narrate herself. As Callie thinks in 'Mysterious Kôr', another of the wartime stories, the loss of her own 'mysterious expectations' about love are as nothing 'beside the war's total of unlived lives'. The great public calamity empties her own story of significance. Bowen's stories depict the inaccessible, unknowable being that emerges from such a diminishment of the personal. And as she described in the *Faber* introduction, it was because the short story allowed her to create characters without recourse to questions of motive – to render experiences that were 'not only not fathomed but not stated' – that she considered it the form best suited to capturing 'this century's emotion, dislocated and stabbing'.[13]

At first glance, one might wonder at this chapter's setting alongside Bowen a writer so distinctly English and *post*-war as V. S. Pritchett. And yet there is a great deal that draws these two together in context of the present discussion, not least their enthusiasm for Chekhov and their conviction that the English had missed a trick when it came to the short story. Here, in a 1966 essay on Flannery O'Connor called 'Satan Comes to Georgia', is Pritchett's version of what will by now be a familiar literary history:

> On the whole, English writers were slow starters in the art of the short story. Until Stevenson, Kipling and then D. H. Lawrence appeared, our taste was for the ruminative and disquisitional; we preferred to graze on the large acreage of the novel and even tales by Dickens or Thackeray or Mrs Gaskell strike us as being unused chapters of longer works. Free of our self-satisfactions in the nineteenth century, American writers turned earlier to a briefer art which learned from transience, sometimes raw and journalistic but essentially poetic in the sense of being an instant response to the exposed human being. Where we were living in the most heavily wind-and-water-proofed society in the world, the American stood at the empty street corner on his own in a world which, compared with ours, was anarchic; and it was the opinion of Frank O'Connor, the Irish master, that anarchic societies are the most propitious for an art so fundamentally drawn to startling dramatic insights and the inner riot that may possess the lonely man or woman at some unwary moment in the hours of their day.[14]

We have heard much of this before, and not just from Bowen, but from O'Faolain and O'Connor, and reaching further back, Henry James, Frederick Wedmore, and G. K. Chesterton. In common with all these commentators, Pritchett's analysis can be read as a description and justification of what he himself was attempting to do in the short form. But Pritchett and Bowen make an especially revealing pair because they were, in the wake of modernism, both regarded as 'middlebrow'. For all their incommensurability in terms of subject matter and style, both were thought to have achieved, and to have sought to achieve, popularity by a highly selective deployment of tropes and techniques of the modernist text – which is to say, by an attenuation of its *difficulty*. They both are perceived as having laboured to steady the unsteadiness of the modernist passage for the repose of the common reader. To borrow terms used by David Lodge in an essay of some years ago, they were 'contemporary' without being wholly 'modern'.[15] While it might be thought unhelpful, or even misleading, to want to group Bowen with Pritchett and, by extension, with a particular strain of post-war traditionalism in English letters as practised by, among others, Angus Wilson, C. P. Snow or Kingsley Amis, there is something to be gained by considering them in quick succession, not just as story writers and theorists of the form, but as fellow travellers in the long shadow or, depending on one's point of view, brilliant afterglow of high modernism.

Pritchett's prolificacy aside, he matters in the history of the short story because, like Bowen, he helps us to understand what became of the form in the inter-war and post-war decades as modernism was, variously, absorbed, distilled, transformed, ameliorated and (never quite convincing, this) rejected. A clue to Pritchett's thinking on this matter lies in an interview given to John Haffenden in 1985. There he remarks that the English writer cannot successfully emulate Chekhov's interrogative, open-ended story style, 'since some sort of practical or responsible instinct works against it'.[16] This suggests that Pritchett regarded the short story, in its modern guise, as fundamentally at odds with the English cultural imaginary, and further, that he considered the 'national taste for the ruminative and disquisitional' to be a phenomenon not just of the nineteenth century, but of his own time as well. Reading Pritchett's short fiction, one has the sense, the critic James Wood suggests, of a modernity tempered with 'English mildness and softened ambition'. As Wood has it, Pritchett was engrossed by an extraordinary and improbable career-long effort to 'blend Dickens and Chekhov', remaining true to what he regarded as the special quality of English comedy while at the same time 'broadening, Russianizing, [and] internationalizing' it. He knew what was important about the 'moderns' – indeed he cherished the 'disorderly, talkative, fantasticating' tradition than ran from Laurence Sterne to James Joyce and Samuel Beckett – but at the same time his fondly satirical wit drew him to portray, often with a theatrical, Dickensian distension of reality, the class-raddled intricacies and absurdities of English society in its age of post-imperial decline.[17]

It is the unlikeliness of Pritchett's 'blend', perhaps, that lends to his fiction a rather confected, at times arch quality. By his own admission he laboured at writing. In the preface to his 1982 *Collected Stories* he describes the process of undertaking multiple revisions of every story, 'perhaps four or five times, boiling down a hundred pages into twenty or thirty'.[18] The sense of short fiction as a 'craft' dominates his appraisals of his own work. 'I have always thought,' the preface continues, 'that the writer of short stories is a mixture of reporter, aphoristic wit, moralist and poet – though not "poetical" . . . He has to be something of an architect'.[19] Reading Pritchett's work, one often senses his wish to be all of these things – reporter, wit, moralist, poet – at once, in the space of a single story. It is this that accounts for the complications that can suddenly and unexpectedly crowd his narratives, particularly as they approach their conclusions. Pritchett is a writer given to second thoughts, and one can usually identify the moment in a story when the Chekhovian gets the better of the Dickensian in him.

One such story, from among his very best, is 'Handsome Is as Handsome Does', which tells of the Corams, a middle-aged couple from England holidaying at a French pension. The pension is owned by a M. Pierre, whom Tom Coram, an industrial chemist risen from humble beginnings, considers a fraud, a poseur and a charlatan. The story is focalized through Coram's wife, a cultured and intelligent woman who has married beneath her class, and traces her gathering feelings of contempt for her inarticulate, boorish husband. During the holiday she develops feelings for Alex, a young Jewish man twenty years her junior who is staying at the pension and who impresses her with his intellectual remoteness and 'serious, considered' conversation. Much of the story is spent elaborating on the differences between Alex and Tom Coram, invariably to the latter's discredit, and reaches a dramatic climax when Alex is forced to save M. Pierre from drowning while Coram, whether out of fear, vengefulness or simple reluctance to help, remains on shore.

From the proverbial flippancy of its title, and from the way in which it mobilizes character in the opening pages, 'Handsome Is as Handsome Does' reads as a somewhat sneering and superior portrait of English provincialism and class anxiety. On the first page we read the following description of Coram's wife: 'She was a short, thin woman, ugly yet attractive. Her hair was going grey, her face was clay-coloured, her nose was big and long, and she had long, yellowish eyes. In this beach suit she looked rat-like, with that peculiar busyness, inquisitiveness, intelligence, and even charm of rats'. Her husband is dispatched with equal brusqueness: 'He was a thick-set, ugly man . . . Surly, blunt-speaking, big-boned, with stiff short fair hair that seemed to be struggling and alight in the sun'; while M. Pierre is summed up as 'a short and vain little dandy . . . given to boastfulness'. There is about these descriptions a cruel vigour and knowingness, a method of efficient capture. Much of Pritchett's humour, as with his English contemporaries, derives from its unflaggingly stylish dispatch, replete with brilliantined metaphors and carefully orchestrated phrasal cadences: 'He was a greasy-looking man, once fat, and the fat had gone down unevenly, like a deflating bladder' ('The Sailor'); 'Margaret's square mouth buckled after her next drink and her eyes seemed to be clambering frantically, like a pair of blatant prisoners behind her heavy glasses' ('Things as They Are'), and so on. But this is only one aspect of Pritchett's technique, for while his narratives are rarely less than emphatic about character types, they always give way to emotional enlargement and some dilation of sentiment, usually by generating contexts that provoke us to sympathy and identification with those types. In the case of 'Handsome Is as Handsome Does', it is not that Coram's wife ceases to be possessed of a rat-like intelligence, but that we are urged to broaden the margins of our tolerance and understanding in order to encompass even as rebarbative a character as she undoubtedly is. For example, towards the end of the story, having been rebuffed by Alex, she retreats to her room and begins to contemplate her husband's failure to come to M. Pierre's aid on the beach. This is the moment for Pritchett to enact one of his characteristically Chekhovian ratios upon the story, for she realizes that her husband's shame and belittlement are what bind her to him:

> Her desire had not gone winged after the rescuer [i.e., Alex], but angry, hurt, astounded, and shocked towards her husband. She knew this.
> She stopped weeping and listened for him. And in this clarity of the listening mind she knew she had not gone into Alex's room to will her desire to life or even to will it out of him, but to abase herself to the depths of her husband's abasement. He dominated her entirely, all her life; she wished to be no better than he. They were both of them like that; helpless, halted, tangled people, outcasts in everything they did.

It is a moment of exhilarating reappraisal, of disorientating second thoughts, and it forces us to revisit the assumptions we had made about the couple, and that the seemingly resolute, impenitent wit of the narrative discourse had drawn us into making. The 'outcasting' prevails, but it is now not simply a comic imposition, a way of mocking oddity or provincialism. In a single move, Pritchett has transformed his story into an internalized, emotionally morbid drama of non-belonging.

It is this sensitivity and seriousness that sets the best of Pritchett's writing apart from that of his contemporaries, particularly Evelyn Waugh, with whom he was often aligned as an exemplar of English comic style. Pritchett was far more self-consciously formalist than Waugh, and as his voluminous criticism makes clear, had read more widely and deeply in European literature of the nineteenth and twentieth centuries than the modest English persona of his work would suggest. He was attracted to the short story because he considered it a 'glancing form of fiction'[20] ideally suited to rendering 'the nervousness and restlessness of contemporary life'. That 'nervousness and restlessness' is intimately bound up in his stories with an apprehension of England and Englishness in the post-war era as a place, and a people, *dis*placed, a nation at odds with a world it had once encompassed.

This perhaps explains why Pritchett's stories are replete with English misfits, like the Corams, or like Hilda in 'When My Girl Comes Home' – individuals nervously, restlessly struggling to assert themselves in a world predisposed to neglect, misunderstand or belittle them. What most of these characters have in common is an intense awareness of ruin, whether of themselves, their families, or their country and its past. The comedy is generated by having these characters fetch up in situations where that sense of ruin, of decadent slump, collides with the breezy indifferent onwardness of the modern world. Albert Thompson, the central figure in 'The Sailor', for example, is a man driven to distraction by the effort to resist 'temptation', be it in the form of 'pubs, cinemas, allotments, chicken-runs, tobacconists'. These misplaced anxieties don't just control his behaviour, but compose his very identity. His account of his own life, the narrator discovers, contains nothing but memories 'of people who hadn't "behaved right", a dejecting moral wilderness with Thompson mooching about in it, disappointed with human nature'.

Similarly fretful and intangible is Charles Peacock in 'The Fall', an account-ant whose identity is so insecure that he adjusts his accent to match that of whomever he is speaking to. At the annual accountancy dinner where the story is set, he is initially able to exploit the interest of the other guests in his actor brother, Shel, owing to whose fame there 'was always praise; there were always questions'. But as the evening progresses, and he drinks too much at dinner, he finds that company deserts him. In a desperate bid to regain attention, he resorts to flinging himself full length across the floor in imitation of his famous brother's stage fall. He does this repeatedly, at first in front of those he knows, then in front of strangers, all of whom drift away from him in embarrassment. Finally, on his own in an empty room of the hotel, he rehearses his fall before a portrait of Queen Victoria.

'The Fall' is more than just a tale of one desperate fantasist, however, but creates the sense of a particularly English cultural disappointment and crisis of identity. Queen Victoria's portrait sets the story against a background of faded imperial grandeur, as does the setting for the dinner – at the Royal Hotel in a 'large, wet, Midland city'. Peacock's display is made all the more pathetic by this provincial situation, as it is by the repeated reminders that his brother, whose style he is trying to mimic, is a star in New York and Hollywood. There is general pride among the guests that Peacock's brother was 'born and bred in this city', but Shel's upbringing in the family's fried fish shop, now bankrupt, suggests that this particular England of the mind was one he would have been glad to escape. It is not insignificant that he should have made that escape through acting, by pretending to be someone he was not.

In an essay on Arnold Bennett, Pritchett asks the question, 'How do people face ruin?' The answer he descries in Bennett's work, and of which he approves, is this: 'Variously, unexpectedly; they traipse, protected by conviction, through their melodramas'.[21] It is a description one might fairly apply to Pritchett's own stories, which typically invest in their melodramas of personal ruin a sense of collective slippage. Of course, it is this melodramatic quality that has contributed to the neglect of Pritchett by a literary academy whose cultural and aesthetic values are very much rooted in modernism; and it seems unlikely that he will ever be considered other than middlebrow by these professional readers of fiction. But in terms of the short story's history and development in the twentieth century, his work matters because, like Bowen's, it marks a decisive turn against modernist subjectivization and formalism, and a guarded restoration of storytelling's social function.

Chapter 10

Angela Carter and Ian McEwan

According to the critic Lorna Sage, 1979 'was Angela Carter's *annus mirabilis* as a writer'.[1] The telling event of that year was the publication of her story collection *The Bloody Chamber*, a book that the novelist Salman Rushdie, a few years after Carter's death, declared a 'masterwork' and 'the likeliest of her works to endure'.[2] In the context of twentieth-century fiction, it is remarkable to see such acclaim bestowed upon a volume of short stories. Perennially regarded as the lesser form, the professional writer's 'private aside', as Henry James called it, the short story continues to be viewed with suspicion by many readers and tolerated by publishers only on the assurance that the author will turn in a novel next time around. *The Bloody Chamber* was not Carter's first venture in short stories nor would it be her last (*Fireworks: Nine Profane Pieces* had appeared in 1974 and *Black Venus* was to follow in 1985), but it was her most significant intervention in the form, and is now regarded as one of the most important works of British fiction to have appeared since the Second World War.

As one might expect of so celebrated a work, *The Bloody Chamber* draws with it a now lengthy comet's tail of scholarly criticism and commentary, ranging from narratological and anthropological studies to readings conducted through the lenses of feminist, Gothic and psychoanalytic theory. By a curious critical oversight, however, the book is rarely, if ever, considered in the context of short story writing in the twentieth century. Given that Carter's text makes so much of its own intertextual dependencies and departures, it is surprising to find it cut off in this way from the history of literary form. Yet I think this oversight reflects the general direction the literary short story, so called, has taken in the post-war era, which has been towards increasingly 'minimalist' forms of realism and away from fabular and fantastic writing of the sort Carter favours. As the critic James Wood explains, the Chekhovian 'slice-of-life' narrative has to a great degree become the default setting for the short story:

> Chekhov may be divine, but he is responsible for much sinning on earth. The contemporary short story is essentially sub-Chekhovian. It is most obviously indebted to what Shklovsky called Chekhov's 'negative

endings': the way his stories expire into ellipses, or seem to end in the middle of a thought . . . This is so invisibly part of the grammar of contemporary short fiction that we no longer notice how peculiarly abrupt, how monotonously fragmentary much of what we read has become.[3]

The 'slice-of-life' story that Wood identifies here has been further bolstered by the development of creative writing as an academic discipline in recent decades. As Andrew Levy has shown, the writing workshop industry has done much to consolidate a teachable, reproducible aesthetic of the short story; and while outright prescriptiveness may not be a feature of such teaching, principles of composition have nevertheless become established through the demands of the classroom situation. In Levy's words, 'A school of fiction such as "minimalism", which promotes literary values such as economy and sparseness and encourages the individual writer to concentrate on each individual sentence, is certainly a logical development in an academic climate where there are currently two hundred graduate writing programmes yearly conferring close to a thousand degrees on would-be short story writers.'[4] It is hardly surprising, then, that Carter's fantastic and mythological collection should be thought of as only nominally a book of short stories, and not related in any significant way to the mainstream of short fiction writing in Britain.

Carter herself, it must be said, actively encourages this sequestering of her work from that of her contemporaries. In an afterword appended to her 1974 collection *Fireworks*, she distinguishes between the 'short story' as it is commonly conceived and the 'tales' that she herself writes:

> Though it took me a long time to realize why I liked them, I'd always been fond of Poe, and Hoffman – Gothic tales, cruel tales, tales of wonder, tales of terror, fabulous narratives that deal directly with the imagery of the unconscious – mirrors the externalized self; forsaken castles; haunted forests; forbidden sexual objects. Formally the tale differs from the short story in that it makes few pretences at the imitation of life. The tale does not log everyday experience, as the short story does; it interprets everyday experience through a system of imagery derived from subterranean areas behind everyday experience, and therefore the tale cannot betray its readers into a false knowledge of everyday experience.[5]

Carter's primary attraction to the tale is its freedom from the restrictive nomenclature of realism; but the tale also clearly appeals because of its difference from what we might think of as broadly modernist cultural and artistic priorities. There is its association with 'low' forms, for example – the Gothic, tales of wonder, terror and the preternatural – and the hackneyed devices such forms use to thrill us – mirrors, forsaken castles, haunted forests. Furthermore, the tale dramatizes the 'externalized self', not the introspective voyagings of the subjective self rendered through stream-of-consciousness. Elsewhere in the same piece Carter describes how the 'limited trajectory of the short narrative *concentrates* meaning' [my italics] in contradistinction to the 'multiplying ambiguities of an extended narrative', the implication seeming to be that shortness focuses rather than disperses meaning.

The impression that Carter is explicitly working against the modernist legacy is reinforced when one considers some of the salient features of her style in *The Bloody Chamber*. The stories demonstrate a pan-cultural eclecticism, freely mixing 'high' and 'low' cultural forms and genres, indulging in Gothic fantasy, tales of wonder, pageants of terror and florid cruelty, and drawing on conventions of oral tale-telling, particularly in their use of ostentatious and often fanciful plot lines. The perfervid prose, too, is anything but scrupulously mean (once asked if she embraced opportunities for over-writing, Carter replied: 'Embrace them? I would say that I half-suffocate them with the enthusiasm with which I wrap my arms and legs around them').[6] Like her American counterparts Donald Barthelme and Robert Coover, and following the example of fabular writers like the Italian novelist Italo Calvino, Carter forges a fictional idiom that clearly cocks a snook at the aesthetic and cultural pieties of high-modernism.

Carter's attitude to authorship and the status of literary texts likewise contrasts sharply with that of the modernists. In her introduction to *The Old Wives Fairy Tale Book*, she describes the difference between the status and origin of the fairly tale and modern ideas about creativity and ownership:

> Ours is a highly individualized culture, with a great faith in the work of art as a unique one-off, and the artist as an original, a godlike and inspired creator of unique one-offs. But fairy tales are not like that, nor are their makers. Who first invented meatballs? In what country? Is there a definitive recipe for potato soup?[7]

Of course, Carter is merely recasting here what any reader familiar with Roland Barthes's famous essay 'The Death of the Author' will know to be the case about any text, that it is, in Barthes's words, a 'tissue of quotations'.[8] But it is significant, I think, that she should choose to describe her own attraction to the fairy tale in these terms, for it challenges the Romantic myth of the author as superlative, non-conformist creative genius, a myth that was renewed and greatly intensified in the modernist period. In this respect, too, Carter presents herself as a *post*-modernist writer of a particularly antagonistic sort.

And yet the condition of being *post* anything always carries within it the sense of indebtedness, the ghostly presence of that past we try to 'other'. As Jacques Derrida puts it, the trace of the expelled thing always remains, 'under erasure'.[9] And so it is with Carter, who, it is worth pointing out, attended university and served her apprenticeship as a writer at the very time when the 'canonization and institutionalization' of modernism were taking place within the academy.[10] Reading *The Bloody Chamber*, one is struck, yes, by the ways in which the stories depart from the practices of other writers we have been looking at in this section under the rubric of post-modernism, but also by the strong resemblances to them.

At a simple level, Carter reproduces many of the disruptive narrative techniques we have witnessed in modernist writing, with the same intention of unsettling the notion of a single, unified or omniscient authority in the text. To take one very clear example, 'The Company of Wolves', as part of its ironic rendition of Red Riding Hood, generates a remarkable fluidity of meaning by the use of free indirect discourse and by dispensing with the markers of direct speech – techniques familiar to us from much modernist writing. Here, for example, is the moment when the wolf arrives at the grandmother's house:

> He rapped upon the panels with his hairy knuckles.
> It is your granddaughter, he mimicked in a high soprano.
> Lift up the latch and walk in my darling.
> You can tell them by their eyes, eyes of a beast of prey, nocturnal, devastating eyes as red as a wound . . .
> His feral muzzle is sharp as a knife; he drops his golden burden of gnawed pheasant on the table and puts down your dear girl's basket, too. Oh, my God, what have you done with her? . . .
> He strips off his shirt. His skin is the colour and texture of vellum. A crisp stripe of hair runs down his belly . . . He strips off his trousers and she can see how hairy his legs are. His genitals, huge. Ah! Huge.

Knowing to whom we should attribute various statements in this passage is highly problematic. Who, for example, makes the comment 'Oh, my God, what have you done with her?'? And is it the same voice that says at the end, 'His genitals, huge. Ah! Huge'? Nor can we readily determine what is meant as speech and what is thought.

More generally, Carter's use of the fairy tale also has many correspondences in modernism. As we have seen, making ironic reinscriptions of familiar story tropes and patterns was a preoccupation of Joyce, Woolf and Beckett in their stories. Carter does something similar with fairy tales, disturbing the narrative conventions and ideological assumptions that control them. As one recent critic explains:

> Fairy tales are informed by closure, a movement from change to permanence. Their plots move from an initial, pernicious metamorphosis to a stable identity that must and will be reached or recaptured. Carter, however, stubbornly moves the other way round, from stability to instability, undermining the closed binary logic of fairy tale ... She takes her reader along the paths of indeterminacy.[11]

In other words, Carter rewrites the fairy tale in ways that challenge the reader's expectations of closure and resolution at the level of plot, and bring into question the values those source texts expressed as well as the educative, morally corrective purposes they were frequently intended to serve.

Among the source texts Carter takes up with in *The Bloody Chamber* are Beauty and the Beast, in 'The Courtship of Mr Lyon' and 'The Tiger's Bride'; Red Riding Hood, in 'The Werewolf' and 'The Company of Wolves'; and Bluebeard, in 'The Bloody Chamber'. In some cases, her purpose is to uncover what was all along buried in the original. In 'The Bloody Chamber', for example, she makes explicit the sadomasochistic subtext in the source text, while in 'The Snow Child' she draws out the hidden patriarchal structure of the Grimm Brothers' original, and in particular its treatment of the vindictive, wicked queen. In her version of that tale, the Countess who kills the beautiful snow child out of jealousy does so not because she is simply wicked, but because she is in thrall to the patriarchal authority of her husband. She kills the child in order to resume the trappings of her power and status, her long furs and diamond brooch and, most important of all, the Count. Carter transforms the source text's unquestioning portrait of female jealousy into an exacting study of the dynamics of female powerlessness in a male-dominated culture.

More often, however, Carter's reworkings attempt to open up the unresolvable, interrogative complexities, both stylistic and moral, that nestle in the fairy tale. 'The Courtship of Mr Lyon', for example, is one of several in *The Bloody Chamber* that recast the story of Beauty and the Beast, in this case the classic eighteenth-century French rendering by Marie Le Prince de Beaumont. Here is how Carter's version begins:

> Outside her kitchen window, the hedgerow glistened as if the snow possessed a light of its own; when the sky darkened towards evening, an unearthly, reflected pallor remained behind upon the winter's landscape, while still the soft flakes floated down. This lovely girl, whose skin possesses that same, inner light so you would have thought she, too, was made all of snow, pauses in her chores in the mean kitchen to look out at

the country road. Nothing has passed that way all day; the road is white
and unmarked as a spilled bolt of bridal satin.
Father said he would be home before nightfall.
The snow brought down all the telephone wires; he couldn't have
called, even with the best of news.
The roads are bad. I hope he'll be safe.

This opening is, as with all of Carter's writing, both familiar and estranging.
The familiarity arises from the embedded references to well-known fairy tales,
specifically Snow White (the lovely girl's flesh) and Cinderella ('her chores in
the mean kitchen'), but also, less directly, to thematic and imagistic tropes we
associate with that genre – the winter landscape, for example, and the bridal
satin. The passage also turns on familiar oppositions between light and dark
and, by extension, good and evil, purity and corruption. The estranging occurs,
however, with the anachronistic juxtaposition of these features of classic fairy
tale (which we usually imagine as occurring at some unspecified moment in the
past) with references to the modern-day paraphernalia of telephone wires and
road transportation. The discontinuity is made all the more stark by the shift
in register from the stylized artifice and metaphoricity of the first paragraph to
the contemporary idiomatic thoughts of the girl.

   This pattern of summoning up the familiar and associative and then defamiliarizing it is characteristic of Carter's narrative procedure, as it is of the
modernist text, and it is the means by which she diverts us away from the
closural pieties of the fairy tale. Or rather, it is more accurate to say that she
releases the repressed energies in the original stories which were sanitized,
cleansed of their lurid or libidinous suggestiveness and moral ambiguity for
the edification and education of children. Carter's versions give expression to
the feelings of vague discomfort and inarticulate misapprehension we often
have when reading fairy tales. In 'The Courtship of Mr Lyon' she does this
most obviously by altering the Beauty character, so that she is no longer the
modest, self-sacrificing and dutiful daughter of Beaumont's rendition who gets
her reward (the prince) for setting virtue ahead of wit and beauty, but is instead
portrayed as vain, narcissistic and thoughtless. The ending, then, becomes not
a moment of resolution and romantic fulfilment, but a troubling, inconclusive
travesty of the source text. The Beast is not transformed into a handsome prince
but into Mr Lyon, 'a man with an unkempt head of hair and, how strange, a
broken nose, such as the noses of retired boxers, that gave him a distant, heroic
resemblance to the handsomest of the beasts'. Mr Lyon is still, it seems, part
Beast: the darkness and snowy whiteness that were held apart in the opening
paragraph appear to merge at the end of the story, as the couple wander, like a
bewildered Adam and Eve after the fall, in the garden.

Of course, one is always conscious of the differences between Carter's use of popular intertexts and the earlier modernists', not least her lack of concern to ascribe them a place within any hierarchy of cultural value. Similarly, her willingness to deploy the debased conventions of fantasy, Gothic and super-naturalism in her work contrasts with the practice of her forebears, and can be read as a refusal of the literary prejudices that informed the modernist project and that have infused the academic discipline of English studies. Yet Carter's work shows enough points of correspondence and creative affinity with modernism that it would be a mistake to view her work, as many commentators do, as a decisive 'breakthrough' against the culture and practices of that movement.

A similar argument can be advanced in the case of Ian McEwan, whose two collections of stories, *First Love, Last Rites* (1975) and *In Between the Sheets* (1978), attracted almost as much critical attention when they were published as *The Bloody Chamber*. Carter's observation, in the afterword to *Fireworks*, that to be living in 1970s Britain was to be living 'in Gothic times', is amply borne out in McEwan's work. Certainly, its roster of main themes is a disturbing one, particularly so when taken in combination: 'dirt, scum, pus, menstrual blood, pathetic obesity, total chinlessness, enforced transvestitism, early teenage incest, child abuse and child murder', in one critic's catalogue.[12] Yet the sensational messiness and social wreckage that is McEwan's subject matter comes to us in tidy ship-shape vessels, brisk narratives notable for their rationality, orderliness and discursive self-control. It may be hell in there, but it isn't bedlam.

Like Carter, McEwan is drawn to adolescence both as a theme and as a condition afflicting his narrators and central characters. For both writers, adolescence figures as a series of baffling initiations, of psychic and bodily crossing points more or less successfully traversed. The eminent critic Christopher Ricks, in an admiring early review of McEwan, sums up the adolescent condition in his work very neatly:

> adolescents are an extraordinary, special case of people; they're close to childhood, and yet they are constantly baffled and irritated by the initiations into what's on the other side – the shadow line, as it were. They are perfect outsiders, in a sense, and fiction – especially short stories, and especially first-person narratives – can thrive on a point of view which is somehow dislocated, removed.[13]

Ricks is clearly nodding here to Frank O'Connor's durable axiom, that the short story specializes in depicting the lonely, isolated and submerged existence. Moreover, he implies that the adolescent sense of estrangement in McEwan's work does not necessarily disperse with maturity, as one crosses over that 'shadow line' (Ricks's essay is entitled 'Adolescence *and After*'). That is to say, McEwan does not so much write about what it is like to be a teenager, as what it is like to have *been* a teenager, and where that experience leaves one as an adult.

This is an important discrimination to make because it takes us to the heart of McEwan's storytelling style. A good place to begin this discussion is with 'Homemade', the opening text of *First Love, Last Rites* and, owing to its depiction of child sexual abuse, the most notorious story in the book. 'Homemade' is narrated in the first person by a man recollecting the occasion on which, as a teenager, he raped his ten-year-old sister, Connie. The event itself is retailed to us in painstaking detail, as part of a witty and cynical portrait of pubescent sexual awakening and initiation. The bulk of the narrative is taken up with the narrator's pursuit of his first sexual encounter, which he is hoping to secure, for a modest financial outlay, from a local girl called Lulu Smith. But before that meeting can take place, he is left home alone with Connie, and, luring her into her favourite game of 'Mummies and Daddies', rapes her.

If that summary is disturbing, it is as nothing compared with reading the story itself, and not just because the full text presents the seduction and rape in detail, which is harrowing, but because it conveys the quality of mind of the perpetrator – cynical, sensuous and emotionally indifferent. McEwan's narration is very sophisticated in the way it presents adolescent experience from a retrospective, adult point of view. The narrator is looking back from some unspecified future point on his younger self, and it is our uncertainty about how the narrator feels *now*, at the point of telling the story, that becomes the most troubled aspect of the whole episode.

To see how this works in practice, consider the following passage in which the narrator recalls first masturbating, egged on by his friend Raymond:

> We were exploring a cellar on a bomb site, poking around to see what the dossers had left behind, when Raymond, having lowered his trousers as if to have a piss, began to rub his prick with a coruscating vigour, inviting me to do the same. I did and soon became suffused with a warm, indistinct pleasure which intensified to a floating, melting sensation as if my guts might at any time drift away to nothing. And all this time our hands pumped furiously. I was beginning to congratulate Raymond on his discovery of such a simple, inexpensive yet pleasurable way of passing the time, and at the same time wondering if I could not dedicate my whole life to this glorious sensation – and I suppose looking back now in many respects I have – I was about to express all manner of

things when I was lifted by the scruff of the neck, my arms, my legs, my insides, haled, twisted, racked, and producing for all this two dollops of sperm which flipped over Raymond's Sunday jacket – it was Sunday – and dribbled into his breast pocket.

The narrator here relies on the technique of defamiliarization in order to convey the ignorance and, so to say, cack-handedness of his younger self. That is to say, the adolescent does not know what he is doing, or what is about to happen, on this first occasion, and the writing mimics his benightedness by communicating the novelty and unfamiliarity of the experience. We, of course, know what he is doing, and so does the narrator, who is able to adopt (as we all might) an ironic distance from the memory. It is this ironic distance that McEwan collapses, however, with the narrator's comment that indeed he has, 'in many respects', dedicated his 'whole life to this glorious sensation'. Suddenly, the impression of a stable, well-adjusted adult looking wryly back on a per-fectly normal stage in his adolescent development breaks down. Moreover, the defamiliarized details – 'rub[bing] his prick with a coruscating vigour'; 'plea-sure which intensified to a floating, melting sensation', and so on – no longer function as elements in an amused and amusing portrait of teenage sexual fumblings, but are reanimated with a lurid sense that the narrator is reliving them with genuine pleasure, that he is fondling the details of his auto-eroticism in front of *us* this time, rather than Raymond.

The key thing to notice here is the way that McEwan's text alludes to some-thing that it refuses to disclose. For all that 'Homemade' is presented as a candid, no-holds-barred confession, the confessor is actually purposely unre-vealing and unrevealed. The questions we want answers to – was this rape the first of many, the first instalment in the *Bildungsroman* of a serial sexual abuser, or was it an aberration of pubescent sexual awakening? – go unanswered. The story advertises what it leaves unsaid. In this respect, McEwan stands squarely in the tradition of modernist short story writing. By techniques of ellipsis, aper-ture and interdiction, he creates a textual world of profound epistemological uncertainty.

The troubling indeterminacy of human motivation is McEwan's abiding subject in his two collections of stories. Not all of his narrators are as disturbed as the one in 'Homemade', but what many of the texts have in common is a tendency to draw a blank on the crucial questions of why a character acts as he (or occasionally she) does. This may be one reason why McEwan has more than once used child narrators in his fiction – narrators like the orphaned boy in 'Last Day of Summer' who is 'not sure how to start off telling someone about myself'.

In that story, the narrator, who lives with his brother in a sort of makeshift commune, speaks with none of the superior, cynical wit we encountered in 'Homemade':

> I am twelve and lying near-naked on my belly out on the back lawn in the sun when for the first time I hear her laugh. I don't know, I don't move, I just close my eyes. It's a girl's laugh, a young woman's, short and nervous like laughing at nothing funny. I got half my face in the grass I cut an hour before and I can smell the cold soil beneath it.

The laugh belongs to Jenny, a cheerful, capable, overweight girl who comes to live with the narrator and his brother and who quickly slips into a surrogate mother role, cooking and keeping house and looking after Alice, the baby daughter of Kate, another of the commune's members. At first the narrator is repulsed by Jenny's size and intrusive manner, but soon the two are firm friends and spending time together on the river in the narrator's rowing boat. One warm evening, the 'last day of summer', the boat capsizes and Jenny and Alice are thrown overboard and the narrator is left swimming slowly back to shore alone. At this climactic moment, however, the narrative withdraws into inscrutability and impercipience, all access to the narrator's feelings, which have gradually been unlocked by Jenny's gentle enquiring, suddenly barred: 'Sometimes great shivers run through my legs and back, but mostly I am calm, hanging on to the green shell [of the boat] with nothing in my mind, nothing at all, just watching the river, waiting for the surface to break and the yellow patches to scatter'.

What connects 'Last Day of Summer' to 'Homemade' is the way it juxtaposes a highly unified and conclusive surface narrative and a deliberately unreflexive and unrevealing narrating intelligence. Motions are resolved, but motives are not; the stories bespeak an inwardness that is incommensurate to outwardness. The same is true of 'Butterflies', another deeply distressing story, this time narrated from the point of view of a child sex abuser and murderer. The narrator's account of his actions is meticulously patterned, artful and suspenseful; his reflections upon it, however, are non-existent. The final paragraph teases us with its allusion to dramatic fulfilment and the revealed truth as the narrator picks up the trope of the butterfly hunt (by which he lured the child to her death) into a parable of his own life: 'The opportunities are rare, like butterflies. You stretch out your hand and they are gone'. The pattern is complete, the irony delicious, but the human substance of the story remains shrouded in incomprehension.

At times, McEwan is guilty of overplaying this card. The metaphorical patterning of 'First Love, Last Rites', for example, is clunking and obvious and unrelieved by any substantive intrigue in the narrating voice. But more often he is able, like Angela Carter in her recasting of the fairy tale, to generate an exhilarating discrepancy between a highly unified story structure and what Elizabeth Bowen termed 'human unknowableness'. One of the most intriguing examples of this is 'Pornography', the opening story of *In Between the Sheets*, which tells of O'Byrne, a self-centred cad who works in his brother's pornographic magazine store and who is cheating on two nurses, Lucy and Pauline, both of whom he has infected with the clap. During intercourse with Lucy, O'Byrne is shocked to discover the pleasure he gets from being dominated and even abused. The climax of the story comes when Lucy one night ties him to her bed as a prelude to sex, only then to introduce Pauline, complete with sterilizer, hypodermic needle and surgical instrument set ready to mutilate his genitals. It ends with O'Byrne still tied to the bed and Lucy instructing Pauline, 'If you'll secure that strap, Nurse Shepherd, then I think we can begin'.

On the face of it, 'Pornography' reads as a thrillingly suspenseful yet ultimately straightforward revenge narrative in which two women betrayed are empowered both physically and symbolically by the emasculation of their betrayer. However, much as Carter does with her fairy tale archetypes, McEwan greatly complicates that familiar narrative at the conclusion to his story, for O'Byrne's prostration and capture by the women appears to be something he is complicit in. As the nurses are preparing for surgery, he continues to feel 'excitement, horrified excitement' and his penis remains erect. At one point he manages to work his hand free from its binding but does not capitalize on this by striking out at his assailants, instead capitulating easily to the timid Pauline, who resecures him. The 'revenge' scenario, then, carries within it a powerful masochistic pleasure for the victim. McEwan opens up the possibility that the punishment the women wish to inflict on O'Byrne, for his particular infidelity and for the sins of men against women in general, as symbolized by his line of work, in fact further feeds the voracious pornographic male imagination. The story we thought we were reading, like the revenge the nurses thought they were taking, flounders on the diversity and incommensurability of the sexual self.

Part IV

Postcolonial and other stories

Introduction: a 'minor' literature?

What connects the writers in this section is that they have all written in the aftermath of colonial disturbance. The question that immediately presents itself is why, of all the interventions we might choose to make in the corpus of twentieth-century short fiction, should we choose to make this one?

The direct answer to this is that the short story is, and always has been, disproportionately represented in the literatures of colonial and postcolonial cultures. The reasons for this are numerous and difficult to determine and they change from culture to culture. But as a starting point, we might want to say that, as in the late-Victorian period, economic considerations have played an important part. In cultures with small or non-existent publishing infrastructures, the low-capital, low-circulation literary magazine tends to be the main outlet for new writing. Such magazines, for reasons of space and means of production, invariably favour the short story over longer forms of fiction.

Beyond that, several critics have attempted to argue that the short story is particularly suited to the representation of liminal or problematized identities – Frank O'Connor's 'submerged population groups' once again – and that in the ruptured condition of colonial and postcolonial societies, the form speaks directly to and about those whose sense of self, region, state or nation is insecure. It is on such grounds that writers from places as far apart geographically as they are socially and historically – from Ireland to Australia to America, France and India – have wanted to claim the short story as their own.

Yet rarely are such accounts satisfactory or even remotely complete, and one immediately begins to make qualifications and demurrals. In the case of a writer like Chinua Achebe, for example, the subject of chapter 12 below, can we really say that his short stories bespeak the postcolonial reality of Igbo culture and Nigerian society any more precisely, suggestively or meaningfully than do his novels? And what of James Kelman? Is his exhilaratingly politicized narrative style any more or less or differently evidenced in his stories than in his award-winning longer fiction? It is extremely difficult to think what generally applicable relationship can be said to exist between the short story and the experience of (post)colonialism per se.

138

However, if it is not possible to argue that the short story is specially or uniquely adaptable or amenable to the colonial or postcolonial context as a whole, we are still able to consider the ways the form has been used by particular writers in particular situations, and the kind of cultural work it has performed thereby. This is some way short of singling the story out as the *nonpareil* form of marginality and otherness, as some critics would like to claim it is, but it nevertheless allows us to demonstrate the special contribution the form has made to the literature of colonial disturbance.

A useful theoretical framework to invoke here is that of the 'minor' literature as it originates in Gilles Deleuze and Felix Guattari's 1975 study *Kafka: Toward a Minor Literature* (*Kafka: Pour une littérature mineure*). There it is defined as the writing 'which a minority constructs within a major language'.[1] 'Minor' literature, the authors argue, occurs in a language which is 'deterritorialized', or displaced, for instance through a process of colonization, and it is this displacement which fits that language 'for strange and minor uses'.[2] Far from trying to compensate for the curiosity of his linguistic inheritance, the 'minor' writer emphasizes and reaffirms the deterritorialization by transgressive and defamiliarizing devices in his work. In the case of Kafka, this involved exploiting the situation of the German language in Prague (where it was 'contaminated' by contact with Czech and Yiddish) by putting its syntactic and stylistic 'poverty' to the service of a 'new sobriety, a new expressivity, a new flexibility, a new intensity'.[3] In other words, 'minor' writing abuses the discursive structures of the 'major' language to its own creative ends. However, Deleuze and Guattari caution against thinking of 'minor' writing as another term for 'regionalism', for regional writing is, by contrast, nostalgic and essentialist, full of 'archaisms that [it is] trying to impart a contemporary sense to'.[4] By the same token, they identify as a danger lurking within all 'minor' writing the desire to become a 'major' form of expression. They therefore propose a new model for understanding the 'minor' writer:

> To make use of the polylingualism of one's own language, to make a minor or intensive use of it, to oppose the oppressed quality of this language to its oppressive quality, to find points of nonculture or under-development, linguistic Third World zones by which a language can escape, an animal enters into things, an assemblage comes into play. How many styles or genres or literary movements, even very small ones, have only one single dream: to assume a major function in language, to offer themselves as a sort of state language, an official language. Create the opposite dream: know how to create a becoming-minor.[5]

The 'minor' is revolutionary because it 'hate[s] all languages of masters';[6] for this reason the 'major' can never be revolutionary. At the moment when 'minor' writing achieves majority status, the authors argue, it loses its radical identity, becoming dominant, 'official' and ultimately imitative of colonial-imperialist ideology: that is, in attempting to 'redo the photos, to remake power and law',[7] it simply follows the course already marked out by imperialism. By arguing that 'minor' writing should have as its ambition the state of 'becoming-minor', the authors are suggesting that it will be a writing which self-consciously maintains its ec-centric, 'minority' position. As Abdul R. JanMohamed and David Lloyd put it in a related essay, 'symptoms of inadequacy can be reread transformatively as indications and figurations of values radically opposed to those of the dominant culture'.[8] What is defined as 'inadequate' or 'minor' about a literature may be the particular hiding places of its power.

The applicability of this theory to the short story is that it provides for a more creative way of thinking about deficit, curtailment, lacking, the markers of 'minority' we have been dealing with throughout this book. It returns us again to Henry James's insistence that we think of the short story not in terms of a confinement or limitation of the full expressive capacity of the novel, but as a form capable of producing its own unique effects of amplitude, or, to use James's word, 'multiplicity'. It answers, too, to Elizabeth Bowen's desire to view the shortness of the short story as a 'positive' quality, and to Beckett's luminous vision of an art of radical indigence in which we read not a 'partial object' but a 'total object, complete with missing parts'. The interrogative story's 'unfinished' economy, its failure literally to express, to extend itself to definition, determination or disclosure, becomes, under the rubric of a theory of 'minor' literature, a positive aversion to the entailment of 'power and law' that defines the 'major' literature.

What is expressly *not* being proposed here is that the short story is uniquely capable of performing this minority function, rather that writers have been able to use it, along with other forms and media, to that end. This gives us a general rubric under which to consider the authors in this section, all of whom have used the interrogative, elliptical properties of the short story to stage a creative resistance to the entailments of 'power and law'.

Chapter 11 deals with two writers from so-called 'settler' societies, the New Zealander Frank Sargeson and the Australian Marjory Barnard. In both cases, they have used the short story as a means of eluding the narrative (an especially powerful one in settler communities) of cultural nationalism. Alice Munro, likewise, has exploited the form in order to show how a range of dominant narratives, from historiography to colonialism to feminism, routinely fall short of adequately representing the live stories of women. In the case of

James Kelman and Chinua Achebe, the subjects of chapter 12, the short story has proven an effective medium for communicating the sense of chronic inconsequence that attends those excluded from the schemes of law and power. None of these writers is wholly contained by the notion of a 'minor' literature, but the theory does allow us to pick out both formal and ideological correspondences among them, and account for their various uses of the short story form.

Chapter 11

Frank Sargeson and Marjorie Barnard

According to one recent critic, Frank Sargeson's work, 'more than that of any other writer . . . signifies New Zealandness in our literature'.[1] Certainly, his writing became, in the 1930s and 40s, synonymous with a particular sort of assertive, masculinist cultural nationalism. Yet Sargeson was also an astute reader of modern European and American writing, and wrote insightfully about Sherwood Anderson, Katherine Mansfield and D. H. Lawrence, to name but three. While he lived and worked during a period of considerable anxiety and agitation around questions of national political identity in New Zealand, and while he and his work were unquestioningly, and to a great degree justifiably, 'claimed' by the nationalist cause, Sargeson's writing is far more ambivalent and artful than such a political affiliation might suggest. They also, as in the case of his key story 'The Making of a New Zealander', resist the kind of political appropriations they were frequently subject to.

Frank Sargeson's short stories were published in three volumes: *Conversation with My Uncle, and Other Sketches* (1936), *A Man and His Wife* (1940) and *That Summer, and Other Stories* (1946). A qualified lawyer, he began publishing in the literary magazine *Tomorrow* in 1935, contributing wry, anecdotal sketches about the undistinguished lives of Depression-era labourers and unemployed itinerants, their unhappy marriages and dislocated families. Regionally specific and conventionally realist, the sketches were also distinctly 'male' in the subjects they treated, and 'masculinist' in the attitudes they expressed.

Considering the slightness of these early sketches – few of them run to more than five pages – it is striking to think that they had as profound and lasting an impact on New Zealand literature as they did. Yet they not only decisively altered the course of fiction written there but made dominant a particular sort of masculine realism which was immediately taken up (and which endured, often oppressively) as the national 'style'. That 'style' is characterized by a severe emotional reticence, a regionally marked working-class vernacular diction, and an aversion to conventions of literary locution. Sargeson's sketches invariably feature economically and intellectually impoverished men who function as both the subjects and narrators of anecdotal yarns about rural working life, poverty, unemployment, and the trials and rewards of 'mateship'. So deeply did this style permeate the New Zealand cultural imaginary thereafter that the novelist C. K. Stead, charged with summing up Sargeson's achievement on the occasion of his seventy-fifth birthday, declared his work to be an 'atmosphere' which had enveloped and nourished the national literature throughout the middle years of the century.[2]

As an example of Sargeson's early style, consider the opening staves of 'I've Lost My Pal':

> It was early summer, shearing time. Tom and me went into the country and we got a job picking up fleeces in a big shed. After we'd pulled the bellies off the fleeces we had to roll them up and put them in the press. It was a good job. We liked it. We had to work hard and we got covered in sheep grease, but I'll tell you a thing about sheep grease. It comes off best in cold water. And that saves a lot of bother.
>
> I could tell you a lot of things about that shed. You know a lot of lambs are beggars for not sitting still when you're shearing them. There was a shearer who used to go maggoty if a lamb wouldn't sit still. He'd heave it back into the pen. But it's not about the shed I want to tell you. I want to tell you about how I lost my pal Tom.

The workings of this passage are very subtle in the way they conjure up not just a narrating character but a condition of mind. Sargeson's fidelity here is, of course, to the spoken rather than the written word, and so one readily detects a manner of spontaneous speech rather than meditated writing in phrases such as 'I'll tell you a thing about sheep grease' or 'I want to tell you about how I lost my pal Tom'. There are always a few grammatical solecisms in Sargeson's stories ('Tom and me', for example, rather than 'Tom and I') which contribute to the impression of an unselfconscious, loosely regulated verbal intelligence at the centre of the narrative; but our impression of the quality of mind addressing us here is mainly gathered from less immediately obvious features of the prose. There is, for example, the extensive repetition. Several successive sentences use the same words and phrases, such as 'fleeces' in the second and third sentences of the first paragraph, or 'I want to tell you' in the second paragraph. The word 'grease', meanwhile, occurs twice in the same sentence in paragraph one. Most of these repetitions are redundancies; or rather, they would be in *written* prose, where our inclination would be to substitute them with synonyms or else take for granted that the reader knows to what we are referring and omit them altogether. Here, however, the repetitions cluster around the key nouns in what is being described – 'fleeces', 'grease', 'lambs', 'shearers' – and around the central act of 'telling', to the extent that the mere mention of a physical object, the sheep grease, or the shed in paragraph two, is enough to loosen the speaker's grip momentarily on the larger, immaterial structure of his own narrative. This under-lexicalization contributes to our sense of a character more at ease with the tactile and material than the emotional or reflective aspects of experience.

An even more striking feature of this passage, and again characteristic of the Sargeson style, is its construction of an implied reader. The narrator repeatedly addresses the imagined reader directly, through the use of the second-person pronoun 'you', and there seems to be an assumption that the reader shares an interest in, or is in some degree curious to know about, for example, sheds and sheep grease, and that the cold water technique for removing the latter will prove useful or informative to him or her. Of course, this is another method by which Sargeson characterizes his narrator, reinforcing our sense of his meandering and skittish intelligence. But in respect of the stories' *actual* first readers, in 1930s New Zealand, this was more than simply a technique of characterization. Rather, it was the means by which Sargeson sought to alter his readers' sense of their relationship to the material reality of New Zealand life. That is to say, by producing a sense of intimate address from these narrators, Sargeson aimed to reveal to his readers, first of all, their connectedness to that distinctively New Zealand voice, and more importantly, the validity of that voice as a means of literary self-expression.

To explain this point more fully we need to consider the literary and cultural context in which Sargeson's stories first appeared. Up until the 1930s, the dominant modes of fiction in New Zealand were romantic and local colourist, with much of what was published palely imitative of English popular literary forms. What is more, it was written to appeal to a British audience rather than an indigenous New Zealand one. By the early 1930s, however, as the nationalist movement became more powerful, there were calls for New Zealand authors to direct their gaze inward, to address a local readership concerned with local issues and questions of regional and national identity. As the literary magazine *Phoenix* put it in July 1932: 'We are hungry for the words that shall show us these islands and ourselves; that shall give us a home in thought'. The use of the word 'home' here is significant, for in common with other 'settler' communities, many New Zealanders at this time still referred to Britain as 'Home'. For professional writers, there were sound economic reasons for preserving this attachment, as one commentator pointed out:

> Some day we shall have stories of New Zealand people by New Zealand people for New Zealand people and, given the requisite art, the beginnings of a truly national literature; but so long as our best writers,

however pardonable the motive of making a living, tell this tale with a telescope to one eye, bearing on the distant market in London, the other eye half-shut to their readers here, that day will be deferred.[3]

Sargeson's stories mark a conscious break with this sense of dependence and belonging elsewhere. Not only do they render an authentic New Zealand voice for the first time in fiction, they allow that voice to take possession of the narrative itself. By proclaiming the local and familiar both valid and valuable, they create the possibility of a literature for, by, and about New Zealanders themselves.

Such a reading as I have given here constructs Sargeson as an unequivocally nationalist writer. But this would be misleading if it were taken to mean that his work was patriotic in any chauvinistic sense, for Sargeson was a fierce critic of the shortcomings of New Zealand society, and in particular of what he called the 'little Bethel' mentality. By 'little Bethel' Sargeson meant the vestigial Puritanism of the culture, which he not only considered a corruption of non-conformist Christian morality but blamed for the sterility and timidity of much of the art produced there. And it is for this reason, I would suggest, that it makes sense to consider Sargeson as a post-modernist writer, operating within an international as well as national context. For, as his essays make clear, Sargeson was, like Marjorie Barnard, well versed in the literature of European and American modernism, and he was able to call upon the stylistic and formal resources of modernism in his endeavour to forge a regionally distinctive writing that was not constrained by any straightforward allegiance to the nationalist agenda. His treatment and understanding of the short story form makes clear how important it is to regard Sargeson within both local and international contexts. As Lydia Wevers and others have pointed out, the short story has long appealed to writers working in colonial or post-colonial situations, in part because 'its very brevity' seems to speak 'for the absence of other, larger certainties'.[4] That may well be so, and I shall return to this subject below. But as we have seen, the notion of the short story's 'shortness' as somehow expressive of the instabilities and uncertainties, the fleetingness and fragility, of experience in the technological age is a distinctly modernist one.

Sargeson's alertness to the aesthetic of the modernist text is amply demonstrated in his essays. In a 1935 piece on Katherine Mansfield, for example, he notes how she achieves a certain expansiveness by maintaining a tight focus in her narratives. Her technique, he discerns, is to concentrate on 'the part rather than the whole' and allow her stories to work out their larger intentions through a depiction of the 'isolated details and moments of life'. Sherwood Anderson he likewise praises for using the 'short, suggestive sentence' in such a way as to liberate the imagination rather than 'restrict and pin it down'. 'Anderson', he goes on, 'expects you to be susceptible to suggestion and implication, to eke out his imagination with your own'. He is also sensitive to the way Anderson narrates in 'commonplace words and phrases' which yet have 'nothing of the flatness of life' but are infused with a sense of 'the third dimension'.[5]

In an interview he gave in 1970, Sargeson was asked whether he had found New Zealand accurately represented in any writing prior to his own. His answer was yes, but not in New Zealand literature. It is a remark that points to an inter-action in Sargeson's mind between a modernist aesthetic of story writing and the creation of a distinctively regional literature. And this, I would suggest, is something we must bear in mind when we read Sargeson's stories and contemplate what he was trying to achieve in them. By way of exemplification consider the 'The Making of a New Zealander'.

'The Making of a New Zealander' employs the same regionally marked narrational discourse as Sargeson's early sketches, creating the same effect of an intimate, confiding, vitalized speaking voice. Also in evidence is the contrary self-referentiality that we observed in 'I've Lost My Pal':

> When I called at that farm they promised me a job for two months so I took it on, but it turned out to be tough going. The boss was all right, I didn't mind him at all, and most days he'd just settle down by the fire and get busy with his crochet. It was real nice to see him looking happy and contented as he sat there with his ball of wool.
>
> But this story is not about a cocky who used to sit in front of the fire and do crochet. I'm not saying I haven't got a story about him, but I'll have to be getting round to it another time.

Later in the story the narrator introduces another alternative narrative, this time concerning his employer, Mrs Crump. But this too is deferred to another, unspecified time of telling. Getting himself back on track, the narrator sets out what his story on this occasion is about. Except that he is unable to say quite what it is about:

> What I want to tell is about how I sat on a hillside one evening and talked with a man. That's all, just a summer evening and a talk with a man on a hillside. Maybe there's nothing in it and maybe there is.

The man in question, it turns out, is his neighbour Nick, a hard-working immigrant farmer from Dalmatia. In a series of oblique and hesitant exchanges Nick and the narrator make observations on the Dalmatian's diseased trees and the lack of sweetness in his grape crop, the fact that neither Nick nor his brother are married or will get married in New Zealand, the shortness of money that makes marrying so difficult, the paradoxical nature of Christ's birth in snow-bound Palestine, a country that never sees snowfall, and Nick's decision to become a Communist. At the end of this perplexing discourse the narrator considers Nick's claim that he is now a New Zealander. The narrator doubts this, and doubts that Nick himself believes it: 'he knew he wasn't a New Zealander. And he knew he wasn't a Dalmatian any more'. The pair part on a promise to meet the next night on the same hillside to drink wine. But the meeting never takes place as the narrator is laid off by Mrs Crump for his dissenting talk and, as she sees it, disrespectful humour. The story ends with the narrator drinking heavily in order to 'get Nick out of my mind. He knew what he was talking about, but maybe it's best for a man to hang on'.

The questions the reader inevitably asks at the end of this story are, What is the narrator referring to when he says that Nick knew what he was talking about? and, Why does he want to get Nick off his mind? It may be that he is referring to the discussion about marrying, and that his comment that 'it's best for a man to hang on' suggests that he is doubtful whether marriage is the right thing for him. But if that is the case, it makes no sense that he thinks Nick knows what he is talking about, since Nick's explanation for not himself marrying is not that he has chosen to hang on, but that 'In New Zealand, everybody says they cannot afford to get married'. Equally beguiling is the narrator's wish to get Nick out of his mind. Which aspect of Nick's conversation or person has he found so unsettling? Is it the conversation about marrying, or about Communism perhaps? Or does the clue lie in the shyness the narrator admits to having felt on first meeting Nick? Whatever is the cause of his distress, we find ourselves thrown back on his earlier comment that this story concerns 'just a summer evening and a talk with a man on a hillside', and that maybe 'there's nothing in it and maybe there is'. It is a 'note of interrogation' sounded at the very heart of Sargeson's text, and it plays intriguingly against the story's title, which summons up the idea that we are reading some kind of pioneer narrative about the making of the national character. Who the New Zealander is meant to be, Nick or the narrator, is impossible to say, but either way the story crucially undermines the nationalistic affirmation of the title with its depiction of a morally deficient money society inhabited by citizens, whether new or native to the place, who are unable to secure either a living or an identity for themselves.

It is a curious irony indeed that 'The Making of a New Zealander' was adjudged joint winner of the 1940 Centennial Literary Competition, an award to commemorate the British annexation of the islands in 1840 and the bringing into being, in effect, of the modern New Zealand state. Yet it reinforces the importance of reading Sargeson's work in contexts other than the national or post-colonial. His reading of D. H. Lawrence is informative in this regard, I think, for what Sargeson was drawn to was the Englishman's self-awareness about the confinements of his provincial background and upbringing. Lawrence, Sargeson says, may have been 'implicated' in that culture, but his saving virtue, as with Sargeson himself, was to have been 'acutely and savagely aware that he was implicated in it' and to have succeeded in 'disentangling himself sufficiently to see it clearly and objectively.'[6]

Marjorie Barnard's short fiction owes an obvious debt to Woolf and Mansfield. And it is clear from the few critical statements she made on the short form that she saw it through modernist lenses. In an essay on Vance Palmer's stories, for example, she distinguishes between the 'potboiler' turned out by the 'hack' writer, and the 'ascetic form' of narrative by which the short story aspires to the status of 'work of art'. Yet one must be careful when making such transnational alignments between writers not to oversimplify the question of how and why texts are transmitted between cultures, or to underestimate the importance of regional or national differences in the reception of those texts. Of course, Barnard wrote in English in an English-speaking 'settler' society, spent time in Britain and Europe and was widely read in anglophone modernism. But that is not to say that she can be unproblematically subsumed within the modernist canon, as a familiar voice from the antipodean outpost. The relationship between Australian cultural production and European modernism is far more tangled than that, not least because many of the artists and writers whom we might wish to categorize as 'modernist' were producing experimental work, not in imitation of European models, but as 'a way of constituting their post-colonial reality' and making a 'creative articulation of Australian difference'.[7]

Writing in 1939, the Australian poet, essayist and literary critic Nettie Palmer described the profound effects that the European struggle against fascism was having on her national literature. From the moment that struggle crystallized into armed conflict, in Spain in 1936, Australian writers were, Palmer argued, unavoidably politicized:

> Perhaps a painter or a musician can cut himself off, in his work, from what is going on around him, but a writer can't. I remember thinking, when we came home from Europe [in 1936] that our writers were trying to do just that, but lately all I know have had this sense of the ground quaking beneath them as acutely as I have.[8]

One of the writers Palmer knew, and whom she had mentored as part of her ongoing efforts to sponsor a tradition of women's writing in Australia, was Marjorie Barnard. Like many of her contemporaries, Barnard had been drawn into political activism in the 1930s, on both national and international fronts. In 1935 she had joined the Fellowship of Australian Writers, which soon became radicalized by Communist members within its ranks. The influence of socialist thinking is evident in her 1936 novel *The Glasshouse* (co-authored, as much of Barnard's work was, with Flora Eldershaw and published under the sobriquet 'M. Barnard Eldershaw'). At the same time she was deeply committed to the Fellowship's wider aims of creating and defining a national literature of Australia and fostering a sense of literary community among writers, and in much of her fiction allied this ambition to an analysis of the role of women in the modern nation. In all these respects, Barnard appears the very embodiment of the politically committed Australian writer Nettie Palmer had envisaged.

And yet, Barnard's association with these interest groups and ideologies was highly problematic for her personally. As early as 1935 she was communicating to Palmer her uneasiness about the socialist affiliations of the Fellowship. She wrote in a letter dated 25 November:

> You say you know nothing of my politics. There is nothing to know. I belong to no party, could be comfortable, with my eclectic mind, in none. As nearly as I can tabulate myself I'm a 19th-century liberal with all sorts of passionate feelings about liberty and free speech. My natural bent is towards an ethical and individualistic outlook, not an economic and social one. I abhor the callousness and cruelty of all reactionaries and 'top dogs'. These things are always settled in one's blood.[9]

At the same time, however, Barnard was well aware of the dangers that the rise of European fascism presented, and recognized the value of collective action in resisting it. But what she could not accept about Communism was its dependence on the repressive apparatus of the state – 'Violence, dictatorship, Machiavellian diplomacy, Realism', as she put it in another letter to Palmer – to enforce its ideology. To Barnard's mind, surrender to such mechanisms of social control was unconscionable. She was eventually able to concoct a solution to this dilemma only by committing herself to a politicized philosophy of non-violence. She joined the Peace Pledge Union in 1940 and throughout the war years protested the virtues of passive resistance and civil disobedience.

The political context of the 1930s and 40s is crucial to any appraisal of Marjorie Barnard's work, and especially so to her one collection of short stories, *The Persimmon Tree*, published in 1943. For those familiar with this remarkable book, it may seem odd to suggest that the ideological upheavals of the era played an important role in its formation, because in many respects its elliptical, understated stories, largely about women's love relationships and the struggle of coming to terms with middle age, seem to represent a shift in

Barnard's work away from the overt political and social commitments of her early novels. As one critic has described it, *The Persimmon Tree* marks a point of rupture between Barnard's artistic and political selves, the moment when 'her exploration of her situation as a woman was intensifying, but could no longer be integrated into the mainstream of her political thought'.[10] What is more, the stories' obvious indebtedness to the earlier generation of modernists, especially Woolf and Mansfield, and in particular their fondness for interrogative effects and interpretative open-endedness, also tend to be seen as a resiling from ideological commitment into aesthetic and formalist concerns, and as such mark a deliberate turning away by Barnard from the overtly nationalistic concerns of her earlier work.

Yet it is in precisely this act of resiling that *The Persimmon Tree*'s significance lies. In terms of Barnard's career, the book did indeed mark something of a departure and can be read as a prelude to her masterpiece (again co-authored with Flora Eldershaw) *Tomorrow and Tomorrow and Tomorrow* (1947) – a novel of profound scepticism that, as one critic has put it, 'condemns capitalism, holds no faith in parliamentary democracy, and raises serious doubts about socialism'.[11] Though far more modest in its ambitions, *The Persimmon Tree* nevertheless shares with that novel a wish to explore scenarios in which individuals conspire in their own oppression by an uncritical regard for the workings of dominant cultural ideologies. Like Elizabeth Bowen, Barnard was particularly drawn to the relationship between the private and the public self. *The Persimmon Tree* exhibits this concern (as it does its indebtedness to modernism) most obviously in the preoccupation with interiority and the female subject. The majority of the stories depict women for whom the preservative space between private and public self has collapsed, or is faltering. These are women who find themselves horribly exposed to the public gaze, often as a result of the actions or conspicuous betrayals of men. Through these scenarios of exposure, Barnard explores the ways in which female identity is mediated by its relationship to significant male others, and the extent to which the private, autonomous self is always already public property.

Barnard sets out the fundamental questions surrounding female identity in the first story in the book, 'Arrow of Mistletoe'. It tells of a lavish party thrown by a flamboyant entrepreneur, Gillespie Munro, who is determined to win over influential backers for a new financial scheme he has concocted, the 'Monopoly Mortgage', and which he is convinced has the potential to make a fortune for him and his devoted young wife, Lisca. Barnard makes the relationship between the couple the main focus of the story, and in particular stresses the way in which Lisca's every characteristic – her shyness, her attentiveness, her naivety – serves a function in the business world in which her husband moves. Indeed, there is no attribute of hers that does not unwittingly promote her husband's interests; she is an entirely public being:

> She was in a quiet way an asset. Some people, a few, thought it a curious aberration that a financial genius, like Gillespie Munro, should openly idolize this slender little thing with the heart-shaped face of a delicate child and the pretty manners of a well trained debutante. Others found it touching. No breath of scandal ever connected his name with any other woman's. The idea got round that because he was faithful to his wife he was a decent sort of chap, and a man you could trust. Astute businessmen were influenced by the fact . . .
>
> She was part of his curious legend, for it was certainly bizarre for such a man to live in respectable felicity with his wife, and to exhibit to the world not diamonds round her neck but trust in her eyes.

It is not his wife's beauty or glamour that Gillespie trades on: he is not so superficial as that. Rather, it is what we might be inclined to call her personal qualities, her 'nature', her modesty, her loyalty, her trust. Her ignorance has its value too – 'She had the best, the most serviceable kind of faith, the faith that did not even try to understand' – and so even, it turns out, does her fear. At the dinner party, the Important Man whom Gillespie most needs to win round regards as the 'crowning touch' to the whole performance 'the white face of Lisca Munro, her anguished eyes, her trembling lips'.

'Arrow of Mistletoe' establishes the public–private gender rubric that will dominate *The Persimmon Tree*. Lisca Munro is the most extreme, not to say docile, manifestation of the publicized female self that we encounter in the book, but many of the other stories explore more complex instances of the same patriarchal distortion in women's identity. In 'The Bride Elect', for example, a young woman attempts to free herself of the subject positions to which she is confined by her husband-to-be and his family. Myra is set to marry Jim, a sheep farmer, but finds that the very qualities he admires in her/his sister Thea despises: 'Thea resented her, Myra knew . . . She hated her delicacy. And it was that that Jim loved, her exquisite frailty, her helplesssness'. Barnard does not allow Myra any release from this dilemma. Instead, she has her inadvertently fulfil the very role that both Jim and his sister assign to her. Deciding to assert herself by packing a suitcase for her honeymoon, she manages to knock herself out as she attempts to wrestle the trunk down from the top of a wardrobe. The story ends with her lying helpless on the floor, being nursed back to consciousness by Thea and Jim.

In 'Beauty Is Strength', a middle-aged woman who has discovered that her husband is having an affair is able to contemplate the affront only in terms of public disgrace. How the betrayal makes her *feel*, about herself and her husband, is repeatedly displaced in the story by her worry about how it will look to others – so much so that she is able to lament the fact that the affair was with 'a woman in their own circle' rather than some 'little dancer'. Barnard's point is not to convict this woman of superficiality, but to reveal the extent to which she depends for her very sense of self on the public persona she inhabits. Her struggle is not to regain control of her feelings, which are never out of her control, but to reassume the 'armour of sophistication' that preserves her from having to deal with feelings at all.

The consequences of infidelity form one of the central themes of *The Persimmon Tree*. It is easy to see why Barnard should have been attracted to this scenario, as a moment of dramatic exposure in which the interactions between public and private realms are revealed. More often than not, the women in her stories experience betrayal as a ghastly violation of their personal security, or 'background', as several of the stories call it; but Barnard is far more interested in showing how that sense of the preciously personal is in fact formed in mistaken dependence upon the *im*personal, public institutions of marriage, propriety and property. In 'It Will Grow Anywhere', for example, she generates considerable sympathy for the wronged woman, Struan Curtice, only then to hint at her culpability in the failure of the marriage. 'She took things too seriously,' we read of Struan. 'All the shibboleths. She really believed in them. She thought a marriage could be made successful by observing all the rules. She was a civilized woman, and that means she'd let go, slipped out of, that secret barbarian life that women lead'.

In *Tomorrow and Tomorrow and Tomorrow*, Barnard describes how, for the early Pioneers, 'liberty was something they could not help having and for which they had no use'. Something similar might be said of the characters in *The Persimmon Tree*, who have liberty yet no notion how to use it, so proficient are they at nurturing the ideologies – of sex, class, and gender – that bind them. Even where circumstances seem most propitious to liberty and escape, as in the title story of the collection, the 'mind-forg'd manacles' – against which Barnard herself so visibly bridled in her own political and cultural life – beleaguer her characters. 'The Persimmon Tree' is narrated by a woman who has recently been released – 'escaped' is the word she uses – from a trying illness. Convalescent, she moves into an apartment in which to enjoy peaceful days and nights and, above all, 'privacy'. From her bedroom window she is able to observe the 'regularity' and 'very correct pattern' by which her neighbours, more encumbered than she, live. Into this ideal world comes suddenly the figure of another woman, into whose apartment the narrator can see. On her window sill the woman is growing a row of persimmons. The trees become the figure of the narrator's feeling of sexual desire for her neighbour, yet she is unwilling to act on her longings, even though she might easily make contact with her. The reason for her reluctance is that she considers her neighbour to be a 'lonely woman', like herself. 'That was a barrier, not a link. Lonely women have something to guard'. The story ends with a powerfully voyeuristic scene in which the woman lets her gown fall to reveal her naked body as the narrator looks on. Confronted with that which she desires, however, the narrator turns away, feeling that her 'heart would break'.

What is it that causes the narrator to look away? What is it that causes her to feel ashamed or saddened, or at any rate to wish to suppress her desire? These are questions that critics continue to turn over in their readings of this most enigmatic of Barnard's stories. According to Bruce Bennett, the narrator's discomfiture signals the timely re-emergence of 'sympathy, sincerity and humane feeling' in her.[12] But that is entirely to ignore the sexual content of the story. Taken in context of the whole collection, it is surely more likely that we are witnessing another example of the internalized public injunction and the unfulfilled private self. That, as I have been arguing, is the dominant theme of *The Persimmon Tree*, and a reflection of Barnard's personal struggle as an artist and citizen of conscience during the war years.

Chapter 12

James Kelman and Chinua Achebe

'I wanted to write and remain a member of my own community'. So declares James Kelman in an essay entitled 'The Importance of Glasgow in My Work'. By his 'own community' Kelman means more than one thing: not just Glasgow, which he believes can be substituted in his case for 'any other town or city in Great Britain', but his class – working class, 'my own background, my own socio-cultural experience'.[1] Beyond that Kelman may mean, too, the community of writers with whom he has collaborated and published since he began writing in the early 1970s and to whom he dedicates his 1994 novel *How Late it Was, How Late*: Alasdair Gray, Tom Leonard, Agnes Owens and Jeff Torrington. Yet nestling within this declaration of vital kinships is an anxiety, namely that writing may carry one away from, rather than towards, community, and not because (or not just because) it is a solitary activity, but because its raw material, language, has such power to estrange and sequester. It is not too much to say that Kelman's life's work is largely about this fretful relationship between language, writing and belonging.

As a means of demonstrating what is at stake for Kelman in the writing project, consider the story 'Street-Sweeper' from his 1991 collection *The Burn*. Like much of Kelman's work, the story makes extensive use of free indirect discourse, by which the third-person narrative voice and the voice of the character blend and merge, at times indistinguishably. The central character is a 47-year-old road sweeper by the name of Peter, and the story, which reads more like an interior monologue, or 'obsessional monologue', as Alasdair Gray more aptly puts it,[2] presents him trying to dodge surveillance by his shift supervisor in order that he can read a few more pages of the book he has been smuggling about in his pocket. Peter's thoughts roam widely, skittishly debating questions about language and literature, about law and authority, religion, politics, colonialism and class, among many other topics. When he stops to check on the condition of a man lying in the street, he is spotted by his supervisor and sacked for neglect of duty.

The preceding summary is selective in the extreme, as always it must be where Kelman's meandering narratives are concerned. Much more informative is a sample of the writing:

> But you've got your brush you've got your brush and he stepped out and was moving, dragging his feet on fast, dragging because his left leg was a nuisance, due to a fucking disability that made him limp – well, it didni *make* him limp, he decided to limp, it was his decision, he could have found some new manner of leg-motoring which would have allowed him not to limp, by some sort of circumlocutory means he could have performed a three-way shuffle to offset or otherwise bypass the limp and thus be of normal perambulatory gait. This was these fucking books he read. Peter was a fucking avid reader and he had got stuck in the early Victorian era, even earlier, bastards like Goldsmith for some reason, that's what he read. Charles fucking Lamb, that's who he read; all these tory essayists of the pre-chartist days, that other bastard that didni like Keats. Why did he read such shite. Who knows, they fucking wreaked havoc with the syntax, never mind the fucking so-called sinecure of a job, the street cleaning. Order Order. Sorry Mister Speaker. But for christ sake, for christ sake.

The critic Cairns Craig has said that Kelman's writing creates 'a linguistic equality between speech and narration which allows the narrator to adopt the speech idioms of his charaters, or the characters to think or speak in "Standard English", with equal status'.[3] We can clearly see that 'linguistic equality' in operation in this passage. Notice how near the beginning of that long first sentence Kelman's third-person narrator describes Peter's movements in the kind of language Peter himself would use: 'he stepped out and was moving, dragging his feet on fast, dragging *because his left leg was a nuisance, due to a fucking disability that made him limp*' (emphasis added). I have italicized the part of this sentence that seems most obviously to be in Peter's idiom, where we most acutely feel the effects of his gravitational field on the language, but in a sense this is to miss the point, for there is in fact nothing attributable to the third-person narrator that we could not attribute to Peter. That is to say, Kelman has closed the gap between the narrator and the character: the narrator is not in possession of a discourse superior to, or capable of encompassing or objectifying, Peter's own.

This point is made clearer still later in the passage, where we encounter the phrase, 'by some sort of circumlocutory means he could have performed a three-way shuffle to offset or otherwise bypass the limp and thus be of normal perambulatory gait'. There is here, we might say, a register shift in the language, into a pedantically grammatical and distinctly dated Standard English, so called. But where in most other fiction, contemporary as well as 'classic', such a shift would signal the resumption of third-person narration, as distinct from the character's voice or thought, here this statement is equally attributable to Peter, since he has been reading eighteenth- and nineteenth-century writers like Oliver Goldsmith and Charles Lamb, whose circumlocutory syntax has infected his own.

What is Kelman trying to achieve by this arresting narrative style? Well, the answer lies at the end of that passage, where Peter thinks about 'the fucking so-called sinecure of a job, the street cleaning'. Immediately he is interrupted, or interrupts himself, with the parliamentary protocol 'Order Order. Sorry Mister Speaker'. We imagine that this interruption relates to his comment on his job, which was, so to say, 'out of order'. But of course, these words are not actually 'spoken', they are self-generated. The point here is that Peter is conscious of limits being placed on his speech and thought, not by his job supervisor but by himself. He has internalized the 'rules'. He is self-policing, bringing himself back into line at the moment when his questioning of the economic and social realities of his life goes too far. For Kelman, the power structures that oppress us work in this way through language, or to use a more precise term, discourse. There is no actual policeman arraigning Peter's speech, but he is still acutely aware that there are limits to the sayable, and that power and authority are exercised through the setting of those limits.

Kelman's purpose in collapsing the space between character and narrational discourses is partly to uncover the power relationship, the hierarchy, that operates, largely unseen, in the bulk of English-language fiction. We tend to assume, Kelman argues, that third-person narrators present us with 'reality', when in fact they are 'saturated with the values of . . . the society within which the author lives and works'. This becomes clear, he goes on, when one considers the representation of working-class characters in the 'classic' English (and indeed Scottish) novel:

> You only ever saw them or heard them. You never got in their mind. You did find them in the narrative but from without, seldom from within. And when you did see them or hear them they never rang true, they were never like anybody I ever met in real life . . . everybody from a Glaswegian or working-class background, everybody in fact from any regional part of Britain – none of the them knew how to talk! What larks! Every time they opened their mouth out came a stream of gobbledygook . . . a strange hotchpotch of bad phonetics and horrendous spelling – unlike the nice stalwart upperclass English hero (occasionally Scottish but with no linguistic variation) whose words on the page were absolutely splendidly proper and pure and pristinely accurate, whether in dialogue or without.[4]

Kelman's writing does not objectify his working-class characters in this way. By dispensing with the paraphernalia of speech marks, his texts 'visually . . . resist the moment of arrest in which the reader switches between the narrative voice of the text and the represented speech of a character'.[5] Moreover, that narrative voice is not qualitatively superior to that of the characters; to adopt some terms from narratology that we have used before, the discourse of the *énonciation* (the narrator) is indistinguishable from the subject of the *énoncé* (the characters).

While Kelman is now best known as a novelist (*How Late it Was, How Late* (1994) won the Booker Prize while *A Disaffection* (1989) was shortlisted for it), it was in the short story that he predominantly worked throughout the 1970s and early 1980s, developing his narrative technique. One can chart that development in the volumes *An Old Pub Near the Angel* (1973, but not published in Britain), *Not Not While the Giro* (1983), *Lean Tales* (1985, jointly authored with Alasdair Gray and Agnes Owens) and *Greyhound for Breakfast* (1987). Kelman's attraction to the short story can be explained on two levels. As I mentioned in the introduction to this section, the short form is often favoured in circumstances where routes to mainstream publishing are, for whatever reason, unavailable, or possibly unsought. The short story, by its very shortness, suits the dissemination of new writing because of its amenability to low-capital periodical publishing and cooperative projects. In Kelman's case, his early work was all published either in literary magazines or joint ventures such as *Three Glasgow Writers* (1976), to which he contributed six stories to stand alongside work by Leonard and Hamilton.

But the short story also attracted Kelman, in his early career, because of its very brevity, which he was able to exploit as a means of conveying the experiential realities of working-class life that were his subject. As we have seen throughout this book, short stories tend to work against the elaboration of character, context and consequence – the kinds of continuities that inevitably emerge over the course of more expansive narratives. This fits perfectly with Kelman's desire to portray lives that were destitute of purpose, that were defined by their very *lack* of consequence. The form, that is to say, became expressive of the content. This point is most easily demonstrated by way of a couple of examples.

'Not Not While the Giro' is a monologue 'spoken' by an unemployed man whose sole task that day is to go to a social security office and 'sign on' for his giro (his benefit cheque). The story is taken up with his ramblings and reflections, his fits of self-doubt, frustration, fantasy and desperation. His life is largely inert, reduced to smoking, drinking tea, urinating and, of course, 'signing on' and awaiting his money. It is a life of seemingly endless postponement and deferral:

Something must be done. A decisive course of action. Tramping around pubs in the offchance of bumping into wealthy acquaintances is a depressing affair. And as far as I remember none of mine are wealthy and even then it is never a doddle to beg from acquaintances – hard enough with friends. Of which I no longer have. No fucking wonder. But old friends I no longer see can no longer be termed friends and since they are obliged to be something I describe them as acquaintances. In fact every last individual I recollect at a given moment is logically entitled to be termed acquaintance. And yet

This passage is representative of much of the story in the way it opens with a declaration of intent, a brief flirtation with verbs of action, only then to disperse intention though a series of qualifications, second thoughts, cancellings out and doublings back. Meanwhile, energies are diverted into a simulation of orderliness and activity – the sorting out of the proper category term for people with whom one is acquainted but not friendly, and so on. Of course, no end point is reached, just a momentary cessation (because the narrator needs to urinate) in the presumably inexhaustible roster of qualifications and corrections. And so on for the remainder of the story: nothing decided, nothing altered, nothing acted upon, the promissory 'And yet' with which this paragraph ends replicated in the 'but' with which the monologue closes. It is a life, in more senses than one, of inconsequence, and Kelman captures its futility in a narrative structure that is itself studiedly inconsequential – its individual paragraphs failing to connect with one another nor leading to anything we might recognize as a resolution of, or conclusion to, what has gone before.

In *Greyhound for Breakfast*, Kelman takes the concept of inconsequence to almost Beckettian extremes. In texts sometimes no more than half a page long he experiments with truncated, abortive, self-cancelling structures. 'An old story', for example, takes us to the brink of a story that cannot be told for reasons that cannot be disclosed, while 'this man for fuck sake' suggests a kind of narrative paralysis. Here it is in its entirety:

This man for fuck sake it was terrible seeing him walk down the edge of the pavement. If he'd wanted litter we would've given him it. The trouble is we didn't know it at the time. So all we could do was watch his progress and infer. And even under normal circumstances this is never satisfactory: it has to be readily understood the types of difficulties we laboured under. Then that rolling manoeuvre he performed while nearing the points of reference. It all looked to be going so fucking straightforward. How can you blame us? You can't, you can't fucking blame us.

We infer that something happens subsequently to the man approaching the litter, something that proves his actions, whatever they are, to be not as 'straight-forward' as they seemed. We do not get that story, however, not because Kelman is playing a narratological game with us, but because a bigger story intervenes, that of the 'difficulties' that the narrator labours under. Here, as in all his work, Kelman shifts our attention away from the story told to the conditions under which the telling proceeds. Once again, the inconsequential narrative implies a narrator whose existence has been rendered inconsequential in other ways.

In 'Pictures' (from *The Burn*), similarly, Kelman establishes multiple narra-tives inside the head of a central character incapable of bringing any of them to fulfilment. A deeply disturbing story, among Kelman's most shocking and pow-erful, it is set in a nearly deserted cinema and revolves around the reflections of a man who, as we find out towards the end, has been a victim of sexual abuse as a child. Before that is revealed to us, however, we witness his hesitant efforts to comfort a woman seated near to him who has been crying since the film began. After 'an eternity of decision making', during which he contemplates the various protocols involved in striking up a conversation with a stranger, especially a woman, he eventually is able to ask her if she wants a cup of coffee. She accepts his offer, but continues to watch the film, leaving him to speculate as to her character and circumstances. The irony in this is that his buying the coffee for her is the one decisive action he is able to take in the story – and it leads to nothing; it supplies no answer to any of the questions he has been asking. Every other scenario of engagement or activity that runs through his head ends in the same way, with his sense of paralysis and inconsequence. He feels anger at the film, for example, but recognizes that his anger is utterly futile. Likewise, he wishes to vent his frustration at his inability to concentrate on the screen, and attract the attention of those around him, but he only knocks his coffee cup over by 'mistake'. All effective agency in the story resides elsewhere: in the hands of the Hollywood director, in the figure of the murderer in the film, and, of course, in the figure of the man who sexually abused him as a boy. That suffocating memory centres on images of helplessness and loss of control as the man easily overpowers him, making resistance futile, just as protest against the film industry peddling images of sexual exploitation and violence is futile, just as his efforts to establish communication with the weeping woman are futile, just as the story of his trauma – 'he just felt so fucking bad, so fucking bad' – renders him incapable of telling any other story.

For many critics, Kelman is a writer squarely in the European tradition of Zola, Kafka and Beckett. But while Kelman himself acknowledges the impor-tance of these writers in shaping his work, he has also spoken of belonging to a larger post-colonial community of artists, which connects him as much to African authors like Ngugi wa Thiong'o and Chinua Achebe as to the European masters. In his Booker Prize acceptance speech he described his position thus:

> There is a literary tradition to which I hope my work belongs. I see it as part of a much wider process, or movement towards decolonisation and self-determination: it is a tradition that assumes two things, 1) the validity of indigenous culture, and 2) the right to defend it in the face of attack. It is a tradition premised on a rejection of the cultural values of imperial or colonial authority, offering a defence against cultural assimilation. Unfortunately, when people assert their right to cultural or linguistic freedom, they are accused of being ungracious, parochial, insular, xenophobic, racist [. . .] My culture and my language have the right to exist, and no one has the cultural authority to deny that.[6]

While there are, of course, many important differences in the situations and experiences of a writer like Kelman, living and working in a politically stable and environmentally secure first-world country like Scotland, and Chinua Achebe, who has lived through periods of revolution, military dictatorship and civil war in the land of his birth, Nigeria, they share a belief in the importance of cultural and linguistic self-determination and have developed their arts of fiction in accordance with these political ideals.

Author of six novels, two collections of short stories, several volumes of poetry as well as books for children, Achebe is also one of the most significant voices in African cultural and literary criticism of the last fifty years. He was born in Ogidi, an Igbo village in eastern Nigeria, the son of a Christian convert, and grew up speaking first his native Igbo and then, from age eight, English, the language in which he was formally educated and in which he writes. Like Kelman, Achebe is convinced of the vital role language and writing have to play in the empowerment and self-realization of countries that have been subject to colonial disruption. In an essay entitled 'The Role of the Writer in the New Nation', published in 1964, shortly after Nigeria gained its independence, he argues for a form of cultural nationalism, the 'fundamental theme' of which will be

> that African peoples did not hear of culture for the first time from Europeans; that their societies were not mindless but frequently had a philosophy of great depth and beauty, that they had poetry and, above all, they had dignity. It is this dignity that many African peoples all but lost in the colonial period, and it is this dignity that they must now regain . . . The writer's duty is to help them regain it by showing them in human terms what happened to them, what they lost.[7]

Among the many aspects of that loss was language, or rather, the relationship between native languages and cultural and political authority (it should be remembered that Nigeria is a country of more than 500 living languages). Writing in English, Achebe sees it as his mission to transform the language of colonial oppression in order to accommodate African experience. As he put it in 1975, 'I feel that the English language will be able to carry the weight of my African experience. But it will have to be a new English, still in full communion with its ancestral home but altered to suit its new African surroundings'.[8]

One of the ways in which Achebe's writing effects that transformation is by its inclusion of forms of non-standard pidgin English and Igbo, not just when characters are speaking, but in the narrative discourse itself. In this respect, Achebe's narrative practice closely resembles that of Kelman. To the mono-lingual English reader (of whom Achebe is often openly critical, pointing out that 'No man can understand another whose language he does not speak'),[9] these unfamiliar words, phrases, and proverbs can feel, as Kelman's Glaswegian *patois* does, like an impediment to comprehension of, or identification with, the writing. But that is rather to miss the point. By not 'translating' or objectifying their so-called 'non-standard' forms, Kelman and Achebe insist first of all on the validity of that cultural vocabulary, and secondly, and moreover, on its *equivalence*. That is to say, they grant that discourse equal status to the 'standard' narrative discourse: neither is able to contain or substitute the other.

One important effect of this discursive equivalence is to challenge the colonialist assumption that its culture marks a higher stage of intellectual, ethical and social development by comparison with the 'primitive', less sophisticated culture it has colonized. In Achebe's work, we are led through language to question this kind of hierarchical thinking. In the story 'Chike's School Days', for example, Achebe uses the word *osu* to refer to the title character and his family. In Igbo culture, the *osu* are the lowest class, socially beneath the level of *ohu* (slaves) and *amadi* (the free-born). The term is applied to those considered outcasts from the community, which in the early days of the colonial period generally meant converts to Christianity. Set at the beginning of the twentieth century, Achebe's story follows the early years of a young boy, Chike, whose parents take on the white man's faith and are accordingly regarded as *osu*. The narrative makes a lengthy diversion in its middle section to describe how Chike's father, Amos, had become a Christian after he visited the white missionary preacher Mr Brown and married a girl called Sarah. On hearing of her son's conversion, Amos's despairing mother visits the village diviner and is instructed to sacrifice a goat in order to appease the spirits of her ancestors in hope of ridding the family of its present insanity, in the shape of Amos. The diversion over, the narrator resumes the account of Chike's early days at infant school and his fascination with the strange English words he learns there, the story concluding with the young boy turning over in his mind sentences and words from his English textbook, the *New Method Reader*.

At first glance, 'Chike's School Days' seems a slight affair. But as one follows through the cultural ramifications of *osu*, the story emerges as a subtle, politically informed analysis of colonial authority and its investment in language. Key to understanding the story's treatment of authority is the parenthetical section that deals with Amos's conversion. Achebe juxtaposes the two men of faith in the village, Mr Brown, the missionary, and the diviner whom Amos's mother visits. I say 'juxtaposes' rather than 'contrasts', because if a contrast exists, it does so only in the mind of the reader. As Achebe describes the two men, there is no qualitative difference between them in terms of what they offer to the people. Both are men of faith and of practical method, for we learn that Mr Brown is 'highly respected by the people, not because of his sermons, but because of a dispensary he ran in one of his rooms'. Like the diviner, he deals both in physics and metaphysics. In the same way as it sets Igbo discourse *alongside*, rather than containing it *within*, the English-language narrative discourse, Achebe's text validates the religious value structures and practices of the both colonizers and the colonized.

The same cannot be said, however, of the Christian missionaries in the story. Chike goes to school when Igbo custom considers him 'old enough to tackle the mysteries of the white man's learning', which is to say, when he is able to reach across his head with his right hand and touch his left ear. Again, Achebe's narrative presents this without evaluative commentary, for it is the culturally valid means of establishing the extent of the child's maturity. Of course, Achebe is perfectly aware of how this differs from European practices and, moreover, of how the enlightened-rationalist English reader is likely to respond to it. But how we deal with cultural differences of this sort is his main subject, and in this story, it is the white missionaries whose ideology is shown to be not only oppressive, but also regressive. Once in school, Chike encounters floggings and rote learning, and much of what is taught is so anglocentric as to be meaningless to the children, such as the refrain 'Ten Green Bottles'. Indeed, meaninglessness becomes a refrain itself in Achebe's story. Chike loves to learn new English words 'even when they conveyed no meaning at all'. It is the sound of words like 'periwinkle' and 'constellation' that he enjoys. And his teacher's learning seems hardly more substantial:

> His favourite pastime was copying out jaw-breaking words from his *Chambers' Etymological Dictionary*. Only the other day he had raised an applause from his class by demolishing a boy's excuse for lateness with

unanswerable erudition. He had said: 'Procrastination is a lazy man's apology'. The teacher's erudition showed itself in every subject he taught. His nature study lessons were memorable. Chike would always remember the lesson on the methods of seed dispersal. According to teacher, there were five methods: by man, by animals, by water, by wind, and by explosive mechanism. Even those pupils who forgot all the other methods remembered 'explosive mechanism'.

The absurdity and idle vanity of much of this teaching naturally impresses Chike, who turns the strange new words into a song: 'It was a meaningless song. "Periwinkles" got into it, and also "Damascus". But it was like a window through which he saw in the distance a strange, magical new world. And he was happy'. It is such happiness as only a child could feel, however – one ignorant of the cultural significance of what he is being subjected to in that classroom. For the adult reader, on the other hand, Chike's is a travesty of learning that far from bringing enlightenment actually triggers regression in the pupil, to a pre-literate, meaningless babble. As the gently sardonic narrator puts it earlier in the story, 'The white man has indeed accomplished many things'.

Similarly, 'The Sacrificial Egg' challenges those monologic assumptions that the colonizer (and by extension, the English reader) brings to bear on Igbo culture. It opens in the offices of a European palm oil trading company which overlook the Nkwo market place on the bank of the Niger. Another cultural juxtaposition is thus established, this time between two different markets – that of the trading company 'which bought palm-kernels at its own price and sold cloth and metalware, also at its own price', and the traditional Igbo one which, despite the encroachment of European technological modernity, 'was still busiest on its original Nkwo day, because the deity who had presided over it from antiquity still cast her spell only on her own day'.

Again, it is important to note how Achebe presents the two markets, not as a contrast but as a juxtaposition of different value systems. And it is as such that they co-exist in the mind of the central character, Julius, who, we are told, sings in the Christian church choir and has passed his Standard Six exams in order that he can work in the trading company offices, yet who, as he looks out the window at the desolate market place, considers the fact that 'not all who came to the great market were real people', because some were mammy-wota, beautiful young women 'who have their town in the depth of the river'. The reason why the market is empty, he further reflects, is owing to the presence of 'Kitikpa, the incarnate power of smallpox'. Julius does not question the reality of the 'dread artist' Kitikpa, nor does his future mother-in-law, a devout Christian. Nor, crucially, does the narrative voice. If we should find ourselves, as readers, questioning the reality of Kitikpa, and seeking a more 'rational' explanation of the smallpox, then we will find ourselves in a minority of one. And it is here that the story's subtlety lies. For enlightened European rationality and 'progress' is in fact very well represented in the story: it has brought the trading company that fills the market with filth and the village with exploitative strangers, induces lawlessness and neglect of duty among the young, and turns the market 'into a busy, sprawling, crowded and dirty river port, a no-man's land'. The white man has indeed accomplished many things.

The challenge Achebe sets his Western readers, to recognize and transcend the limitations of their own world-view, is one he also sets his characters in several of the stories in *Girls at War*. His principal device throughout the collection is the figure of the outsider, the person or group of persons on the powerless margins of Nigerian society. Indeed, as C. L. Innes remarks, Achebe largely reserves the short form for the study of such subjects: 'Whereas the novels have told the stories of those who aspired to be central to their communities or their nation, these stories [in *Girls at War*] dwell on the perspectives and situations of those who have never seen themselves as holders of power – for the most part they are concerned with physical and psychological survival.'[10] And it is not only power as wielded by the colonizer that concerns Achebe, but authority in all its forms. He repeatedly stages scenarios in which the relationship between the centre and the periphery is disturbed, even if only temporarily, and in which the value structures that sustain authority and produce meaning are brought into question. In 'The Madman', which is the first story in the volume, a man of 'high standing . . . wealth and integrity' is stripped bare first of his clothes, then of his power as a result of his relentless need to define himself by his difference from the outcast title character. 'Vengeful Creditor', similarly, targets the complacency of a wealthy and powerful middle-class couple whose pursuit of their own interests leads them to deny education to the young babysitter who works for them, with near-disastrous results in which they are unable to recognize their own culpability. Meanwhile, in 'Akueke', a young sick woman abandoned in the bush by her own brothers acting in unquestioning accordance with patriarchal law, inexplicably survives and reappears to them at the house of her grandfather. The enigma of her survival serves to expose the ignorance of her brothers in their blind obedience to authority. In all these stories, as in his tales of colonial disruption, Achebe gives expression to what, in an essay on Igbo cosmology, he describes as his culture's 'belief in the fundamental worth and independence of every man and of his right to speak on matters of concern to him and, flowing from it, a rejection of any form of absolutism which endangers those values'.[11] It is a belief, as we have seen, to which James Kelman would also happily subscribe.

Chapter 13

Alice Munro

Alice Munro is considered by many to be the finest short story writer now working in English. A native of Ontario, Canada, where she presently lives, the first of her (to date) eleven volumes of short fiction, *Dance of the Happy Shades*, was published in 1968, the most recent, *The View from Castle Rock*, in 2006. Munro is a rare thing among writers of short fiction, an international bestseller. She is also widely acclaimed in the academy, and her work has been the subject of several critical monographs. Yet despite the attention Munro's stories have deservedly received in recent years, there persists a marked reluctance to deal with them *as* short stories. Even among enthusiastic readers of her work, one detects a desire to explain away the negative connotations of the 'short story' genre-mark. Hence the dust jackets of her books overflow with testimony to the novel-like quality of the stories, their satisfying range and depth and complexity of characterization. It is as though Munro is to be considered a great writer *in spite of* the fact that she *only* writes short stories.

Munro is not much given to commenting on her own writing, but in an interview in 1983 she made a comment that provides a useful starting point for the student new to her large body of work. Looking back on the style she had adopted in her first collection, she made the following observation:

> I've never been an innovator or an experimental writer. I'm not very clever that way. I'm never ahead of what's being done at the time. So in those stories in *Dance of the Happy Shades* there's an awful lot of meaningful final sentences. There's an awful lot of very, very important words in each last little paragraph. And that's something that I felt was necessary at the time for the stories to work. It was the way I felt that you made a story most effective. And now, I would go back, if I could rewrite most of those stories, and I would chop out a lot of those words and final sentences. And I would just let each story stand without bothering to do the summing up, because that's really what it amounts to.[1]

Munro here narrates the major shift in her work that took place in the early 1980s, around the time of her collection *The Moons of Jupiter* (1983). It was a shift from impressionism towards what one commentator has characterized as an 'art of indeterminacy' in which 'the possible meanings of a story are unsettled at every stage in the process of its telling',[2] and it took the form, as she suggests here, of 'chopping out' what may amount to crucial orientational material from her narratives, in an effort to avoid this effect of 'summing up'.

An example of one such 'meaningful' conclusion will make clear the kind of summary gesture she had in mind. Here is the final paragraph of 'Walker Brothers Cowboy', from *Dance of the Happy Shades*:

> So my father drives and my brother watches the road for rabbits and I feel my father's life flowing back from our car in the last of the afternoon, darkening and turning strange, like a landscape that has an enchantment on it, making it kindly, ordinary and familiar while you are looking at it, but changing it, once your back is turned, into something you will never know, with all kinds of weathers, and distances you cannot imagine.
>
> When we get closer to Tuppertown the sky becomes gently overcast, as always, nearly always, on summer evenings by the Lake.

It is deliberately beautiful writing, its hypotactic constructions, balanced phrases, euphonious repetitions and slightly precious parentheses ('always, nearly always') contributing to the air of wistful 'enchantment'. As we have seen throughout this book, some stories end in soft focus, some in a harsh light. This is very much of the former variety.

The change Munro effected in her writing in the early 1980s was to do away with 'meaningful' moments like this. Put baldly, her prose became more sparing, elliptical and indirect. At the same time, she began to experiment with complex, indeterminate and multi-layered story structures, in which various narrative strands were kept in play simultaneously, often qualifying or even cancelling one another out. The overall effect on her mature work, particularly the collections *Friend of My Youth* (1990) and *Open Secrets* (1994), has been to create a sense of chronic misapprehension and irresolution.

What is particularly interesting about this change is its relationship to what has emerged as a central subject in Munro's work, namely the experience of women in Canada's colonial and postcolonial history. Munro's interest in this topic can be traced back to the beginning of her career, but it is in her more recent volumes that she has begun to utilize the indeterminate, interrogative short story to stage an alternative history of Canada's 'settler' past, one that recognizes and accommodates the private life stories of women.

A key early text in Munro's treatment of the colonial past, and one that has many connections to later stories, is 'Heirs of the Living Body' (from *Lives of Girls and Women*, 1971). In this story, the female narrator, Del Jordan, contemplates male models of history and historicizing as well as her own role as an imaginative rewriter of her community's Scottish and Irish cultural inheritance. Her Uncle Craig is the clerk of Fairmile Township and author of a meticulous factual history of Wawanash County, as well as a personal family tree reaching back to ancestral roots in Ireland and Scotland. Munro's narrative sets up an opposition between two sorts of storytelling: on the one hand Uncle Craig's painstaking, faithful, accretive style, a crude but sturdy carpentry of facts, and on the other Del's creative, selective, and potentially disloyal imaginative interventions in private life. Del knows she would be criticized by Uncle Craig for her 'inaccurate notions of time and history', but she is just as aware of the shortcomings of *his* vision, the way his faith in 'public events' and the 'structure of lives supporting us from the past' overlooks the importance of the intimate personal, the 'individual names'. It is thus her ambition to make sense of the gaps in his 'whole history' of county and family.

Del's secret disdain of Uncle Craig's narrative authority aligns her briefly in the story with her aunts who, although inhibited by their brother's 'authoritative typing', nevertheless enjoy a kind of squeamish uproar among themselves behind his back:

> They respected men's work beyond anything; they also laughed at it. This was strange; they could believe absolutely in its importance and at the same time convey their judgment that it was, from one point of view, frivolous, non-essential. And they would never, never meddle with it; between men's work and women's work was the clearest line drawn, and any stepping over this line, any suggestion of stepping over it, they would meet with such light, amazed, regretfully superior laughter.

The aunts' brilliant non-combativeness intrigues Del, whose narration mimics what it describes here. That first sentence does not allow an adversative 'but', even by implication, between its two clauses, so emphasizing that the aunts' laughter does not qualify their respect for Uncle Craig's work but rather coexists with it. The aunts are capable of an 'absolute' belief in the importance of what men do, while at the same time treating it as frivolous; and their frivolity, in Del's telling, is not placed in any syntactical relation to their belief: it neither follows from it nor contradicts it. The importance of maintaining this doubleness explains why any vivid protest, any 'stepping over of the line', is viewed with regret by the aunts, because it obliterates the source of their power, which is their difference from men and their independence of male schemes of authority. For as long as Uncle Craig believes he is in charge and engaged in serious, solitary work, the aunts need not compete with him, and can continue in their own more effectual and superior organization of the household.

Del Jordan's observation of her aunts in this passage can be readily translated into a characterization of Munro's short story aesthetic generally, a translation one may feel justified in making given that *Lives of Girls and Women* is so conspicuously about the act of writing. I light on this particular passage because of the way in which it determines to protect and sustain the male historian in the figure of Uncle Craig, rather than threaten him into conflict or prosecute him out of existence. Despite the fact that Del rejects Uncle Craig's 'heavy and dull and useless' chronicle – refusing to carry on his project and indeed destroying the manuscript by her neglect of it when it is bequeathed to her after his death – she nevertheless reflects that she found his '[m]asculine self-centredness . . . restful to be with', compared to the agitated company of her mother and aunts. Later in *Lives of Girls and Women*, she concludes that, like Uncle Craig, she 'would want to write things down'. At the end of 'Heirs of the Living Body', Del experiences a 'brutal, unblemished satisfaction' in finally ridding herself of the burden of Uncle Craig's history, yet feels too a 'tender remorse' over its loss. She at once needs to be free of Uncle Craig, and yet is comforted and instructed by his presence. Her loss of his chronicle is not, therefore, the figure of Del's outright rejection of him and all he stands for, and its destruction the displacement of his kind of narrative by hers. In fact, his fidelity to 'daily life' is something Del wishes to emulate in her writing. She is taking up a position akin to the one she so marvelled at in her aunts, in which she does not seek to vanquish the masculine narrative (for that would be just another struggle for supremacy on male terms of contest) but allows it to coexist alongside and even within her own narrative. To return to the terms I introduced above, Del has no desire to produce a 'major' literature, availing of 'power and law', for that would be to play one more game by the old rules, to reproduce by merely inverting the male hierarchy. Del has learned from her aunts the source of a different kind of power.

I dwell on 'Heirs of the Living Body' first of all because its account of Del Jordan's encounter with both male and female narratives is applicable to Munro's writing generally, particularly the later stories which touch on Canada's settler history. But it is also an important text because Munro has revisited it obliquely throughout her career in stories such as 'The Stone in the Field' (from *The Moons of Jupiter*, 1982), the title story and 'Meneseteung' from *Friend of My Youth* (1990) and 'A Wilderness Station' (from *Open Secrets*, 1994). From its original conception as an episode in the life of the author as girl and woman, 'Heirs of the Living Body' has become a text by which we can trace the development of Munro's short story art. Just as Del Jordan perceives her own subject matter in the blind spots and occlusions of Uncle Craig's chronicle, so Munro has herself returned to various details of 'Heirs' in order to make new imaginative interventions in the history described there. What is particularly interesting, however, is that these revisitings do not intend to clarify or authenticate the portrait of the past, but are in fact marked by an increasing obliqueness and scepticism concerning the authority of historical narrative itself. In her work from the early 1980s onward, Munro has explored Canada's colonial history only to question the truth-value of the historical enterprise and even of her own narrative acts.

An early example of how Munro curtails narrative authority in her fiction is 'The Stone in the Field' (from *The Moons of Jupiter*, 1982). It is worth looking briefly at this text because it has many points of contact with 'Heirs of the Living Body' and so can usefully be read as an intermediate text between the early and mature styles. At the story's centre is a group of presbyterian spinster aunts on the father's side of the family about whom the narrator experiences conflicting emotions. Like Del Jordan, she feels 'guilt' at her neglect of these women, yet knows that their life in Mount Hebron is one she has to 'think twice about regretting'. Another repeated figure in story is that of the early settler in the town killed by a falling tree: in 'Heirs' the victim is the young man after whom Jenkin's Bend is named; in 'The Stone in the Field' he is the brother of the narrator's great-grandfather. The earlier story also makes mention of a man of Austrian origin whom the narrator's grandfather hired for work and allowed to sleep in the granary on his farm. His counterpart in 'The Stone in the Field' is the reclusive labourer Mr Black, who is thought to have come 'from some European country' and who is likewise accommodated in a shack on the family property. Both men are said to mutter and curse under their breaths in a foreign tongue.

The narrators of both stories are interested in finding their own mode of telling about the settler community's past. In 'Heirs', as we saw, Del Jordan objected to the style of Uncle Craig's heartless chronicle and so refused her aunts' commission to 'copy his way', instead pursuing her own writing in the form of an unfinished novel and poems. The narrator of 'The Stone in the Field', similarly, wishes to 'figure out a story' that will provide access to an alternative history of the Huron Tract district. However, her narrational model is her father, who makes precisely the kind of imaginative reconstructions of the lives of the early settlers that Del Jordan might have appreciated:

> [I]t's a wonder how those people had the courage once, to get them over here. They left everything. Turned their backs on everything they knew and came out here. Bad enough to face the North Atlantic, then this country that was all wilderness. The work they did, the things they went through. When your great-grandfather came to the Huron Tract he had

his brother with him and his wife and her mother, and his two little kids. Straightaway his brother was killed by a falling tree. Then the second summer his wife and her mother and the two little boys got the cholera, and the grandmother and both the children died. So he and his wife were left alone, and they went on clearing their farm and started up another family. I think the courage got burnt out of them. Their religion did them in, and their upbringing. How they had to toe the line. Also their pride. Pride was what they had when they had no more gumption.

Such an account exceeds the bare facts of the case that sufficed for Uncle Craig by admitting a level of self-reflection and interpretation to the telling. For the narrator's father, history is no simple matter of what happened, but a discursive event in which the past is disposed by the present. His comments on his ancestors' theocratic nature, and the powerful forces of social and religious conformity that secured their community in the midst of moral wilderness, reflect his own personal history of estrangement from such values. Freed up by this example of an imaginative, self-affirming narrative style, the narrator decides to investigate further the life of the mysterious Mr Black. She comes across a newspaper report of his death and, mimicking Del Jordan's ambition to liberate the lives between the lines of Uncle Craig's cuttings, goes in search of the stone in the field in Huron County under which Mr Black was buried. However, this is where the story diverts from the pattern of the earlier work. Instead of uncovering something meaningful about Mr Black, the narrator is unable even to locate the one remaining trace of him, the stone in the field. Realizing now that the story of Mr Black cannot be told as she imagined it might be, she is forced to reflect on the nature of her interest in him and to question the legitimacy of the storytelling vocation itself:

> Now I no longer believe that people's secrets are defined and communicable, or their feelings full-blown and easy to recognize. I don't believe so. Now, I can only say, my father's sisters scrubbed the floor with lye, they stooked the oats and milked the cows by hand. They must have taken a quilt from the barn for the hermit to die on, they must have let water dribble from a tin cup into his afflicted mouth . . . However they behaved they are all dead.

This gesture of resiling from the story that has just been told will become the defining characteristic of Munro's mature fiction. What for the narrator of 'The Stone in the Field' is a recognition of the limits of her own narrative art becomes, in the context of Munro's postcolonial stories, a deliberate refusal to recover the inarticulate figure from the margins of history by writing out his or her experience. There is no 'summing up' of Mr Black in the final paragraph of 'Stone', I would suggest, because Munro wishes to maintain his membership of that 'submerged population group' in which Frank O'Connor says the short story specializes. She does not seek to recover him from obscurity, or to compensate for his neglect, but rather confirms his eccentricity by preserving his insusceptibility to the narrational act. The interrogative nature of the story's ending, its questioning of its own narrative authority, is an early indication of how Munro will develop the short story as a 'becoming-minor' form – a form through which, as Deleuze and Guattari imagine, the ambitions towards 'power and law' which lie behind literary production can be disclaimed.

The significance of Munro's disclaiming narrative authority in this way is apparent in those texts which deal with the legacy of Canada's settler history. In 'Friend of My Youth', 'Meneseteung' and 'A Wilderness Station', Munro ostensibly sets out on a mission to recover what Helen Tiffin calls 'those aspects of culture that have been subject to historical erasure'[3] as a result of colonial disruption. In particular, Munro focuses on the legacy of presbyterianism in Canada and how this religious discourse both structures an understanding of the past and, by extension, arrests the development of postcolonial self-identification and interpretation. The specific challenge Munro sets herself, however, is to find a way of articulating this 'erased' history that does not entail taking possession of it all over again by repeating the subjection dynamic of colonialism in narrative form. Feminism largely fails this test in Munro's writing when it requisitions the female subject for its own political purposes. Hence Munro's development of the interrogative short story as a narrative form which concedes narrative authority, a 'minor' literature that does not seek to 'remake power and law'.

In 'Friend of My Youth' (1990), Munro takes up with the legacy of sectary presbyterianism in Canada, but the story quickly moves to questioning its own procedures and the legitimacy of the representations it is making. In an interview with Chris Gittings, Munro has described how the presbyterian church to which her family in Canada was connected emanated not from the moderate established kirk in Scotland, but from what she calls a 'radical fundamentalist wing' that crossed the Atlantic in the form of the Glasgow Missions of the 1840s and 1850s.[4] The missions, which sent ministers and schoolteachers to British North America throughout the first half of the nineteenth century, were sponsored by the strongly evangelical Glasgow Colonial Society. Under the guidance of figures such as Robert Burns (1789–1869), an evangelist and missionary enthusiast who founded Knox College in Toronto, the presbyterian church took on a radical character in the colony. 'Friend of My Youth' centres around the narrator's mother's encounter, as a young woman, with two sisters, Flora and Ellie Grieves, whose family belong to a severe and, historically at least, violent presbyterian sect, the Cameronians, so called after their leader, Richard Cameron (1648–80). The Cameronians, whom the narrator's mother describes as a 'freak religion from Scotland', were unyielding in their adherence to the Covenants of 1638 and 1643 which declared the Scottish people and their church bound to Christ alone, rather than to the English king, and were among those radical factions pursued by the English in what came to be known as the 'Killing Times' of the late seventeenth century. The murder of the 'haughty Bishop of St Andrews' mentioned in the final paragraph of Munro's story refers to the murder of James Sharp, then Archbishop of St. Andrews, whose assassination (on 3 May 1678) was the most notorious of the Cameronians' acts of guerilla warfare and resulted in the execution of many of the movement's leading figures.

In Munro's story, Flora Grieves is the character most closely associated with the Cameronian legacy. She is initially engaged to Robert Deal, a farm labourer recently arrived from Scotland, but their attachment is broken when he gets Flora's younger sister, Ellie, pregnant. The child is stillborn, and several miscarriages follow for Ellie before it is discovered that she has cancer. In the final months of her life, Ellie is nursed by the brash and self-seeking Audrey Atkinson, who comes to live in the house. Nurse Atkinson drives a car, smokes cigarettes, wears make-up and considers the Grieveses' way of life the most 'primitive' she has ever encountered. After Ellie's death, Robert Deal, to the surprise of the townsfolk, marries not Flora, his original intended bride, but Audrey Atkinson.

As is typical of Munro's mature writing, the story of Flora Grieves is conducted through a complex of narrative perspectives, beginning with the narrator's version according to the account given by her (the narrator's) mother. This initial portrait of Flora is further complicated by the fact that the narrator is telling the story as a retrospective on how she *used* to feel about the way her mother spoke of Flora, and by the fact that her mother is now dead. So, in telling of Flora, the narrator is also telling of herself and her guilt over the way she behaved towards her mother in her final, sickly years. This array of distorting and conflicting points of view indicates how the narrative as a whole will proceed, by presenting a version of the story of Flora only to qualify or even cancel it out as a fabrication or misapprehension arising from the troubled relationship between the narrator and her mother.

A conspicuous point of conflict between the narrator and her mother concerns their shared literary ambition to tell the story of Flora's life. The mother plans to write a novel about Flora called *The Maiden Lady*, but the narrator, looking back on her younger self, recalls her irritation at what she supposed her mother's novel would entail. In particular, she remembers being repulsed by the solemnity and sentimentality implied in the title, with its 'hint of derision turning to reverence':

> That was what I believed my mother would make of things. In her own plight her notions had turned mystical, and there was sometimes a hush, a solemn thrill in her voice that grated on me, alerted me to what seemed a personal danger. I felt a great fog of platitudes and pieties lurking, an incontestable crippled-mother power, which could capture and choke me. There would be no end to it. I had to keep myself sharp-tongued and cynical, arguing and deflating. Eventually I gave up even that recognition and opposed her in silence.

The narrator remembers how, in order to counter her mother's version, she composed in her mind her own novel in which Flora appeared not as noble and self-sacrificing, but as a 'Presbyterian witch, reading out of her poisonous book'. In that text, Flora was condemned to a life of crippling arthritis, and the story climaxed with the burning of her books – 'The elect, the damned, the slim hopes, the mighty torments – up in smoke' – by the triumphant Audrey Atkinson. By inflicting on Flora what was in fact her mother's crippled state, the narrator (who was a teenager at the time she plotted out this version of Flora's life) was bringing the two women together as a way of expressing her anger at her mother's overbearing prudishness, her latter-day puritanical 'turning away from sex'.

What we have in this story, then, are two competing novelistic accounts of the life of Flora. In that respect the story resembles 'Heirs of the Living Body' and 'The Stone in the Field', both of which are also structured around differing ways of narrating their subjects. However, what happens in 'Friend of My Youth' is that the subject herself, Flora, slips from the grasp of both of her would-be narrators. This process begins early on in the story with the recollection of a letter which Flora sent to the narrator's mother. In this letter, Flora reports that she no longer lives on the family farm and has taken a house and a job as a store clerk in town. To the narrator this is an 'unsettling' correspondence as it 'leav[es] so many things out'. In particular, it omits to explain *why* Flora left Robert and Audrey on the farm, and how matters were settled financially between them. Nor does it contain the expected mention of 'God's will', or state whether Flora still attends her church. For the narrator, the frustration of this letter is that it forces her to review her understanding of Flora's life and challenges her desire to make Flora into a representative of religious and moralistic severity. In other words, Flora as subject *to* and *of* her narrative becomes unruly: she refuses to be appropriated for the story the narrator wishes to tell. The narrator is therefore forced to release Flora's past from this possessive narrational present.

Where the father figure in 'The Stone in the Field' was prepared unconscionably to inscribe his own predilections on the history he told, the narrator of 'Friend of My Youth' concedes that her knowledge of Flora is little more than a series of unanswered and unanswerable questions about how she lived, what she looked like, what she felt, feared or believed:

> I would have wanted to tell her that I knew, I knew her story, though we had never met. I imagine myself trying to tell her. (This is a dream now, I understand it as a dream.) I imagine her listening, with a pleasant composure. But she shakes her head. She smiles at me, and in her smile there is a degree of mockery, a faint, self-assured malice. Weariness, as well. She is not surprised that I am telling her this, but she is weary of it, of me and my idea of her, my information, my notion that I can know anything about her.

Flora's liberation from the storytelling interests of the narrator also entails her breaking free from the idea that her Cameronian inheritance defines her. The narrator's 'information' on this matter is proven incomplete and useless. Flora thus escapes into a kind of intractability at the end of the story; she 'gets loose', in Deborah Heller's phrase, from 'knowledge and control'.[5]

In fact, there have been suggestions all along in the story that Flora is subtly subversive of the Cameronian doctrine that others use to define her. For example, her fondness for playing crokinole and reading comic stories of Scottish life belies the severity of her creed and its 'configuration of the elect and the damned' and runs counter to the narrator's mother's expectations of her. Similarly, when the mother writes to Flora to express her sympathy and outrage at the conduct of Robert Deal and Audrey Atkinson, she is surprised to receive back a letter which contains no trace of judgement of the new couple and politely deflects the mother's enquiries into her feelings. The narrator is likewise at a loss over the nature of Flora's life and faith once she has moved to her new job in town: 'How could she go on being a Cameronian? How could she get to that out-of-way church unless she managed to buy a car and learned to drive it?' It is only at the end of the story that the narrator comes to recognize the pointlessness of these questions, motivated as they are by a desire to confine Flora within a novelistic narrative that she now understands will not hold her.

In the story's final startling move, another woman gets loose too – the narrator's mother. Again she is aligned with Flora, but this time in order to show how she also finally exceeds the definition which the narrator, in her resentment, would impose on her. Moving 'rather carelessly out of her old prison', the mother reveals 'options and powers' that the narrator 'never dreamed she had', and in so doing 'changes more than herself'. Like Flora, whose letter seemed to leave so much out, so the mother concealed much in her unfinished letters. Only now that the narrator admits the limitation of her knowledge can she appreciate the extent and nature of both women's freedom. And it is a freedom akin to that of the aunts in 'Heirs of the Living Body' – not a conspicuous act of resistance, a contesting of power by power, but the preservation of an identity which exceeds that 'reserve-discourse' which would name and know it.

The luminous final paragraph of the story, which appears as a coda to the main text, brings the issue of Flora's covert dissidence from her Cameronian inheritance together with the problematic matter of narrative authority which the text has raised:

> The Cameronians, I have discovered, are or were an uncompromising remnant of the Covenanters – those Scots who in the seventeenth century bound themselves, with God, to resist prayer books, bishops, any taint of popery or interference by the King. Their name comes from Richard Cameron, an outlawed, or 'field' preacher, soon cut down. The Cameronians – for a long time they have preferred to be called the Reformed Presbyterians – went into battle singing the seventy-fourth and seventy-eighth Psalms. They hacked the haughty Bishop of St. Andrews to death on the highway and rode their horses over his body. One of their ministers, in a mood of firm rejoicing at his own hanging, excommunicated all the other preachers in the world.

Coral Ann Howells suggests that the ending to 'Friend of my Youth' presents the narrator's 'steadfast rejection of coercion' by her mother and Flora, whom Howells sees as women deploying 'stratagems of secrecy and silence'.[6] But this is to read Flora as unproblematically aligned with the Cameronian world-view, when, as we have seen, there is much in the story to indicate that Flora, by her character and conduct, circumvents that severely judgemental ideology. I would argue, rather, that the story represents various modes of female eman-cipation from the confinements of patriarchal discourse. Flora's life of tolerant forgiveness, her refusal to condemn or criticize, and her final remarkable will-ingness to change beyond recognition or expectation, is the measure of how she exceeds not only the doctrines of her ancestors, but, crucially, the pos-sessive ambitions of the narrator. Flora is no rebel, but she has produced an identity radically exceeding those which are offered to or imposed upon her. In contemplating Flora, the narrator comes to recognize that she must pursue a kind of writing that is capable of registering and valuing the often inarticulate nature of women's difference. She realizes at the end of the story that she has misread the nature of her mother's and Flora's individuality; in her way she has attempted to 'excommunicate' these two women for what she took to be their slavish prudery and hostility to her way of life. In so doing, she has, like the Cameronian who believes himself justified in killing for Christ and the Covenants, sought to obliterate their difference by imposing on them a unity of like-mindedness. The narrator was in fact the one trapped within patriarchal ideology, not her mother or Flora, and her development in the story involves her coming to doubt the authority and legitimacy of her own narrative.

Significantly for the present discussion, the narrator figures her development in her abandonment of the novel in favour of the short story. The novels which the narrator and her mother proposed to write both aimed to take possession through knowledge and disclosure of their subject, Flora. The short story which is finally produced proceeds differently, towards non-disclosure and the questioning of knowledge. The pattern of 'Friend of My Youth', as is the case in many of Munro's mature stories, is one of qualification or even cancellation of what has earlier been declared in the narrative, a process of working backwards from accepted truth or assumed knowledge towards contradiction and uncertainty. The mature stories are anti-narratives in the sense that they present one or more versions of an event or a character only to begin a process of endless revision of the 'facts' that the story has itself presented. To adopt the terms we met in the introduction, we can say that Munro writes a 'minor' literature by resiling from the imposition of authority in her narratives. She looks to tell women's stories in terms other than those offered by male narrational models, hence the interest in all her work (right back to the aunts in 'Heirs of the Living Body') in types of female alterity which resist patriarchy not by open opposition on male terms, but in ways that patriarchy itself does not conceive of. The narrator of 'Friend of My Youth' comes to understand that she has been guilty of judging her mother and Flora against the very values she rejects, doing to these women what the Cameronians in their way did to all the other preachers in the world. The kind of narrative she then learns to write is one in which she surrenders the novelistic will-to-knowledge in favour of the interrogative story's poetics of obscurity and marginality, its condition of 'becoming-minor'.

Notes

Introduction

1. E. M. Forster, *Aspects of the Novel* (Harmondsworth: Penguin, 1990), p. 41.
2. Elizabeth Bowen, 'The Faber Book of Modern Short Stories', *Collected Impressions* (London: Longmans, 1950), p. 39.
3. G. K. Chesterton, *Charles Dickens* (London: Methuen, 1906), p. 69.
4. Nadine Gordimer, 'The International Symposium on the Short Story: South Africa', *Kenyon Review* 30 (1968): 459.
5. H. E. Bates, *The Modern Short Story: A Critical Survey* (London: Thomas Nelson, 1941), p. 21.
6. Ibid., p. 43.
7. Ibid., p. 48.
8. Frank O'Connor, *The Lonely Voice: A Study of the Short Story* (London: Macmillan, 1963), p. 13.
9. Ibid., p. 45.
10. Ibid., p. 45.
11. Ibid., p. 18.

Part I: Introduction: publishers, plots and prestige

1. V. S. Pritchett, 'Satan Comes to Georgia', *The Tale-Bearers: Essays on English, American and Other Writers* (London: Chatto and Windus, 1980), p. 164.
2. Henry James, 'Guy de Maupassant', *Partial Portraits* (London: Macmillan, 1905), p. 264.
3. Peter Keating, *The Haunted Study: A Social History of the English Novel 1875–1914* (London: Secker, 1989), p. 40.
4. Henry James, 'The Science of Criticism', *New Review* 4 (1891): 398.
5. Henry James, 'Ivan Turgenieff', *Partial Portraits* (London: Macmillan, 1905), pp. 314–15.
6. Henry James, 'The Lesson of the Master', *Critical Prefaces*, ed. R. P. Blackmur (New York and London: Charles Scribner's Sons, 1934), p. 231.
7. Henry James, 'The Story-Teller at Large: Mr. Henry Harland', *Fortnightly Review* 63 (April 1898): 652–3.

8. Frederick Wedmore, 'The Short Story', *The Nineteenth Century* 43 (March 1898): 406–9.
9. G. K. Chesterton, *Charles Dickens* (London: Methuen, 1906), p. 69.

1 Charles Dickens and Thomas Hardy

1. Charles Dickens, Preface to *Christmas Stories* [1852], *The Christmas Books*, vol. I, ed. Michael Slater (Harmondsworth: Penguin, 1971), p. xxix.
2. H. E. Bates, *The Modern Short Story: A Critical Survey* (London: Thomas Nelson, 1941), pp. 22–3.
3. V. S. Pritchett, *The Tale-Bearers: Essays on English, American and Other Writers* (London: Chatto and Windus, 1980), p. 164.
4. See Tzvetan Todorov, 'Language and Literature', in Richard Macksey and Eugenio Donato (eds.), *The Languages of Criticism and the Sciences of Man* (Baltimore and London: Johns Hopkins Press, 1970), pp. 125–33.
5. Quoted in Debirah A. Thomas, *Dickens and the Short Story* (London: Batsford, 1982), p. 11.
6. George Gissing, *Charles Dickens: A Critical Study* (London: Blackie, 1898), p. 30.
7. Charles Dickens, 'Frauds on the Fairies', *Household Words* (1 October 1853), quoted in Thomas, *Dickens*, p. 13.
8. Quoted in Florence Emily Hardy, *The Life of Thomas Hardy 1840–1928* (London: Macmillan, 1962), p. 252.
9. Roland Barthes, *S/Z*, trans. Richard Miller (Oxford: Blackwell, 1990), p. 76.
10. Quoted in William Archer, *Real Conversations* (London: Heinemann, 1904), pp. 369–70.
11. E. M. Forster, *Aspects of the Novel* (London: Edward Arnold, 1927), p. 42.
12. Bates, *Modern Short Story*, p. 41.
13. Wendell V. Harris, 'Vision and Form: The English Novel and the Emergence of the Short Story', in Charles E. May (ed.), *The New Short Story Theories* (Athens, OH: Ohio University Press, 1994), pp. 182–91.
14. Samuel Beckett, *Dream of Fair to Middling Women* (London and Paris: Calder Publications, 1993), pp. 119–20.
15. Henry James, *Partial Portraits* (London: Macmillan, 1888), p. 251.

2 Rudyard Kipling and Joseph Conrad

1. Frank O'Connor, *The Lonely Voice: A Study of the Short Story* (London: Macmillan, 1963), p. 103.
2. H. E. Bates, *The Modern Short Story: A Critical Survey* (London: Thomas Nelson, 1941), pp. 115–17.

3. George Orwell, 'Rudyard Kipling', in *Essays* (Harmondsworth: Penguin, 2000), p. 14. Orwell's essay first appeared in *Horizon* in Februrary 1942.
4. Rudyard Kipling, *Something of Myself* (London: n.p., 1937), p. 207.
5. Ernest Hemingway, *A Moveable Feast* (London: Arrow, 1994), pp. 63–4. (First published 1964.)
6. William Empson, *Seven Types of Ambiguity* (London: Chatto and Windus, 1947), p. 31.
7. Henry James, 'The New Novel', in *Essays on Literature, American Writers, English Writers* (New York: Library of America, 1984), p. 151. ('The New Novel' was first published in 1914.)
8. Joseph Conrad, 'Author's Note' to *A Set of Six* (London: Methuen, 1908), p. vii.

3 The *Yellow Book* and the 1890s avant-garde

1. [Henry Harland], 'Dogs, Cats, Books, and the Average Man', *The Yellow Book* 10 (July 1896): 15–16.
2. Henry James, *Partial Portraits* (London: Macmillan, 1888), pp. 314–15.
3. James, 'The Story-Teller at Large: Mr. Henry Harland', *Fortnightly Review* 63 (April 1898): 652–3.
4. James, *The Art of the Novel: Critical Prefaces*, ed. Richard P. Blackmur (London: Macmillan, 1935), pp. 218–20.
5. Henry James, 'Hubert Crackanthorpe', in Hubert Crackanthorpe, *Last Studies* (London: William Heinemann, 1897), pp. xv, xvii.
6. H. D. Traill, 'Literature', *New Review* 8 (1893): 607–8.
7. Hubert Crackanthorpe, 'Reticence in Literature', *Yellow Book* 2 (July 1894): 261.
8. Andrew Lang, 'Realism and Romance', *Contemporary Review* 52 (November 1887): 684–5.
9. Unsigned, 'He, She, and the Library List', *Academy* 54 (31 December 1893): 553.
10. Arthur Morrison, 'How to Write a Short Story', *The Bookman* 5 (March 1897): 45–6.

Part II: Introduction: 'Complete with missing parts'

1. Katherine Mansfield, letter to Dorothy Brett, 11 November 1921, *The Collected Letters of Katherine Mansfield*, ed. Vincent O'Sullivan and Margaret Scott, 4 vols. (Oxford: Oxford University Press, 1984–96), vol. IV, p. 316.
2. James Joyce, *Stephen Hero*, ed. Theodore Spencer (London: Cape, 1950), p. 188.
3. James Joyce, letter to Grant Richards, 5 May 1906, *Selected Letters of James Joyce*, ed. Richard Ellmann (London: Faber and Faber, 1975), p. 83.
4. Virginia Woolf, 'Tchehov's Questions', *The Essays of Virginia Woolf*, ed. Andrew McNeillie, 6 vols. (London: Hogarth Press, 1986–), vol. II, p. 245.

5. J[ohn] M[iddleton] M[urry] and K[atherine] M[ansfield], 'Seriousness in Art', *Rhythm* 2, 2 (1912): 49.
6. Katherine Mansfield, letter to Virginia Woolf, 27 May 1919, *Collected Letters*, vol. II, p. 320.
7. Walter Benjamin, 'The Work of Art in the Age of Mechanical Reproduction', in *Illuminations*, tr. Harry Zorn (London: Pimlico, 1999), pp. 211–44.
8. Fredric Jameson, *The Political Unconscious: Narrative as a Socially Symbolic Act* (Ithaca and London: Cornell University Press, 1981), p. 236.
9. Georg Lukács defines the modernist text by its techniques of 'negation'. See 'The Ideology of Modernism', in *The Meaning of Contemporary Realism*, tr. John and Necke Mander (London: Merlin Press, 1963), pp. 17–46.
10. James Joyce, 'The Day of the Rabblement', in *Occasional, Critical, and Political Writing*, ed. Kevin Barry (Oxford: Oxford University Press, 2000), p. 50. Joyce is here paraphrasing the Italian philosopher Giordano Bruno.
11. Tim Armstrong, *Modernism: A Cultural History* (Cambridge: Polity, 2005), p. 55.
12. Frederick Wedmore, 'The Short Story', *The Nineteenth Century* 43 (March 1898): 409.
13. For an extended treatment of this topic see Leonard Diepeveen, *The Difficulties of Modernism* (New York and London: Routledge, 2003).
14. Umberto Eco, *The Open Work*, tr. Anna Cancogni (Cambridge, MA: Harvard University Press, 1989), p. 8.
15. Henry James, 'The Story-Teller at Large: Mr. Henry Harland', *Fortnightly Review* 63 (April 1898): 653.
16. José Ortega y Gasset, 'Notes on the Novel', in *The Dehumanization of Art and Other Essays on Art, Culture and Literature*, tr. Helen Weyl (Princeton, NJ: Princeton University Press, 1968): 65. (First published as *La Deshumanización del arte e Ideas sobre la Novela* (Madrid: Revista de Occidente, 1925).)

4 James Joyce

1. Quoted in Richard Ellmann, *James Joyce*, rev. edn. (Oxford: Oxford University Press, 1982), p. 163.
2. See Katherine Mullin, 'Don't Cry for Me, Argentina: "Eveline" and the Seductions of Emigration Propaganda', in Derek Attridge and Marjorie Howes (eds.), *Semicolonial Joyce* (Cambridge: Cambridge University Press, 2000), pp. 172–200.
3. Dominic Head, *The Modernist Short Story: A Study in Theory and Practice* (Cambridge: Cambridge University Press, 1992), pp. 70–1.
4. Colin MacCabe, *James Joyce and the Revolution of the Word* (Basingstoke and London: Macmillan, 1979), p. 30.
5. Virginia Woolf, *The Death of the Moth and Other Essays* (London: Hogarth Press, 1942), p. 126.
6. William Empson, *Seven Types of Ambiguity* (London: Chatto and Windus, 1947), p. 31.

7. Hugh Kenner, *Joyce's Voices* (London: Faber and Faber, 1978), p. 16.
8. Clare Hanson, *Short Stories and Short Fictions: 1880–1980* (Basingstoke: Macmillan, 1985), p. 58.
9. Head, *Modernist Short Story*, p. 50.
10. M. M. Bahktin, *The Dialogic Imagination: Four Essays*, ed. Michael Holquist, trans. Carl Emerson and Michael Holquist (Austin and London: University of Texas Press, 1981), p. 276.
11. Margot Norris, 'Narration Under a Blindfold: Reading "Clay"', in Harold Bloom (ed.), *James Joyce's* Dubliners: *Modern Critical Interpretations* (New York: Chelsea House, 1988), p. 146.
12. Ezra Pound, 'Dubliners and Mr James Joyce', in *Literary Essays of Ezra Pound*, ed. T. S. Eliot (London: Faber and Faber, 1960), pp. 400–1.

5 Virginia Woolf

1. Mary Louise Pratt, 'The Short Story: The Long and the Short of It', in Charles E. May (ed.), *The New Short Story Theories* (Athens, OH: Ohio University Press, 1994), pp. 91–113.
2. John Barth, interview with Frank Gado, in Frank Gado (ed.), *First Person: Conversations on Writers and Writing* (New York: Union College Press, 1973), p. 123.
3. Virginia Woolf, 'Modern Fiction', *The Essays of Virginia Woolf*, ed. Andew McNeillie, 6 vols. (London: Hogarth Press, 1986–), vol. IV, pp. 160–1.
4. Virginia Woolf, 'Mr Bennett and Mrs Brown', *The Essays of Virginia Woolf*, vol. III, p. 385.
5. Sean Latham, *'Am I a Snob?': Modernism and the Novel* (Ithaca, NY: Cornell University Press, 2003), p. 115.
6. Virginia Woolf, 'Tchehov's Questions', *The Essays of Virginia Woolf*, vol. II, p. 245.
7. Virginia Woolf, 'The Russian Point of View', *The Essays of Virginia Woolf*, vol. IV, p. 185.
8. Ibid., p. 185.
9. Ibid., p. 185.
10. Woolf, 'Tchehov's Questions', p. 245.
11. Woolf, 'The Russian Point of View', p. 184.

6 Katherine Mansfield

1. Elisabeth Schneider, 'Katherine Mansfield and Chekhov', *Modern Language Notes* 50 (1935): 394–7. For a response to this piece see R. Sutherland, 'Katherine Mansfield: Plagiarist, Disciple, or Ardent Admirer?', *Critique* 5, ii (1962): 58–76. Claire Tomalin reprints correspondence from the *Times Literary Supplement* on the plagiarism charge in her *Katherine Mansfield: A Secret Life* (New York: Alfred A. Knopf, 1988), pp. 261–72.

2. Katherine Mansfield, letter to Virginia Woolf, 27 May 1919, *Collected Letters of Katherine Mansfield*, ed. Vincent O'Sullivan with Margaret Scott, 4 vols. (Oxford: Oxford University Press, 1984–96), vol. II, p. 320.
3. Mansfield, letter to S. S. Koteliansky, [6 June 1919], *Collected Letters*, vol. II, p. 324.
4. Mansfield, letter to S. S. Koteliansky, [21 August 1919], *Collected Letters*, vol. II, p. 353.
5. Mansfield, letter to Dorothy Brett, [11 November 1921], *Collected Letters*, vol. IV, p. 317.
6. Katherine Mansfield, *The Critical Writings of Katherine Mansfield*, ed. Clare Hanson (Basingstoke and London: Macmillan, 1987), pp. 99–100.
7. Ibid., p. 68.
8. Ibid., p. 73.
9. Katherine Mansfield, *Journal of Katherine Mansfield*, ed. John Middleton Murry (London: Constable, 1962), p. 121.
10. Mansfield, letter to J. M. Murry, [8 November 1919], *Collected Letters*, vol. III, p. 77.
11. Angela Smith, *Katherine Mansfield: A Literary Life* (Basingstoke: Palgrave, 2000), p. 103.
12. Mansfield, letter to Dorothy Brett, [11 October 1917], *Collected Letters*, vol. I, p. 331.
13. Smith, *Katherine Mansfield*, p. 116.
14. Mansfield, *Journal of Katherine Mansfield*, pp. 93–4.
15. Sydney Janet Kaplan, *Katherine Mansfield and the Origins of Modernist Fiction* (Ithaca, NY, and London: Cornell University Press, 1991), p. 113.
16. Angela Smith, *Katherine Mansfield and Virginia Woolf: A Public of Two* (Oxford: Clarendon Press, 1999), p. 100.
17. Arthur Symons, *The Symbolist Movement in Literature* (London: Constable, 1908), p. 8.
18. J[ohn] M[iddleton] M[urry] and K[atherine] M[ansfield], 'The Meaning of Rhythm', *Rhythm* 2, 5 (1912): 18.
19. Ibid.: 20.
20. J[ohn] M[iddleton] M[urry] and K[atherine] M[ansfield], 'Seriousness in Art', *Rhythm* 2, 2 (1912): 46–9.
21. Mansfield, *Journal of Katherine Mansfield*, p. 21.
22. Nicholas Daly, *Modernism, Romance and the* Fin de Siècle: *Popular Fiction and British Culture, 1880–1914* (Cambridge: Cambridge University Press, 1999), p. 118.

7 Samuel Beckett

1. John Harrington, 'Beckett's "Dubliners" Story', in Phyllis Carey and Ed Jewinski (eds.), *Re: Joyce'n Beckett* (New York: Fordham University Press, 1992), p. 36.

2. Linda Hutcheon, *A Poetics of Postmodernism: History, Theory, Fiction* (New York and London: Routledge, 1988), pp. 26, 35.
3. Hugh Kenner, *A Reader's Guide to Samuel Beckett* (Syracuse, NY: Syracuse University Press, 1996), p. 54.
4. Robert Cochran, *Samuel Beckett: A Study of the Short Fiction* (New York: Twayne, 1991), p. 18.
5. John Fletcher, 'Joyce, Beckett, and the Short Story in Ireland', in *Re: Joyce'n Beckett*, p. 27.
6. Hugh Kenner, 'Progress Report, 1962–65', in John Calder (ed.), *Beckett at Sixty. A Festschrift* (London: Calder and Boyars, 1967), p. 61.
7. Samuel Beckett, 'German Letter of 1937', trans. Martin Esslin, in *Disjecta: Miscellaneous Writings and a Dramatic Fragment*, ed. Ruby Cohn (London: John Calder, 1983), p. 172.
8. Hutcheon, *a Poetics of Postmodernism*, p. 121.
9. Samuel Beckett, 'Three Dialogues', in *Disjecta*, p. 138.

Part III: Introduction: theories of form

1. Elizabeth Bowen, 'Introduction to *Ann Lee's*, in *After-Thought: Pieces about Writing* (London: Longmans, 1962), p. 94.
2. V. S. Pritchett, 'Preface' to *Collected Stories* (London: Chatto and Windus, 1982), p. xi.

8 Frank O'Connor and Sean O'Faolain

1. Sean O'Faolain, *The Short Story* (London: Collins, 1948), pp. 198–200.
2. Clare Hanson, *Short Stories and Short Fictions, 1880–1980* (Basingstoke: Macmillan, 1985), p. 82.
3. O'Faolain, *The Short Story*, pp. 32–8.
4. Sean O'Faolain, 'Foreword', *Stories of Sean O'Faolain* (Harmondsworth: Penguin, 1970), p. 12.
5. Ibid., p. 11.
6. Declan Kiberd, *Inventing Ireland: The Literature of the Modern Nation* (London: Vintage, 1995), p. 6.
7. Frank O'Connor, *The Lonely Voice: A Study of the Short Story* (London: Macmillan, 1963), p. 103.
8. Ibid., pp. 20–1.
9. Frank O'Connor, *The Mirror in the Roadway* (New York: Alfred A. Knopf, 1956), p. 305.
10. O'Connor, *The Lonely Voice*, p. 13.
11. Ibid., p. 19.

12. Ibid., p. 18.
13. Ibid., p. 115.
14. For a comparison of Corkery's Civil War writing with that of O'Faolain and O'Connor see Michael Storey, '"Not To Be Written Afterwards": The Irish Revolution on the Irish Short Story', *Eire-Ireland: Journal of Irish Studies*, 28, 1 (1998): 32–47.
15. Frank O'Connor, *An Only Child and My Father's Son* (Harmondsworth: Penguin, 2005), p. 143.
16. Ibid., p. 147.
17. Ibid., p. 164.
18. Ibid., p. 177.
19. Ibid., p. 177.
20. Ibid., p. 191.
21. Michel Foucault, 'Of Other Spaces', trans. Jay Miskowiev, *Diacritics* 16, 1 (1986): 24.

9 Elizabeth Bowen and V. S. Pritchett

1. Elizabeth Bowen, *English Novelists* (London: William Collins, 1945), p. 7.
2. For a useful overview of this period see Keith Williams and Steven Matthews (eds.), *Rewriting the Thirties: Modernism and After* (London and New York: Longman, 1997).
3. Maud Ellmann, *Elizabeth Bowen: The Shadow Across the Page* (Edinburgh: Edinburgh University Press, 2003), p. 16.
4. Frederick Wedmore, 'The Short Story', *The Nineteenth Century* 43 (March 1898): 406–9.
5. Elizabeth Bowen, 'The Faber Book of Modern Short Stories', *Collected Impressions* (London: Longmans, 1950), p. 40.
6. Ibid., p. 39.
7. Ibid., p. 38.
8. Elizabeth Bowen, 'Introduction to *Ann Lee's*', in *After-Thought: Pieces About Writing* (London: Longmans, 1962), p. 94.
9. Virginia Woolf, 'Modern Fiction', *The Essays of Virginia Woolf*, ed. Andew McNeillie, 6 vols. (London: Hogarth Press, 1986–), vol. IV, p. 160.
10. Adam Piette, *Imagination at War: British Fiction and Poetry 1939–1945* (London: Papermac, 1995), p. 2.
11. Bowen, 'The Faber Book of Modern Short Stories', p. 43.
12. Philip Larkin, *The Whitsun Weddings* (London: Faber and Faber, 1964), p. 29.
13. Bowen, 'The Faber Book of Modern Short Stories', p. 45.
14. V. S. Pritchett, 'Satan Comes to Georgia', *The Tale-Bearers: Essays on English, American and Other Writers* (London: Chatto and Windus, 1980), p. 164.

15. David Lodge, 'The Modern, The Contemporary, and the Importance of Being Amis', in *Language of Fiction: Essays in Criticism and Verbal Analysis of the English Novel* (London: Routledge and Kegan Paul, 1966), pp. 243–67.
16. John Haffenden, *Novelists in Interview* (London: Methuen, 1985), p. 219.
17. James Wood, 'V. S. Pritchett and English Comedy', in Zachary Leader (ed.), *On Modern British Fiction* (Oxford: Oxford University Press, 2002), pp. 8–19.
18. V. S. Pritchett, 'Preface' to *Collected Stories* (London: Chatto and Windus, 1982), p. ix.
19. Ibid., pp. x–xi.
20. Ibid, p. xi.
21. V. S. Pritchett, 'Arnold Bennett', in *A Man of Letters: Selected Essays* (New York: Random House, 1985), p. 115.

10 Angela Carter and Ian McEwan

1. Lorna Sage, 'Angela Carter: The Fairy Tale', in Danielle M. Roemer and Christina Bacchilega (eds.), *Angela Carter and the Fairy Tale* (Detroit, MI: Wayne State University Press, 2001), p. 65.
2. Salman Rushdie, 'Introduction', in Angela Carter, *Burning Your Boats: Collected Short Stories* (London: Chatto and Windus, 1995), p. xi.
3. James Wood, 'A Long Day at the Chocolate Bar Factory', *London Review of Books* 26, 4 (2004): 26.
4. Andrew Levy, *The Culture and Commerce of the American Short Story* (Cambridge: Cambridge University Press, 1993), p. 124.
5. Angela Carter, 'Afterword to *Fireworks*', in *Burning Your Boats: Collected Short Stories* (London: Chatto and Windus, 1995), p. 459.
6. John Haffenden, 'An Interview with Angela Carter', in John Haffenden (ed.), *Interviews with Writers* (London: Methuen, 1985), p. 91.
7. Angela Carter, 'Introduction', in *Angela Carter's Book of Fairy Tales* (London: Virago, 2005), p. xii.
8. Roland Barthes, 'The Death of the Author', *Image Music Text*, trans. Stephen Heath (London: Fontana, 1977), p. 46.
9. Jacques Derrida, *Of Grammatology*, trans. Gayatri Chakravorty Spivak (Baltimore, MD: Johns Hopkins University Press, 1976), passim.
10. Christina Britzolakis, 'Angela Carter's Fetishism', in Joseph Bristow and Trev Lynn Broughton (eds.), *The Infernal Desires of Angela Carter: Fiction, Femininity, Feminism* (London and New York: Longman, 1997), p. 50.
11. Anny Crunelle-Vanrigh, 'The Logic of the Same and Différance: "The Courtship of Mr Lyon"', in Roemer and Bacchilega (eds.), *Angela Carter and the Fairy Tale*, p. 128.

12. Robert Towers, 'In Extremis: *The Cement Garden*', *New York Review of Books* (8 March 1979): 8.
13. Christopher Ricks, 'Adolescence and After', *Listener* (12 April 1979): 526.

Part IV: Introduction: a 'minor' literature

1. Gilles Deleuze and Felix Guattari, *Kafka: Toward a Minor Literature*, trans. Dana Polan (Minneapolis and London: University of Minnesota Press, 1986), p. 16.
2. Ibid., p. 17.
3. Ibid., p. 23.
4. Ibid., p. 24.
5. Ibid., p. 25.
6. Ibid., p. 26.
7. Ibid., p. 86.
8. Abdul R. JanMohamed and David Lloyd, 'Toward a Theory of Minority Discourse: What Is To Be Done?', in Abdul R. JanMohamed and David Lloyd (eds.), *The Nature and Context of Minority Discourse* (New York and Oxford: Oxford University Press, 1990), pp. 1–16; 8.

11 Frank Sargeson and Marjorie Barnard

1. Lydia Wevers, 'The Short Story', in Terry Sturm (ed.), *The Oxford History of New Zealand Literature in English* (Oxford: Oxford University Press, 1991), p. 222.
2. C. K. Stead, 'A Letter to Frank Sargeson', in *In The Glass Case: Essays on New Zealand Literature* (Auckland: Auckland University Press, Oxford: Oxford University Press, 1981), p. 48.
3. 'Quivis', review of John Guthrie, *So They Began*, *Evening Post* (18 January 1936).
4. Wevers, 'The Short Story', p. 203.
5. Frank Sargeson, 'Katherine Mansfield', in *Conversations in a Train and Other Critical Writing* (Auckland and Oxford: Auckland University Press and Oxford University Press, 1983), p. 29.
6. Frank Sargeson, 'D. H. Lawrence', in *Conversations in a Train*, p. 48.
7. Bill Ashcroft and John Salter, 'Modernism's Empire: Australia and the Cultural Imperialism of Style', in Howard J. Booth and Nigel Rigby (eds.), *Modernism and Empire* (Manchester and New York: Manchester University Press, 2000), p. 294.
8. Nettie Palmer, *Fourteen Years: Extracts from a Private Journal* (Melbourne: Meanjin Press, 1948), p. 250.
9. Quoted in Drusilla Modjeska, *Exiles At Home: Australian Women Writers 1925–1945* (London and Sydney: Sirus, 1981), p. 108.
10. Ibid., p. 241.

11. Ibid., p. 114.
12. Bruce Bennett, *Australian Short Fiction: A History* (St Lucia, Queensland: University of Queensland Press, 2002), p. 119.

12 James Kelman and Chinua Achebe

1. James Kelman, 'The Importance of Glasgow in My Work', *Some Recent Attacks: Essays Cultural and Political* (Stirling: AK Press, 1992), p. 81.
2. Alasdair Gray, quoted on the dustjacket of Kelman's 1987 collection *Greyhound For Breakfast*.
3. Cairns Craig, *The Modern Scottish Novel* (Edinburgh: Edinburgh University Press, 1999), p. 101.
4. Kelman, 'The Importance of Glasgow in My Work', pp. 79–80.
5. Ibid.
6. Quoted in H. Gustav Klaus, *James Kelman* (Devon: Northcote House, 2004), p. 9.
7. Chinua Achebe, 'The Role of the Writer in a New Nation', *Nigeria Magazine* 81 (1964): 157.
8. Chinua Achebe, 'The African Writer and the English Language', in *Morning Yet on Creation Day* (London: Heinemann, 1975), p. 62.
9. Achebe, *Morning Yet on Creation Day*, p. 48.
10. C. L. Innes, *Chinua Achebe* (Cambridge: Cambridge University Press, 1990), p. 123.
11. Achebe, '*Chi* in Igbo Cosmology', in *Morning Yet on Creation Day*, p. 67.

13 Alice Munro

1. J. R. (Tim) Struthers, 'The Real Material: An Interview with Alice Munro', in Louis K. MacKerdrick (ed.), *Probable Fictions: Alice Munro's Narrative Acts* (Toronto: ECW Press, 1983), p. 9.
2. Coral Ann Howells, *Alice Munro* (Manchester and New York: Manchester University Press, 1998), p. 85.
3. Helen Tiffin, 'Post-Colonialism, PostModernism and the Rehabilitation of Post-Colonial History', *Journal of Commonwealth History* 23 (1988): 172.
4. Chris Gittings, 'The Scottish Ancestor: A Conversation with Alice Munro', *Scotlands* 2 (1994): 85.
5. Deborah Heller, 'Getting Loose: Women and Narration in Alice Munro's *Friend of My Youth*', in Robert Thacker (ed.), *The Rest of the Story: Critical Essays on Alice Munro* (Toronto: ECW Press, 1999), p. 67.
6. Howells, *Alice Munro*, p. 105.

Guide to Further Reading

Anthologies

Achebe, Chinua, and Innes, C. L. (eds.). *African Short Stories*. London: Heinemann, 1985.
The Heinemann Book of Contemporary African Short Stories. Oxford: Heinemann, 1992.
Atwood, Margaret, and Weaver, Robert (eds.). *The Oxford Book of Canadian Short Stories in English*. Toronto and Oxford: Oxford University Press, 1986.
Bradbury, Malcolm (ed.). *The Penguin Book of Modern British Short Stories*. Harmondsworth: Penguin, 1988.
Byatt, A. S. (ed.). *The Oxford Book of English Short Stories*. Oxford: Oxford University Press, 1998.
Dolley, Christopher (ed.). *The Penguin Book of English Short Stories*. Harmondsworth: Penguin, 1967.
Dunn, Douglas (ed.). *The Oxford Book of Scottish Short Stories*. Oxford: Oxford University Press, 1995.
Goldsworthy, Kerryn (ed.). *Australian Short Stories*. Melbourne and London: Dent, 1983.
Hudson, Derek (ed.). *Modern English Short Stories*. Oxford: Oxford University Press, 1956.
Kravitz, Peter (ed.). *The Picador Book of Contemporary Scottish Fiction*. London: Picador, 1997.
O'Connor, Frank (ed.). *Classic Irish Short Stories*. New York and Oxford: Oxford University Press, 1985.
O'Sullivan, Vincent (ed.). *The Oxford Book of New Zealand Short Stories*. Auckland and Oxford: Oxford University Press, 1992.
Trevor, William (ed.). *The Oxford Book of Irish Short Stories*. Oxford: Oxford University Press, 1989.

Volumes of short stories by individual author, and related critical works

Achebe, Chinua

The Sacrificial Egg and Other Short Stories. Omitsha: Etudo, 1962.
Girls at War and Other Stories. London: Heinemann, 1972.
Hopes and Impediments: Selected Essays. London: Heinemann, 1988.
Carroll, David. *Chinua Achebe: Novelist, Poet, Critic.* Second edition. London: Macmillan, 1990.
Innes, C. L. *Chinua Achebe.* Cambridge: Cambridge University Press, 1992.

Barnard, Marjorie

The Persimmon Tree and Other Stories. Sydney: Clarendon, 1943; London: Virago, 1985.
Bennett, Bruce. *Australian Short Fiction: A History.* St Lucia, Queensland: University of Queensland Press, 2000.
Modjeska, Drusilla. *Exiles at Home: Australian Women Writers 1925–1945.* London and Sydney: Sirius, 1984.

Beckett, Samuel

More Pricks Than Kicks. London: Chatto and Windus, 1934; London: John Calder, 1970.
The Complete Short Prose, 1929–1989, ed. S. E. Gontarski. New York: Grove, 1995.
Carey, Phyllis, and Jewinski, Ed (eds.), *Re: Joyce'n Beckett.* New York: Fordham University Press, 1992.
Cochran, Robert. *Samuel Beckett: A Study of the Short Fiction.* New York: Twayne, 1991.
Kenner, Hugh. *A Reader's Guide to Samuel Beckett.* New York: Farrar, Straus and Giroux, 1973.
Pilling, John. *Beckett Before Godot.* Cambridge: Cambridge University Press, 1997.

Bowen, Elizabeth

Collected Stories. London: Jonathan Cape, 1980.
Collected Impressions. London: Longmans, 1950.
After-Thought: Pieces About Writing. London: Longmans, 1962.
Bennett, Andrew, and Royle, Nicholas. *Elizabeth Bowen and the Dissolution of the Novel: Still Lives.* Basingstoke: Palgrave Macmillan, 1995.

Ellmann, Maud. *Elizabeth Bowen: The Shadow Across the Page*. Edinburgh: Edinburgh University Press, 2003.
Piette, Adam. *Imagination at War: British Fiction and Poetry 1939–1945*. London: Papermac, 1995.

Carter, Angela

Burning Your Boats: Stories. London: Chatto and Windus, 1995.
Expletives Deleted: Selected Writings. London: Vintage, 1993.
Bristow, Joseph, and Broughton, Trev Lynn (eds.). *The Infernal Desires of Angela Carter: Fiction, Femininity, Feminism*. London and New York: Longman, 1997.
Roemer, Danielle M., and Bacchilega, Christina. *Angela Carter and the Fairy Tale*, Detroit, MI: Wayne State University Press, 2001.
Sage, Lorna. *Angela Carter*. Plymouth: Northcote House, 1994.
   (ed.). *Flesh and Mirror: Essays on the Art of Angela Carter*. London: Virago, 1994.

Crackanthorpe, Hubert

Wreckage: Seven Studies. London: William Heinemann, 1893.
Sentimental Studies and A Set of Village Tales. London: William Heinemann, 1895.
Last Studies. London: William Heinemann, 1897. (This edition includes an essay on Crackanthorpe by Henry James.)
Beckson, Karl. *London in the 1890s: A Cultural History*. New York and London: W. W. Norton, 1992.
Crackanthorpe, David. *Hubert Crackanthorpe and English Realism in the 1890s*. Columbia and London: University of Missouri Press, 1977.

Conrad, Joseph

The Complete Short Fiction of Joseph Conrad, ed. Samuel Hynes. 2 vols. London: William Pickering, 1992.
Carabine, Keith. 'Introduction', in Joseph Conrad, *Selected Short Stories*. Hertfordshire: Wordsworth Edition, 1997, pp. vii–xxvi.
Erdinast-Vulcan, Daphna. *The Strange Short Fiction of Joseph Conrad*. Oxford: Oxford University Press, 1999.
Fraser, Gail. 'The Short Fiction', in J. H Stape (ed.), *The Cambridge Companion to Joseph Conrad*. Cambridge: Cambridge University Press, 1996, pp. 25–44.

Dickens, Charles

Selected Short Fiction, ed. Deborah A. Thomas. Harmondsworth: Penguin, 1976.
Orel, Harold. *The Victorian Short Story: Development and Triumph of a Literary Genre*. Cambridge: Cambridge University Press, 1986.
Smith, Grahame. *Charles Dickens: A Literary Life*. Basingstoke: Macmillan, 1996.
Thomas, Deborah A. *Dickens and the Short Story*. London: Batsford, 1982.

Egerton, George (Mary Chavelita Dunne)

Keynotes and Discords. London: Virago, 1983. (First published London: Matthews and Lane, 1893 and Boston: Roberts Bros., 1894.)
A Leaf from The Yellow Book: The Correspondence of George Egerton, ed. Terence de Vere White. London: The Richards Press, 1958.
Chrisman, Laura. 'Empire, "Race" and Feminism at the *Fin de Siècle*: The Work of George Egerton and Olive Schreiner', in Sally Ledger and Scott McCracken (eds.), *Cultural Politics at the Fin de Siècle*. Cambridge: Cambridge University Press, 1995, pp. 45–65.
Cunningham, Gail. '"He-Notes": Reconstructing Masculinity', in Angelique Richardson and Chris Willis (eds.), *The New Woman in Fiction and in Fact: Fin de Siècle Feminisms*. Basingstoke and London: Palgrave, 2001, pp. 94–106.

Hardy, Thomas

Wessex Tales. London and New York: Macmillan, 1888.
Life's Little Ironies. London and New York: Macmillan, 1894.
Selected Stories of Thomas Hardy, ed. John Wain. London: Papermac, 1966.
Brady, Kristin. *The Short Stories of Thomas Hardy*. Basingstoke and London: Palgrave Macmillan, 1982.
Orel, Harold. *The Victorian Short Story: Development and Triumph of a Literary Genre*. Cambridge: Cambridge University Press, 1986.

Joyce, James

Dubliners. London: Grant Richards, 1914; London: Jonathan Cape, 1967.
Bloom, Harold (ed.). *James Joyce's Dubliners: Modern Critical Interpretations*. New York: Chelsea House, 1988.
Bollettieri Bosinelli, Rosa M., and Mosher, Harold F., Jr (eds.). *ReJoycing: New Readings of Dubliners*. Lexington, KY: University Press of Kentucky, 1998, pp. 13–40.

Gottfried, Roy. "'Scrupulous Meanness" Reconsidered: *Dubliners* as Stylistic Parody', in Vincent J. Cheng (ed.), *Joyce in Context*. Cambridge: Cambridge University Press, 1992, pp. 153–69.

Head, Dominic. *The Modernist Short Story: A Study in Theory and Practice*. Cambridge: Cambridge University Press, 1992.

Leonard, Garry. *Reading Dubliners Again: A Lacanian Perspective*. Syracuse, NY: Syracuse University Press, 1993.

McCabe, Colin. *James Joyce and the Revolution of the Word*. Basingstoke: Macmillan, 1979.

Mullin, Katherine. 'Don't Cry for Me, Argentina: "Eveline" and the Seductions of Emigration Propaganda', in Derek Attridge and Marjorie Howes (eds.), *Semicolonial Joyce*. Cambridge: Cambridge University Press, 2000, pp. 172–200.

Kelman, James

Not Not While the Giro and Other Stories. London: Polygon, 1983.

Greyhound for Breakfast. London: Secker and Warburg, 1987.

The Burn. London: Secker and Warburg, 1991.

The Good Times and Other Stories. London: Secker and Warburg, 1998.

Some Recent Attacks: Essays Cultural and Political. Stirling: A. K. Press, 1992.

'And the Judges Said–': Essays. London: Secker and Warburg, 2002.

Craig, Cairns. *The Modern Scottish Novel*. Edinburgh: Edinburgh University Press, 1999.

Klaus, H. Gustav. *James Kelman*. Tavistock: Northcote, 2004.

Kipling, Rudyard

Collected Stories, ed. Robert Gottlieb. London: D. Campbell, 1994.

Something of Myself and Other Autobiographical Writings, ed. Thomas Pinney. Cambridge: Cambridge University Press, 1990.

Kemp, Sandra. *Kipling's Hidden Narratives*. Oxford: Basil Blackwell, 1988.

Mallett, Phillip. *Rudyard Kipling: A Literary Life*. Basingstoke: Palgrave Macmillan, 2003.

Sullivan, Zohreh. *Narratives of Empire: The Fictions of Rudyard Kipling*. Cambridge: Cambridge University Press, 1993.

McEwan, Ian

First Love, Last Rites. London: Jonathan Cape, 1975.

In Between the Sheets. London: Jonathan Cape, 1978.

Childs, Peter (ed.). *The Fiction of Ian McEwan*. Basingstoke: Palgrave Macmillan, 2006.
Malcolm, David. *Understanding Ian McEwan*. Columbia: University of South Carolina Press, 2002.
Ryan, Kiernan. *Ian McEwan*. Plymouth: Northcote House, 1994.
Slay, Jack. *Ian McEwan*. New York: Twayne; London: Prentice Hall, 1996.

Mansfield, Katherine

The Collected Stories of Katherine Mansfield. London: Constable, 1945; Harmondsworth: Penguin, 1981.
Dunbar, Pamela. *Radical Mansfield: Double Discourse in Katherine Mansfield's Short Stories*. Basingstoke: Macmillan, 1997.
Kaplan, Sydney Janet. *Katherine Mansfield and the Origins of Modernist Fiction*. Ithaca and London: Cornell University Press, 1991.
Smith, Angela. *Katherine Mansfield and Virginia Woolf: A Public of Two*. Oxford: Clarendon Press, 1999.
Katherine Mansfield: A Literary Life. Basingstoke: Palgrave, 2000.

Morrison, Arthur

Tales of Mean Streets. London: Methuen, 1894.
'What is a Realist?', *New Review* (March 1897): 326–36.
Greenfield, John. 'Arthur Morrison's Sherlock Clone: Martin Hewitt, Victorian Values, and London Magazine Culture, 1894–1903', *Victorian Periodicals Review* 35, 1 (2002): 18–36.
Keating, P. J. *The Working Classes in Victorian Fiction*. London: Routledge and Kegan Paul, 1971.

Munro, Alice

Dance of the Happy Shades. Toronto: Ryerson Press, 1968.
The Moons of Jupiter. London: Allen Lane, 1982.
The Progress of Love. Toronto: McClelland and Stewart, 1986.
Friend of My Youth. London: Chatto and Windus, 1990.
Open Secrets. London: Chatto and Windus, 1994.
The Love of a Good Woman. London: Chatto and Windus, 1998.
Hateship, Friendship, Courtship, Loveship, Marriage. London: Chatto and Windus, 2001.
Runaway. London: Chatto and Windus, 2005.
Heble, Ajay. *The Tumble of Reason: Alice Munro's Discourse of Absence*. Toronto, Buffalo and London: University of Toronto Press, 1994.

Howells, Coral Ann. *Alice Munro.* Manchester and New York: Manchester
    University Press, 1998.
Thacker, Robert (ed.). *The Rest of the Story: Critical Essays on Alice Munro.*
    Toronto: ECW Press, 1999.

O'Connor, Frank

The Stories of Frank O'Connor. New York: Knopf, 1952.
My Oedipus Complex and Other Stories, ed. Julian Barnes. Harmondsworth:
    Penguin, 2005.
An Only Child. London: Macmillan, 1961.
The Lonely Voice: A Study of the Short Story. London: Macmillan, 1963.
My Father's Son. London: Macmillan, 1968.
Lennon, Hilary (ed.). *Frank O'Connor: New Critical Essays.* Dublin: Four Courts
    Press, 2007.

O'Faolain, Sean

Stories of Sean O'Faolain. Harmondsworth: Penguin, 1970.
Selected Stories of Sean O'Faolain. London: Constable, 1978.
The Short Story. London: Collins, 1948; revised, 1972.
Harmon, Maurice. *Sean O'Faolain: A Life.* London: Constable, 1994.
Storey, Michael. "'Not To Be Written Afterwards": The Irish Revolution on the
    Irish Short Story', *Eire-Ireland: Journal of Irish Studies* 28, 1 (1998):
    32–47.

Pritchett, V. S.

Collected Stories. London: Chatto and Windus, 1982.
The Complete Essays. London: Chatto and Windus, 1991.
Treglown, Jeremy. *V. S. Pritchett: A Working Life.* London: Chatto and Windus,
    2004.
Wood, James. 'V. S. Pritchett and English Comedy', in Zachary Leader (ed.), *On
    Modern British Fiction.* Oxford: Oxford University Press, 2002, pp. 8–19.

Sargeson, Frank

The Stories of Frank Sargeson. Auckland: Longman Paul, 1974.
Conversation in a Train and Other Critical Writing, ed. Kevin Cunningham.
        Auckland: Auckland University Press; Oxford: Oxford University Press,
        1983.

King, Michael. *Frank Sargeson: A Life.* London: Viking/Allen Lane, 1995.
Lay, Graeme, and Stratford, Stephen (eds.). *An Affair of the Heart: A Celebration of Frank Sargeson's Centenary.* Auckland: Cape Catley, 2003.
Murray, Stuart. *Never a Soul at Home: New Zealand Literary Nationalism and the 1930s.* Wellington: Victoria University Press, 1998.

Woolf, Virginia

The Complete Shorter Fiction of Virginia Woolf, ed. Susan Dick. London: Hogarth Press, 1985; revised and expanded, 1989.
Beer, Gillian. *Virginia Woolf: The Common Ground.* Edinburgh: Edinburgh University Press, 1996.
Hanson, Clare. *Virginia Woolf.* Basingstoke: Macmillan, 1994.
Roe, Sue, and Sellers, Susan (eds.). *The Cambridge Companion to Virginia Woolf.* Cambridge: Cambridge University Press, 2000.
Smith, Angela. *Katherine Mansfield and Virginia Woolf: A Public of Two.* Oxford: Clarendon Press, 1999.
Snaith, Anna. *Virginia Woolf: Public and Private Negotiations.* Basingstoke: Palgrave Macmillan, 2000.

General critical works on the short story

Allen, Walter. *The Short Story in English.* Oxford: Clarendon Press, 1981.
Aycock, Wendell M. *The Teller and the Tale: Aspects of the Short Story.* Lubbock: Texas Tech Press, 1982.
Bates, H. E. *The Modern Short Story: A Critical Survey.* London: Thomas Nelson, 1941.
Bayley, John. *The Short Story: Henry James to Elizabeth Bowen.* Brighton: Harvester, 1988.
Burke, Daniel. *Beyond Interpretation: Studies in the Modern Short Story.* New York: Whitston, 1991.
Flora, Joseph M. (ed.). *The English Short Story 1880–1945: A Critical History.* Boston: G. K. Hall, 1985.
Hanson, Clare. *Short Stories and Short Fictions: 1880–1980.* Basingstoke: Macmillan, 1985.
    ed. *Re-Reading the Short Story.* London and Basingstoke: Macmillan, 1989.
Head, Dominic. *The Modernist Short Story: A Study in Theory and Practice.* Cambridge: Cambridge University Press, 1992.
Lohafer, Susan. *Coming to Terms with the Short Story.* Baton Rouge and London: Louisiana State University Press, 1983.
    and Clary, Jo Ellen, eds. *Short Story Theory at a Crossroads.* Baton Rouge and London: Louisiana State University Press, 1989.

May, Charles. *The Short Story: The Reality of Artifice*. New York: Twayne, 1995.
  ed. *The New Short Story Theories*. Athens, OH: Ohio University Press, 1994.
O'Connor, Frank. *The Lonely Voice: A Study of the Short Story*. London:
  Macmillan, 1963.
O'Faolain, Sean. *The Short Story*. London: Collins, 1948.
Reid, Ian. *The Short Story*. London and New York: Routledge, 1977.
Shaw, Valerie. *The Short Story: A Critical Introduction*. London and New York:
  Longman, 1983.

Index

Titles in this series: